Selected
Political Writings

NICCOLÒ MACHIAVELLI

Selected
Political Writings

Edited and Translated by
DAVID WOOTTON

Hackett Publishing Company, Inc.
Indianapolis/Cambridge

17 16 15 14 13   6 7 8 9 10 11 12

For further information, please address
  Hackett Publishing Company, Inc.
  P.O. Box 44937
  Indianapolis, Indiana 46244-0937
  www.hackettpublishing.com

Text design by Dan Kirklin

Library of Congress Cataloging-in-Publication Data

Machiavelli, Niccolò, 1469–1527.
  [Selections. English. 1994]
  Selected political writings/Niccolò Machiavelli: edited and translated by David
Wootton.
      p.   cm.
  Includes bibliographical references (p.   ).
  ISBN 0-87220-248-8   ISBN 0-87220-247-X (pbk)
  1. Political science—Early works to 1800. I. Wootton, David, 1952– . II. Title.
JC143.M1463   1994
320.1'01—dc20   94-21202
                                                        CIP

ISBN-13: 978-0-87220-248-1 (cloth)
ISBN-13: 978-0-87220-247-4 (pbk.)

CONTENTS

INTRODUCTION

As a method of torture, the *strappado* is simple but efficient. The prisoner's hands are tied behind his back; a rope is thrown over a pulley or beam; the prisoner is lifted into the air by his wrists. This is acutely painful and undignified, particularly if he is left dangling for hours or days. But from time to time he is dropped and allowed to fall a few feet before the rope goes taut; the sudden stop tears at his shoulders, even dislocating them. The pain is excruciating.

Torture was legal in most sixteenth-century states as part of the investigation of a crime. Machiavelli presented himself to the authorities, knowing what was in store, on 12 February 1513. Two acquaintances of his had been arrested for plotting against the new government of Florence, now controlled by the Medici family. In their possession was a list of names, of which Machiavelli's was one. He was presumably tortured fairly soon after his arrest—but not until he had heard the screams of other victims, and their cries of "Too high! Too high!" as they waited for the drop, for the torturer was not supposed to inflict permanent damage, and calculating the drop was not easy. Had he confessed under torture—and presumably people often confessed to crimes they had not committed—he would have been executed, as his two associates were. (One of them was, like Machiavelli, all too enamored of ancient Rome: he died begging the priest to help him get Brutus out of his head, so that he might die a Christian.) Machiavelli held out, in fact, through six drops and over several days. The torturers persisted longer than usual (four drops was the normal allowance), perhaps because they were persuaded he was guilty; or perhaps they felt his small, wiry frame had enabled him to get off lightly. In a letter to his friend Francesco Vettori, Florence's ambassador in Rome, Machiavelli was later to boast that he was proud of his own resilience.[1]

Was he guilty? We do not know. His torturers did not conclude he was innocent. Sixteenth-century Italian judges knew of degrees of guilt and innocence. One could be convicted, for example, of having given grounds for suspicion.[2] So Machiavelli was locked up. He wrote a poem to Giuliano de' Medici, who had once been a friend, asking, with what dignity he could muster, for him to arrange his release. His network of contacts was set in motion, in the hope someone had enough influence to come to his rescue. By good luck, as it happened, Cardinal

Giovanni de' Medici, Giuliano's brother, was elected pope, taking
the name Leo X. On 12 March Machiavelli, along with all the other
prisoners, was released. The prison gates had been thrown open so
that even the most unfortunate could join in the public celebrations.
But he was still confined to the lands of Florence, he was still under
suspicion.

The lands of Florence: Draw a circle with a radius of twenty-five
miles (forty kilometers) around Florence, and you will have a rough
idea of the limits within which he was confined. Less than a day's ride
from the city, and you would arrive at the frontier. Sixteenth-century
Italy was divided into a patchwork of independent states, each linked
to the others by a complicated and ever-shifting network of enmities
and alliances. Forty miles to the south of Florence was the independent
city of Siena; fifty miles to the north, the papal city of Bologna; rather
nearer, to the west, and controlling Florence's trade routes down the
river Arno to the sea, Pisa was sometimes independent, but now (since
1509, and thanks in large part to Machiavelli) under Florentine control.
Three or four potentially hostile states were thus in a position to place
an army outside Florence's walls within the space of a few days. Under
such circumstances diplomats had to be constantly alert, and political
and military advisers could never be sure what crisis they would face
tomorrow.

Released from jail, Machiavelli retreated to his farm in the country.
He could still see the dome of Florence's cathedral (designed by
Brunelleschi in 1420) seven miles in the distance, but the city itself
was small (perhaps seventy thousand inhabitants) and confined within
medieval walls. The line between town and country was a sharp one,
and Machiavelli was lost in the depths of the country. There, in the
evening, he read his favorite authors, especially Livy, and he imagined himself dressed in a toga, an ancient Roman. This was not a very
difficult feat of imagination, for farm life in the sixteenth century was
not very different from life two millennia before. Hammers, saws and
nails, plows and sickles differed little from their Roman prototypes.

Of course there had been some significant changes. Christianity had
been the official religion of Italy for twelve hundred years, though
Machiavelli seems to have had little faith in it: his friends teased him
about his unbelief, and he joked to them about his failure to attend
Church.[3] The printed book had been invented around 1440, but the
full impact of the print revolution was only just beginning to be felt
when Machiavelli was a young man.[4] He probably owned only a few
books, for they were still expensive. He went to the trouble of transcrib-
ing long volumes for his own use: the entire text, for example, of Lucre-

tius's famous atheistical poem *De rerum natura*.[5] Wars were now fought with guns, though Machiavelli thought the military importance of gunpowder was greatly overestimated. The Battle of Ravenna, 1512, is sometimes said to be the first field battle whose outcome was decided by artillery.[6] And in 1492 Columbus had discovered the New World: Machiavelli compares his own discoveries in politics to the discovery of a new continent.

Of these differences the religious difference was, to Machiavelli's mind, much the most important. But more important than any differences were the similarities between his own city state and those of ancient Greece and ancient Rome. That he should have had such a strong sense of the relevance of antiquity is not surprising, for all the most interesting intellectual advances in art, in law, in philosophy, in medicine over the past hundred and fifty years had been grounded in the principle of imitating the ancients, of rediscovering lost techniques and forgotten ways of thinking. These discoveries were still going on as Machiavelli wrote: Tacitus's *Annals*, for example, were first published in 1515. The theories of Polybius to which Machiavelli refers in the *Discourses on the First Decade of Titus Livius* were normally available only to a few scholars who knew Greek. Since Machiavelli did not, he must have laid his hands on a manuscript translation or listened to Greek scholars describe Polybius's views.[7] For the intellectuals of Machiavelli's day progress was intimately linked to classical scholarship, for discovery was nearly always believed to be rediscovery. It was natural for Machiavelli to assume that, in his own subject, politics, the imitation of "my Romans," as he called them, was the path to follow.

In 1513 Machiavelli was forty-four. Of his life between 1469 and 1498 we know almost nothing, beyond the fact that his father was a poor lawyer ("I was born to penury") who went to some trouble to ensure that his son was decently educated. Machiavelli's father was probably illegitimate, which would explain why Niccolò was never entitled to participate in Florentine politics in his own right.[8] He was always an employee, never a politician. In 1498 when the radical, almost democratic, regime inspired by a reforming monk, Savonarola, was thrown into crisis and Savonarola himself was executed, there was a purge of government officials, and Machiavelli suddenly appears in the records as second chancellor of the Florentine republic. As such he was, from the start, a senior bureaucrat. The same year he was elected secretary to a key committee, the Ten of War, which meant he had much to do with military planning, with procurement and logistics.

As a civil servant, his most important achievement was the organization, in 1505–6, of a militia, a Florentine conscript army to replace or at least supplement the mercenaries on whom Florence, like other Italian states, had traditionally relied. At the same time, Machiavelli was frequently employed on diplomatic missions. He journeyed all over Italy, made four trips to France, and one to the court of the Holy Roman Emperor in Austria.

As a consequence of his professional experience, Machiavelli saw politics from the point of view of the technician. His job was to predict wars, preserve alliances, prepare defenses, raise taxes. Of wars there was no shortage.[9] In 1494 Ludovico Sforza, ruler of Milan, had invited the French, as his allies, to invade Italy. The French troops had swept all before them (Machiavelli himself quotes the famous aphorism that they had conquered Italy with a piece of chalk: the piece of chalk that the quartermaster carried to mark the soldiers' billets) and had discovered in Italy a land ripe for conquest, rich in plunder. The resources of the little city states of Italy were no match for those of the larger territorial states of France, Spain, and the Empire, while Italian mercenaries were easily defeated by Swiss ones. For the rest of Machiavelli's life, one foreign invasion was followed by another, and the Italian states competed to find strong foreign allies. The trick was to be the invader's ally, not his victim.

If the military defenses of the various Italian states had proved weak, Italian governments were politically, as Machiavelli boasted, much more skillful than their northern neighbors. For over a century five Italian states (Florence, Milan, Naples, Rome, Venice) had been locked in a struggle for dominance. They were used to forming networks of shifting alliances and kept resident ambassadors (like Machiavelli's friend Francesco Vettori) in the key cities to keep them abreast of the latest developments. In these men's dispatches we can trace the growth of the professionalized political skills that Machiavelli was trained to deploy. Along with those skills came a particular set of moral values. Around 1490 Ermolao Barbaro, Venice's ambassador in Rome, wrote a little handbook for professional diplomats such as himself. "The first duty of an ambassador," he says, "is exactly the same as that of any other servant of a government, that is, to do, say, advise and think whatever may best serve the preservation and aggrandizement of his own state."[10] Machiavelli spent fourteen years faithfully serving the Florentine state, thinking only about power, never, or hardly ever, about principle.

Between 1494 and 1512 Florence's government was controlled by a Great Council of three thousand citizens (perhaps twenty percent of the adult males) who held office for life and could expect to pass it on to their children. The wealthy and influential resented the broad social basis of this regime, dismissing the majority of the Council's members as *popolani*, but, despite this hostility, the middling and poorer citizens gained increasing control after 1499, when appointments to the key committees that ran the city's day-to-day business began to be made by a process that gave an important role to selection by lot. These committees had a constantly changing, and increasingly inexperienced, membership, and in 1502 it was decided to introduce an element of continuity into government by the election of Piero Soderini to the new office of gonfaloniere for life. From the beginning the powers and role of the gonfaloniere were ambiguous, but the *popolani* seem to have gained more from his appointment than the elite.

Soderini believed in a policy of alliance with France, but in 1512 France proved unable to protect Florence from attack by the papacy and the Spanish (who possessed the Kingdom of Naples). Defeat at Prato led to the expulsion of Soderini and the return to the city, and to effective control of its politics, of the Medici family, who had governed Florence, while nominally being no more than private citizens, from 1434 to 1494. Early September 1512 saw widespread debate about constitutional reform among the Medici's supporters. On 17 September a coup d'état placed emergency powers in the hands of a large committee dominated by Medici supporters, the Balìa, and the Great Council was deprived of its powers. It was against this new regime that Machiavelli, who had been dismissed in November, was suspected of conspiring. In August 1513 Lorenzo de' Medici, nephew of the pope, arrived in Florence to take control, leaving his uncle Giuliano in Rome. On 22 November the Balìa agreed that in future routine power should be in the hands of a committee of seventy, although it continued to keep emergency powers in its own hands. Florentine government was thus nominally in the hands of a close-knit oligarchy, effectively in the hands of Lorenzo de' Medici. A few days later Machiavelli described to Vettori the first draft of his little book *The Prince*.

The first question we want to ask in reading *The Prince* is: What assumptions did Machiavelli bring to the study of politics as a result of his years of government service from 1498 to 1512? It is easy to show that *The Prince* draws largely on Machiavelli's personal experience (on his meetings, for example, with Cesare Borgia, the illegitimate son of Pope Alexander VI, who had conquered the Romagna in 1499–1501 and threatened to invade Florence), and key themes from it are already found in a letter known as the Caprices, written in 1506.[11] In

particular *The Prince* lays great stress on the need for a ruler to establish
a militia, and the formation of a militia had been Machiavelli's main
personal achievement as a civil servant.

In recent years, however, particularly since an important article by
Carlo Dionisotti, which first appeared in 1967, has begun to attract
attention, there has been a good deal of disagreement among scholars
about how to interpret Machiavelli's politics in these years of public
service.[12] Dionisotti points out that some contemporaries saw Machiavelli as Soderini's personal agent, and feared that the militia would be
used in a coup d'état to concentrate power in Soderini's hands. Two
features of it were particularly disturbing. It was recruited from the
countryside, not from Florence itself (it was thus not a *citizen* militia, but a *subject* militia),[13] and Don Micheletto, an extremely unsavory
professional soldier, a former henchman of Cesare Borgia, and a spe-
cialist in strangulation, was placed in charge of it. We know from the
Discourses that Machiavelli later felt that Soderini should have taken
extralegal action to secure his hold on power and crush the supporters
of the Medici.[14] One can thus argue that in the years before Soderini's
fall Machiavelli's goal was the establishment of a dictatorship. If one
takes this view, Machiavelli in *The Prince* was simply advising the Medici
to do what he thought Soderini ought to have done. Machiavelli's later
contempt for Soderini as a political baby would thus have been born
of the conviction that he had missed an opportunity to seize power.[15]

Against this view it has been stressed that Machiavelli was a servant
of the republic, not of Soderini. The militia was never answerable to
Soderini personally, but only to committees on which his opponents
were represented. In the *Discourses* (which some believe Machiavelli
began to write in 1513) he appears as a committed supporter of republican, participatory government. These counterarguments have had
considerable success in undermining Dionisotti's case, but it is difficult
to believe Machiavelli was either an apolitical civil servant or an admirer
of government by the Grand Council and its appointees. John Najemy
has shown Machiavelli was in constant trouble for failing to keep the
politicians properly informed of what he was up to.[16] One cannot help
but feel his behavior suggests a professional civil servant's contempt
for the amateurs from whom he was obliged to take his instructions,
an attitude that could easily have led him to long for more authoritarian
government.[17]

The second question we need to ask is: What was Machiavelli's
purpose in writing *The Prince*? There is no doubt Machiavelli was
seeking to gain employment from the Medici. He sent the manuscript
of *The Prince* to his friend Francesco Vettori in Rome, saying that he

was planning to dedicate it to Giuliano de' Medici, and asking for
Francesco's advice on how to proceed. The conventional view seems
to follow naturally: Machiavelli in *The Prince* was advising the Medici
on how to govern Florence.[18] He hoped his advice would be recognized
as good advice, and he would be offered employment, presumably with
a view to putting his policy recommendations into effect. A minority
view holds that the real position is much more complicated: Machiavelli knew the advice he was giving was bad advice, and he hoped the
Medici, by adopting it, would bring about their own ruin.[19]

In my view both the conventional and the minority views are fundamentally misconceived. In fact, the real subject of *The Prince* is not
Florence, and in it Machiavelli discusses Florentine politics only in
passing.[20] A number of texts about how to govern Florence were produced during the crisis of September 1512 and during the months
prior to the reform of November 1513. These canvassed a wide range
of options, including dictatorial government. But if Machiavelli
intended to write a text of this sort, he missed the boat. By December,
the key decisions had been made. Moreover, if he wanted to be hired
to play a part in the government of Florence, he was going about it
the wrong way. By August 1513 it was clear Lorenzo, not Giuliano,
was to be in charge of Florence, and it was he whom Machiavelli
should have been seeking to contact, not Giuliano, who was far away
in Rome.

In any case, *The Prince* fails to discuss the key problems that exercised
those concerned with governing Florence. Their debates revolved
around questions such as whether the pre-1494 constitution should be
restored, whether the *popolani* should be allowed a role in government,
whether the interests of the elite and the Medici were the same. Except
for a brief aside in chapter twenty, Machiavelli is not, in *The Prince*,
concerned with these practical questions.[21] It is simple to compare *The
Prince* in this respect with a letter of advice to the Medici of 1512, the
"Ricordo ai Palleschi," or with an essay Machiavelli wrote in 1519 or
1520, the *Discursus florentinarum rerum*, which is about how to restore
republican government to Florence.[22] It is also hard to reconcile the
claim that *The Prince* provides advice on how to govern Florence with
Machiavelli's letter of early 1514 about Lorenzo's administration.
There he praises policies sharply at odds with those recommended in
The Prince.[23] Either this letter is hypocritical, or he thinks the question
of how the Medici should behave in Florence is quite different from
the questions discussed in *The Prince*.

The Prince is an essay on how a prince who is new to power should
rule. But the Medici were not new to power in Florence in 1513. They

were merely newly restored to power. They had an existing body of support, traditional policies, a party ideology. Their problems are not the problems Machiavelli is addressing when talking about new princes: Indeed, he never even mentions the history of the Medici family.

One response among readers who have recognized some of these problems has been to conclude that *The Prince* is about new rulers in general, that it is an abstract analysis, not a practical guide.[24] But there is a more convincing alternative that ought to be apparent to anyone who reads the letters exchanged between Machiavelli and Francesco Vettori in 1513 and 1514. Machiavelli may, in the autumn of 1513, have hankered after a job in Florence, but he knew he had virtually no prospect of getting one, because those in charge of governing Florence regarded him with suspicion.[25] His best hope of a job was in Rome, where the Medici pope was proving a liberal patron to Florentines and where he had a well-placed contact, Francesco Vettori. In December 1513 Vettori was hoping Machiavelli might be employed to accompany Cardinal Giulio de' Medici as legate in France, but this came to nothing.[26] A year later, in December 1514, Vettori arranged what looks very like a serious consideration of the possibility of hiring Machiavelli. Machiavelli was asked to file a report on what papal policy should be in the event of a war between France and Spain for possession of Milan—he recommended allying with France. The report was read by the pope and Giuliano de' Medici, but, as in so many cases when Francesco tried to place a friend, no job resulted.[27] A role in shaping papal foreign policy would have allowed Machiavelli to put his professional skills to work without there being much reason to suspect him of having opinions or interests at odds with those of the government—although Soderini had always favored an alliance with France, so Machiavelli was afraid his advice would not seem impartial.[28]

Both Machiavelli and Vettori believed, at the time *The Prince* was being written, that there was another possibility for employment. They assumed the pope—a young and vigorous man—would take the necessary steps to ensure the Medici family acquired an hereditary state.[29] In the summer of 1513, the pope was thought to have his eye on Parma and Piacenza. In the autumn, the talk was of the French helping him to seize Naples from Ferdinand of Spain in order to give it to Giuliano: Hence, one may suspect, the prominent place Ferdinand occupies in *The Prince*. In early 1515 the pope, no longer on good terms with the French, negotiated with Spain and the emperor to acquire Parma, Piacenza, Modena, and Reggio for Giuliano. Francesco Vettori's brother Paolo was to become governor of one of the cities, and Machiavelli evidently hoped to acquire employment there, too.[30]

It is this papal objective of acquiring a state for Giuliano that provides the context for *The Prince*. In it, Machiavelli offers advice that would be suitable for any ruler of a newly acquired principality in Italy. The advice had to be general, for Vettori had warned him there was no knowing what territory Giuliano would acquire.[31] But it had to be advice for someone coming in from outside to rule territory within which he had no preexisting power base, and, in all probability, territory that had no tradition of urban self-government to overcome. Chapters one to twenty-five of *The Prince* are thus an advice book for a papal brother about to acquire a state of his own. Machiavelli originally hoped, I believe, that he might end up with the job he soon argued Paolo Vettori should have, the job of overall administrator of a new territorial state. Indeed, Machiavelli was considered by Giuliano for an appointment in February 1515, but he was vetoed by Cardinal Giulio de' Medici.

There has been a good deal of speculation as to whether chapter twenty-six, an excited, rhetorical call to free Italy from the barbarians, was added later. It would seem it must have been, for two reasons. In the first place, Machiavelli's letters to Vettori of 1513 show no hint of a desire to drive the foreigners out of Italy, and we have already seen that in 1514 Machiavelli positively recommended an alliance with one of the foreign powers. In the second, only when it seemed clear that Giuliano was likely to end up with a state in North Italy could such a policy appear remotely realistic. We should therefore accept Hans Baron's argument that chapter twenty-six was written between January and August 1515, which is the only period when such an outcome seemed likely. After September 1515, when the French secured Milan by defeating the Swiss at Marignano, there was no longer any prospect of driving out the foreigners.[32] Finally, the Introduction, a letter to Lorenzo, postdates the rest of the book, which we know was originally intended for Giuliano. It must predate Lorenzo's election as Duke of Urbino in October 1516, since Machiavelli addresses him as *Magnificus*, not (as would have been appropriate in writing to a duke) *Eccellenza*.[33] Contemporaries (and many modern commentators) thought he was encouraging Lorenzo in his known aspirations to become sole ruler of Florence. But this seems unlikely, for soon after Lorenzo's death in 1519 Machiavelli advised Cardinal Giulio de' Medici that it would never be possible to establish princely government in Florence. It is much more likely Machiavelli was responding to news of the plans to make Lorenzo Duke of Urbino, which took shape in early 1516. *The Prince* thus appears to have been written in three stages: Chapters one through twenty-five were written between July and December 1513;

chapter twenty-six, probably in early 1515, when Machiavelli once again hoped for employment; and the dedication, in 1516.

At none of these stages was Machiavelli primarily concerned with Florentine politics. It is striking there are very few references to Florence and the Florentines to be found in *The Prince*. Remarkably, there are no references at all to the Medici until the final, prophetic chapter. Two chapters, however, look at first sight as if they are directly relevant to the situation of Florence in 1513: chapter five ("How you should govern cities or kingdoms that, before you acquired them, lived under their own laws"), and chapter seven ("About new principalities that are acquired with the forces of others and with good luck"). In addition, chapter nine ("Of the citizen-ruler": *De principatu civile*) is clearly about city government. On closer inspection, chapter five is about free cities that are annexed by an existing state. Since the Medici had no preexisting state, the chapter would hardly appear to be relevant to their position in 1512–13. Yet it is hard not to suspect Machiavelli is also hinting at the situation of the Medici as rulers of Florence. He offers three alternative policies: to leave a formerly free city a large measure of independence, and collect tribute from it; to govern it oneself; or to destroy it. He never discusses what would be involved in governing it oneself—precisely what he ought to have discussed if he was advocating princely rule in Florence—but instead advocates destruction as the only sure policy, for otherwise, no matter how much time passes, previously free cities will always rebel as soon as they see their opportunity. If *The Prince* is really about Florence, then this chapter implies Machiavelli has no useful advice to offer (for what would be gained by destroying the city?), and Florence will eventually win back her freedom. Rather than conclude, as some have done, that Machiavelli is deliberately giving bad advice (surely he would not be so obvious about it?) or writing a satire (why then propose presenting it to the Medici?), we ought to recognize that Machiavelli is advising the Medici to concentrate, not on Florence, but on their other, safer opportunities for territorial acquisition. And, indeed, many Florentines complained that this was exactly what the Medici were doing in 1513, that Florence was far from being their first priority.[34]

Chapter seven appears to be about the position of the Medici in Florence only if one imagines they had been put there by Spanish arms and were dependent on Spanish favor. In reality the Medici had deep roots of support in the city, had received only half-hearted support from the Spanish, and were certainly no longer dependent on them. This chapter is not about the position of the Medici in Florence in

1513, but about the position in which Giuliano might find himself in Naples.

Chapter nine, on the other hand, evidently does have Florence as its subject. But is its discussion of "the citizen-ruler" who is chosen by his fellow citizens about the Medici? The Medici were not officially rulers of Florence. Technically they were merely private citizens; in practice, it is true, they were Florence's rulers, but they had selected themselves for the position, not been elected. It was Soderini who had become a ruler by the favor of his fellow citizens, and what this chapter primarily provides is an analysis of Soderini's position.[35] Soderini had, as Machiavelli later complained in the *Discourses*, failed to act decisively against his opponents. It was he who should have followed the example of Nabis of Sparta. As advice to the Medici, chapter nine is almost useless, for it recommends that the citizen prince establish a power base in the populace, without discussing how the Medici should set about doing this. Above all, it insists it is almost impossible to transform elected office into absolute, hereditary authority, and, although it suggests there might be some policy that would enable such a ruler to consolidate support, it never says what this policy is. At the very moment when he seems on the verge of giving some practical advice, Machiavelli says everything depends on specific circumstances, and that he will therefore put the question to one side. Machiavelli, both here and in chapter twenty, may be criticizing the reforms of November 1513 by insisting on the need to build a popular power base, but such criticism was scarcely opportune, and he seems aware his recommendations will not be welcome *(e però si lasceranno indrieto)*. In practical terms he is advising Giuliano to turn his thoughts elsewhere, if he does not want the Medici's position to be as temporary as Soderini's had been.

A key chapter any interpretation of *The Prince* must explain is chapter eight, "Of those who come to power through wicked actions." Throughout *The Prince* Machiavelli recommends what others would have rejected as wicked policies, for all that matters is success. Yet here he makes a clear distinction between effective policies and admirable ones. Agathocles of Syracuse and Oliverotto of Fermo are examples of rulers who are effective and, indeed, Machiavellian. But "one ought not, of course, to call it *virtù* [virtue or manliness] to massacre one's fellow citizens, to betray one's friends, to break one's word, to be without mercy and without religion." What distinguishes Agathocles from Cesare Borgia, whose example Machiavelli insists one should follow?[36] It is easy to show that Agathocles is not an ideal ruler, in Machiavelli's own terms. He does not simulate goodness, but then neither does Borgia. He does not found a new order, but neither does Borgia. In fact, it is clear he has every good quality Borgia has. He has a good and loyal army (which means a great deal in Machiavelli's scheme of things), and, like Borgia, he is an example of how cruelty can be well used to win the loyalty of the population. He is no Philip of Macedon, who treated his subjects like cattle, for we are told he made every effort to ensure his subjects benefited in the long run.[37] Why, then, is he not admirable? Victoria Kahn, facing up to the problem, has cleverly argued that Machiavelli is here deliberately confusing or testing the reader. By making his advice ambiguous, he is placing his reader in the position of a subject, unable to make sense of his prince's policies.[38]

Such an interpretation would be compelling if there were no real difference between Borgia and Agathocles, but in fact there is one, and a very simple one. Both Agathocles and Oliverotto destroyed free states, murdering their friends and fellow citizens. This is the one crime Machiavelli will not forgive. Where it is concerned, success is irrelevant, for Caesar is no better than Catiline.[39] As he says in the *Discursus florentinarum rerum*, "to establish a principate where a republic could do well, or a republic where a principate would flourish, is difficult, inhuman, and unworthy of anyone who wants to be thought pious and good."[40] Machiavelli may appear to teach the immoral pursuit of power by any means. In fact, he clearly teaches two sets of moral values: one deals with relations between states, where only success counts;[41] the other, much more complex, concerns one's dealings with one's fellow citizens, where the means must be justified by the purposes they serve.[42] To seize power, as Agis and Cleomenes did, in order to strengthen the republic is admirable; to seize it in order to establish a lasting tyranny, however benevolent, is shameful.

Machiavelli, I would suggest, is telling the Medici that if they were to concentrate all power in Florence in their own hands by means of a coup d'état the act would be shameful; they will have no difficulty finding competent advice, if this is their intent, but he is not the man for the job. In short, here he declares himself to be a principled republican who holds the view that republics should not be forcibly destroyed by their own citizens; in the next chapter he argues that there is no pacific way for a citizen to acquire long-lasting power. The conclusion is obvious: A new prince ought to seize territory that is accustomed to princely rule. It is only the false assumption that Machiavelli in *The Prince* is advising the Medici to seize absolute power in Florence that has prevented this chapter, whose meaning is clear enough, from being understood.

A good deal of recent criticism has argued that *The Prince* provides deliberately bad advice, is satirical, or is so ambiguous it provides no clear guidance. These interpretations all presume the true subject of *The Prince* is Florentine politics. Placed back in the context of Medici concerns in 1513, Machiavelli's argument reappears as relatively straightforward: He is offering himself as an adviser to a future ruler of an as yet unspecified Italian state, a state to be acquired through papal influence. The temptation to read *The Prince* as if it were written about Florence is a strong one, because we know so much about Florentine politics in this period, and Machiavelli, of course, knew even more. But in 1513 Machiavelli had little prospect of employment in Florence, and he knew it. In *The Prince* he was intelligently pursuing his own interests, as well as trying to interpret theirs to the Medici in terms he had reason to believe they would find acceptable. Any other interpretation makes *The Prince* incoherent, ambiguous, self-contradictory, and unlikely to benefit either Machiavelli or the Medici.

One of the advantages of this interpretation is that it greatly simplifies the vexed problem of the relationship between *The Prince* and the *Discourses*. One view, which goes right back to the sixteenth century, is that *The Prince* is a manual for tyrants, while the *Discourses* is a book by a lover of liberty. How, then, to explain the relationship between the two? The simplest explanation would be that Machiavelli had simply changed his mind. But most scholars used to think Machiavelli wrote the two works at almost the same time. This view seemed almost inescapable, for *The Prince* appears to contain a reference to the *Discourses* ("I will leave behind me any discussion of republics, for I discussed them at length on another occasion"), while the *Discourses* contains references to *The Prince*.[43] So, it was argued, the *Discourses* must have been begun before *The Prince* and finished later.

Most scholars, consequently, argued that the differences between *The Prince* and the *Discourses* are not as great as they might seem. One view holds that *The Prince* does not advocate tyranny, but attacks it. This argument places great emphasis on chapter eight, which on most accounts appears as a peculiar exception to the overall thrust of the book. It also emphasizes that Machiavelli insists a ruler is only secure if he has the support of his subjects and that he urges him to pursue policies from which they will benefit.[44] Another view takes as its starting point Machiavelli's recurring preoccupation in the *Discourses* with dictatorial legislators who seize power in order to institute reforms and construct a long-lasting political order.[45] Matters would be straightforward if the prince was intended to be such a man. But Machiavelli never discusses in *The Prince* the problem of how to construct a political system that will depend, not on the *virtù* of one man, but on impersonal institutions. A third view argues that Machiavelli believes republics can only be established under favorable conditions. The absence of such conditions in Florence makes republican politics idealistic, princely politics realistic.[46] This view seems to be at odds with Machiavelli's own *Discursus florentinarum rerum*, which insists that, in a Florentine context, republicanism is the practical option. A fourth view argues that the underlying values of both books are the same, for what Machiavelli wants is a state capable of conquering others, whether the state itself be republic or tyranny.[47] This is clearly true, but it sidesteps the question of whether Machiavelli is advocating princely rule or participatory self-government for his fellow citizens.

In an important series of essays, Hans Baron argued that *The Prince* and the *Discourses* were indeed incompatible, but the simplest solution was after all the right one: Machiavelli had written *The Prince* first and then the *Discourses*, changing his mind in between.[48] Internal evidence shows the bulk of the *Discourses* was written around 1517.[49] Machiavelli, in his foreword, says he would never have written the *Discourses* but for Zanobi Buondelmonti and Cosimo Rucellai, and we know he did not meet them until 1515. Cosimo died in 1519, so, since one does not write letters, even letters of dedication, to the dead, the work as we have it must have been written between 1515 and 1519. For 1513, when we know Machiavelli was working on *The Prince*, we have Machiavelli's extensive correspondence with Vettori. Had he been working on another project at around the same time, he would surely have mentioned it. In Baron's view the conclusion is simple: *The Prince* was written, with the exception of the foreword and the last chapter, in 1513; the *Discourses* after 1515. The crucial sentence in *The Prince* that appears to suggest otherwise can only be a later interpolation, added in 1516 when Machiavelli wrote the foreword dedicating the book to Lorenzo.

I happen to think this argument is fundamentally correct, but I want first to point out that the interpretation of *The Prince* that I have defended provides an alternative way of reconciling *The Prince* and the *Discourses*. If *The Prince* is not about how to acquire power in a free city, then it is perfectly possible Machiavelli could have written it while at the same time writing a book in praise of republican politics. He could quite reasonably hold that feudal Naples and bourgeois Florence would benefit from quite different sorts of government.[50]

Baron is right to insist there is nothing about the *Discourses* to suggest any part of it was written by 1513. Must we then conclude that the key sentence in *The Prince* that suggests otherwise (*"Io lascerò indrieto el ragionare delle republiche, perché altra volta ne ragionai a lungo")* is an interpolation? Commentators have been nearly unanimous in taking this to be a reference to the *Discourses*, and all have agreed it is a reference to a written work. But this need not be the case.[51] Machiavelli was writing for Giuliano de' Medici, who was, he believed, favorably disposed towards him, and Giuliano knew full well that Machiavelli was suspected of being an enemy of the Medici government in Florence, had been tortured, and had recently been released from prison. Machiavelli, one might suspect, would have felt obliged to acknowledge this problem, if only to deflect criticism. Our sentence does not say Machiavelli had ever written about republics, merely that he had discussed them. And it insists he wants to leave this discussion, not to one side, but behind: What is past is past. What discussion of republics could Machiavelli have been thinking of, a discussion that, in the winter of 1513, he was unquestionably eager to consign to oblivion, but bound also to acknowledge? A discussion that had gone on too long? The answer is so straightforward that I am puzzled no one has thought of it. The discussion Machiavelli is referring to is the one that took place as he dangled at the end of a rope in the city jail. What were his interrogators interested in, if not his attitude to republics, and his commitment to the republican cause?

This one sentence, which has misled generations of scholars, was, I suspect, originally intended as nothing more than a wry, private joke on Machiavelli's own ill fortune. Indeed, Machiavelli felt a compulsive need, in the autumn of 1513, both to reenact his own torture by catching birds in snares (an activity he describes as *dispettoso et strano*, which I have translated as "nasty and peculiar"), and to joke about what had happened to him. For example, in the sonnet he sent Giuliano in 1513 accompanying a gift of thrushes caught with his own hand, he apologizes for the fact that the birds are scrawny, but adds that his own scrawniness had not prevented the interrogators from getting their teeth into him.[52] And to Vettori he writes, "This letter of yours terrified me more than the rope."[53] In *The Prince*, putting a brave face on things, he talks, not of his tortured body or the rope, but of reasonable discussions about abstract problems in political theory: But he expects Giuliano to understand at once what he is referring to.

Buondelmonti and Rucellai were members of a group that met to discuss politics and history in the *Orti Oricellari*, the gardens owned by the Rucellai family, a group of wealthy young men with anti-Medicean and republican commitments (Buondelmonti was to be condemned to exile after the failure of a plot to murder Cardinal Giulio de' Medici in 1522). The praise of freedom in the *Discourses* is exactly what we would expect in a work written to be discussed in such a circle. If Machiavelli was not a committed republican in 1513, he clearly was one in 1517. But this leads to another problem that has not attracted the attention it deserves, that of Machiavelli's intentions in writing a work that appears alongside *The Prince* in its earliest editions, the *Life of Castruccio Castracani*. While on a visit to Lucca in 1520, he wrote this brief biography of Castracani, a Lucchese tyrant who had made extensive conquests in the early fourteenth century.

The *Life* is a puzzling work in two respects. In the first place, much of it is fiction, not fact. Machiavelli invents the story that Castracani was a foundling, reared by a priest; he denies Castracani had children, when in fact he had many; he fabricates accounts of battles in order to illustrate the theories of his *Art of War*. These fictions might escape a reader unfamiliar with the details of Castracani's life, but, as if to incite the reader's suspicions, Machiavelli ends the *Life* with a long series of aphorisms that he attributes to Castracani, but that come for the most part from well-known classical sources. That these had been imported into the story from elsewhere was apparent to his first readers, members of the Rucellai circle.

Second, the *Life* offers nothing but praise for a man who had, in fact, seized power in Lucca from her citizens, destroyed the republic, and (on Machiavelli's account) massacred his fellow citizens in cold blood. Castracani thus appears as another Agathocles, and the *Life* is often compared with *The Prince* as an essay in praise of successful tyranny. Had it been written at the same time as *The Prince*, this would be bound to affect our interpretation of that work; as it is, it seems a very strange book for the republican author of the *Discourses*. Castracani so wants to be like Caesar that he is even keen to die like him; in the *Discourses* Machiavelli had expressed nothing but contempt for Caesar.[54]

Fortunately, a fairly straightforward explanation is available. By 1520 Machiavelli had established himself in literary circles as the author of *Mandragola* and *The Art of War*. His friends continued to seek employment for him with the Medici, as his financial needs continued to be pressing. Their plan in 1520 was to arrange for him to be hired to write a history of Florence.[55] In writing the *Life* Machiavelli must have been primarily concerned to show he could indeed write a history, something he had never done before. But secondly, he had to face the fact he still had a reputation for moving in anti-Medicean circles. He needed to find some way of demonstrating that he would not turn a history of Florence into an attack on the Medici. When, during his visit to Lucca, he came across the life of Castracani written in 1496

by a Lucchese citizen, Nicolao Tegrimi, he must have been delighted
to see a simple solution to his problem. Tegrimi was an ardent republican, but he had written in praise of a despot as an indirect way of
flattering the Sforza Dukes of Milan, Lucca's allies, to whom he had
been appointed ambassador.[56] Machiavelli set out to imitate him by
using praise of Castracani to indicate the flexibility of his republican
values. At the same time, though, by clearly indicating that his history
was fiction, not fact, he distanced himself from the views expressed
in it. If Castracani was a fiction, might not the narrator also be an
invention?

On this interpretation, the *Life* is not an honest presentation of
Machiavelli's views, which are much more clearly expressed in chapter
eight of *The Prince*. Rather it is a parody of the more cynical of Machiavelli's arguments, as is *Mandragola* (where a young man, assisted by a
cunning adviser, tricks an old man into letting him sleep with his wife).
Machiavelli is amusing himself by portraying "Machiavellism" in its
most blatantly immoral form. *The Prince*, I have argued, is not a satire; the *Life*, however, comes close to being one. But we may suspect
that Machiavelli took little pleasure in distorting his convictions in order
to curry favor.[57] Borrowing from Diogenes Laertius, he reports that
Castracani once spat upon someone who sought a favor from him.
The courtier's response was, "Fishermen are prepared to get soaked
with seawater in order to catch a tiny fish; there's no reason why I
shouldn't get soaked in spit in order to catch a whale."[58] Machiavelli, trying to curry favor, must have felt plainly how shameful his own
position was.

Shameful or not, the strategy succeeded. Machiavelli landed the job
of historian of Florence, a project on which he worked until he presented the completed volume to Giulio de' Medici, by then Pope
Clement VII, in May 1525. Although written under Medici patronage, there was little need for Machiavelli in the *History* to compromise
his principles to the extent that he had done in the *Life of Castruccio
Castracani*. As he explained to a friend, he simply had to place his
criticism of the Medici into the mouths of their opponents.[59] By this
elementary expedient he could write for Medici consumption a history that made clear why one should be hostile to their rule, and could
be read with pleasure by his anti-Medicean friends. Unfortunately,
though, the fact that he had been a beneficiary of Medici patronage
was to count against him when, in 1527, the Medici were overthrown.
Machiavelli died that year, still denied any position of political
significance.

I have argued so far that *The Prince* was largely written in the second

half of 1513, when Giuliano was expected to acquire a new state of
his own to rule. The *Discourses* was written later, between 1515 and
1519, and is concerned with republican self-government. These arguments are at odds with the traditional view, which holds that *The Prince*
and the *Discourses* were written more or less simultaneously. They are
also at odds with the generally accepted belief that both address the
problems of Florentine politics. Most scholars assume both works were
intended to be taken seriously, but some believe *The Prince* is a satire,
while others hold that Machiavelli is deceptive and disingenuous
throughout his work.[60] This latter view seems to me hardly plausible
as an account of works written for private circulation, not for publica-
tion, but I have suggested that there is something distinctly fishy about
the *Life of Castruccio Castracani*.

I want now to turn to a question that has much exercised scholars
in recent years, that of Machiavelli's language. In order to understand
Machiavelli, we need to bear in mind that his vocabulary for discussing
politics is very different from ours. Sixteenth-century Italian has no
words for "selfish" or "selfless," for "egotistic" or "altruistic," for
"anarchy" or "alliance."[61] It does not even have a word for "politics"
as we understand the term. By "politics" Machiavelli's contemporaries
mean the theory of good government, usually of a city-state.[62] For the
policies required to seize or secure power they use the phrase "*l'arte
dello stato*," or statecraft. But Machiavelli has words or phrases that
enable him to discuss most of the issues we want to discuss when we
talk about politics (and where necessary he can invent a phrase, such
as "self-charity" for selfishness), and it would often be artificial to
avoid using modern terminology when translating him into twentieth-
century English.

However, there are a number of words Machiavelli uses that at first
sight appear easy to translate, but are in fact problematic. The first we
should note is *principe*. Machiavelli's title is always translated *The Prince*,
but by *principe* Machiavelli never means a king's son. His term usually
means "ruler" (so that the book ought to be called *The Ruler*), and a
principato is any system of government where power is concentrated
in the hands of one man (e.g. monarchy, tyranny). But Machiavelli
sometimes uses the word to mean "leader," so the general of an army
can be *un principe*, as can an elected official in a republic; and he also
occasionally calls the Medici, who held no official position in Florence,
but for long periods of time effectively controlled its politics, "princes," meaning "de facto rulers." A republic can be *principe di se stesso*, i.e.
self-governing. Machiavelli's "princes" have "states." When he is

discussing a king as head of state, or as ruling over a state, or when he is talking about statecraft, this presents no problems. Sometimes Machiavelli uses *stato* where we would use "government" or "power," to talk, for example, of a new government, or acquiring power. But *stato* sometimes means something closer to status: The Medici were not heads of state, but they had *uno stato*, a particular, private power, authority, status within Florence. To be *un principe* is to have *un stato*, but Machiavelli uses both terms to cover a wider range of cases than our terms "ruler" and "state."

In approving of someone, Machiavelli standardly refers to their *virtù*. By this he does not normally mean virtue in a Christian sense, for he has little time for humility or chastity. It might be thought his virtues are pagan ones, and he is surely aware of the origin of the word in *vir*, man. His virtues might be expected to be the manly ones of courage, prudence, temperance, honesty, and justice. But this is not the case. Machiavelli approves of rash actions when they are successful; he advocates the stratagems of the coward when they are necessary to ensure survival or are likely to lead to victory; he believes rulers must be prepared to lie, murder, and act unjustly. They must therefore master the arts of deception, appearing to be one thing while in fact being another, cultivating a public image at odds with the facts. In taking this view Machiavelli is deliberately going against the arguments of Cicero, who had insisted honesty, justice, etc. are always the best policy.[63] Machiavelli's virtuous man is much nearer to being a virtuoso (and *virtuoso* is, of course, the adjective in Machiavelli's vocabulary, *virtù* the noun). Just as a virtuoso violinist can play music that defeats others, so in Machiavelli's world a virtuous general will win battles others would lose, a virtuous politician secure power where others would lose it. Virtue is thus role-specific: Virtuous soldiers are strong and brave, virtuous generals intelligent and determined. The virtuous man is the man who has those qualities that lead to success in his chosen activity.

The virtuous man will know when to seize his chances and will recognize what needs to be done. He will identify opportunities where others see only difficulties, and recognize necessity where others believe they have freedom of choice. But even virtue cannot guarantee success: He may be unlucky, circumstances may change, someone with greater virtue may get the better of him. Virtue thus finds itself in a constant struggle with fortune. The wise man limits the scope of fortune by taking appropriate precautions, but he also recognizes that bold, apparently rash actions often pay off. If *virtù* is in part the quality of manliness, then fortune is a woman who can be mastered. This is Machiavelli's way of saying that nothing succeeds like success and that one makes one's own good luck.

Machiavelli, however, unlike these aphorisms, is offensive, and deliberately so: Modern readers notice only the violence between man and woman in chapter twenty-five of *The Prince*, but sixteenth-century readers would have been acutely conscious that fortune is a *lady* and would have been particularly shocked at the violence between social inferior and superior.[64] It would be wrong, I think, to jump too quickly from Machiavelli's gendered language to a simple reading of Machiavelli as a patriarchal chauvinist.[65] If anything he seems to be exceptionally prepared to recognize that women can legitimately exercise power. Lucrezia is the hero of *Mandragola*, capable, indeed, "of ruling a kingdom."[66] *Clizia* can be read as a critique of masculinity, and as portraying "a protofeminist community."[67] Machiavelli seems to have nothing but admiration for the Countess of Forlì, who, ruthless as any man, is prepared to sacrifice her children in order to hold on to power.[68] Given this wider context, it is perhaps worth remembering that when he wrote *The Prince* Machiavelli had himself recently been beaten and abused. Usually he portrays Lady Fortune as mastering him, not he her. Fortune, like the thrushes he captures, embodies not Machiavelli's sense of masculine power but rather his experience of powerlessness. It is not surprising, then, that she also evokes fantasies of revenge.

Success, mastery of fortune, is important, but not all ends are worth pursuing, not all means justifiable. Machiavelli's virtuous man seeks not merely fame, but glory. There is nothing glorious or virtuous about unnecessary cruelty and bloodshed; on the other hand, a squeamish distaste for violence may make things worse in the long run. Machiavelli thus advocates "an economy of violence."[69] Since history reflects the views of the victors, success, even if it involves murder or treachery, is likely to lead to glory, not infamy. There are some goals, however, that are in themselves shameful. No one should want to destroy good government in order to establish anarchy or tyranny; no one should want to be Caesar. Politicians should all aspire to establish sound government that enables the mass of society to live in security. This is the best recipe for success, but also the only goal that is morally admirable.

Machiavelli thus aspires to the creation of order; the term *ordini*, meaning those constitutional provisions and institutional arrangements that make stable government possible, runs as a recurring refrain through the *Discourses*. To establish and preserve government, however, "extraordinary" measures are often necessary: Rulers, and even private individuals, may have to act outside the law in order to restore good government or ensure stability. If Machiavelli believes strongly in the sort of order that makes justice possible, he does not believe one must always act within the law.

Virtue and fortune, opportunity and necessity, shame and glory, constitutional order and extraordinary measures: These are the key polarities around which Machiavelli's thought revolves, and many of the tensions in his work come from his attempts to balance them, one against the other.[70] But there is a further preoccupation that lies at the heart of the *Discourses*, a preoccupation with liberty. Orderly government provides what Machiavelli sometimes calls *il vivere civile* or *il vivere politico*. Kings can provide this; indeed, Machiavelli repeatedly praises France, where royal despotism and aristocratic tyranny are kept within the law by the *parlements*. This is the least one can hope for, although it is more than can be found in a tyranny or despotism. But better still is *il vivere libero*, or self-government.[71] Most men, the *plebs*, want only security. A minority, the *popolo*, those who are true citizens, want to participate in political life. A few, the *grandi*, want to be leaders. Where there is great social inequality, particularly where the *grandi* are a landed aristocracy, with castles and armed retainers, popular self-government is impossible. But where there is a reasonable degree of equality, where the wealthy and privileged do not have things all their own way, then, in a city-state, popular self-government is possible, and wherever it is possible, it is desirable.

Machiavelli writes eloquently about the superiority of popular self-government to the rule of one man. The people, he believes, are a better judge than any individual, and where there is freedom, prosperity follows. Above all, the people can change their leaders to adapt to changing circumstances. No other system of government is thus as well placed to adapt to changes in fortune. A virtuous people has those qualities that make self-government successful: courage, self-sacrifice, integrity. At this point it seems Machiavelli's cynicism is turning into idealism.[72] But it must always be remembered that Machiavelli believed people were easily corrupted and always inclined to be selfish. No system of government that relied on altruism could hope to succeed, even where young people were trained from childhood to seek glory in public service and avoid shameful behavior at all costs. Indeed, Machiavelli has very little to say about obligations and duties, for the simple reason that he does not expect people to take them very seriously.

What, then, makes successful self-government possible? Machiavelli's answer to this question was profoundly original. It was, he believed, the clash of interests, particularly the clash between the interests of *grandi* and *popolo*. As long as individuals pursued genuine collective interests, not merely private ones, good government could result, even if the collectivity with which they identified was only one social group within the city. In his *Discourses* Machiavelli broke new ground by approving of the conflicts between the senate and the people in Rome; in his *History of Florence* he placed a new emphasis on the guilds as the legitimate representatives of interest groups, and he even expressed sympathy with the revolt in 1378 of the *ciompi*, the poorer workers whose interests were not adequately represented in the guilds.[73] Machiavelli consequently views conflicts that are founded in divergent economic interests and differing social statuses as inevitable, and indeed healthy. Where these conflicts result in a balance of power and a mixed constitution, something resembling the general good, *il bene commune*, will result, and selfish, short-sighted individuals will end up behaving like virtuous citizens.

Florentine history was certainly a history of internal conflict.[74] Why, then, had Florence proved a miserable failure, while Rome had experienced success on a scale unparalleled in history? Machiavelli's answer to this question depends on distinguishing between productive conflict and destructive conflict. What he terms *sette* (sects, parties, factions) unite individuals across economic and status groups, appealing to supposed issues of principle (in Florence, Guelfs versus Ghibellines, and supporters of the Medici versus opponents). Such conflicts resulted merely in pork-barrel politics, in the attempt to monopolize the benefits of political power for an unrepresentative minority. Members of political factions might think they were seeking a greater good, but in fact their actions always proved in practice to be narrowly corrupt and self-interested. Machiavelli sees conflicts between factions as destructive, while conflicts between classes are constructive.

Machiavelli thus held that, under the right conditions, successful, virtuous self-government was possible, although it was bound to be accompanied by conflict, tumult, and the occasional resort to extraordinary measures. Machiavelli's cynicism legitimized a cautious optimism, but it is important to recognize the narrow limits within which he was optimistic. If the clash of interests within a city could have beneficial consequences, Machiavelli could see no way of mediating the conflict of interests between states. Governments would always be driven to go to war against each other. A successful city would be one well prepared for war. Since attack was the best form of defense, the liberty of one city would necessarily be based on the servitude of others.[75] At the best, conquered cities might enjoy a limited *vivere civile*, like the subjects of a monarch. Freedom could be the privilege of no more than a few. In the clash of city against city, state against state, only the fittest could hope to survive. In Rome the energy generated by internal conflict had spilled outward to fuel external conquest. Only such a martial liberty was worth having. Participatory politics was possible only where there was also military discipline. Machiavelli, who had seen cities looted, crops burned, and populations starving, could imagine no alternative to a world of wars and rumors of wars.[76] The trick was simply to be on the winning side.

Machiavelli is a brilliant author, and we need to give some thought to the way he presents his views in his work. Both of Machiavelli's major works, *The Prince* and the *Discourses*, begin with references to artists, and Machiavelli clearly believes there is a point of comparison between his own science of politics and the art of his day.[77] *The Prince* begins with Machiavelli comparing himself to an artist painting a landscape in which mountains rise from the plain: Only from a distance can you see the shapes and forms of the land. Machiavelli is writing almost a century after the discovery of perspective, and Machiavelli's artist is painting depth and distance. One should compare the painting of Machiavelli's own day with Machiavelli's insistence that he does not want to write an ornamental, decorative prose; instead he wants to portray the facts as they are.[78] Just as one looks *into* a Renaissance painting, seeing a world one feels one could step into and move about in, rather than regarding the painting as a decorative surface, so Machiavelli wants you to think of his books as windows on the world of politics. *The Prince* is intended to be like the bird's-eye maps Leonardo da Vinci drew for Cesare Borgia, enabling him to envision his newly conquered territories. Here, laid out before one, are the routes along which troops may advance, here the natural strongholds toward which to retreat when under attack. Machiavelli probably knew these maps and marveled at them.[79]

Machiavelli only once names an artist in his works. In *The History of Florence* he praises the great architect and sculptor Brunelleschi.[80] Brunelleschi had been involved in a plan to divert a river in order to cut off the city of Lucca so it could be the more easily besieged. The plan had been a dismal failure, as had Machiavelli's own attempt—on which he worked in collaboration with the greatest of all artist-engineers, Leonardo himself—to divert the river Arno in order to cut off Pisa from the sea. But I do not believe Machiavelli admired Brunelleschi simply because he was a military engineer (he uses of him his highest word of praise, *virtù*, which he normally applies only to politicians and generals). Brunelleschi's sculptures were supremely lifelike, so that, looking at them, one could forget one was looking at works of art and imagine one was looking at real people. So, too, Machiavelli aims to conceal his own artistry behind the appearance of realism. Realism, of course, is as much a contrived effect as any other, for the appearance of fidelity to nature is itself an illusion. But in order to achieve this effect, Machiavelli writes always about people and actions, rarely about authors and words. His *Discourses on Livy* have little to say on Livy, for what interests Machiavelli is Roman politics, not Roman authors.[81]

Machiavelli had been educated as a humanist, and conventional humanism was a discipline centered upon texts. Great authors were imitated, quoted, and paraphrased, learning paraded. Machiavelli expects his readers to have a humanist education and to recognize implicit references to Cicero or Dante. The core of a humanist education was the study of rhetoric, and students practiced rhetorical figures until they became second nature. Machiavelli would expect his readers to recognize that chapters sixteen to eighteen of *The Prince* are a virtuoso exercise in *paradiastole*, the redescription of behavior in order to transform its moral significance.[82]

Many humanists before Machiavelli had written essays on how to educate a prince, essays in which they displayed their learning and rhetorical skill and urged the prince to become, like them, learned and eloquent. Machiavelli is different. Both *The Prince* and the *Discourses* reject the humanists' preoccupation with the text and with it the humanists' concern with rhetoric, the art of persuasion, as the supreme political skill.[83] Of course Machiavelli often reports the speeches of politicians and generals, and acknowledges their importance, and *The Prince* echoes with imaginary, implicit conversations: between Machiavelli and his prince, Machiavelli and the reader, subjects and their rulers, princes and their advisers.[84] But in Machiavelli's view, words are less important than deeds; rhetoric is insignificant beside armed force.[85] His own writing is presented, not as a form of political activity, but as an inadequate substitute for it.[86] Machiavelli thus attacks the traditional hierarchy of values upheld by humanism. In place of ornate eloquence he offers simplicity; in place of learning, experience; in place of words, deeds; and in place of integrity, deception. All the literary techniques of the humanist are brought to bear, but one of the chief casualties is intended to be humanism itself.

It has, I think rightly, been argued that this is one of the reasons why Machiavelli seems to usher in the modern age.[87] But Machiavelli's claim to portray practical realities has provoked a number of postmodern readings.[88] Scholars have been eager to argue that his texts, like all other texts, fail to refer to anything outside themselves, that Machiavelli's arguments double back on themselves, his words shift their meaning, until in the end, the reader, far from being orientated, as by a map, is disorientated.[89] To use Machiavelli's works as a guide to how one should act is, on this view, as pointless as trying to step into a painting.

Machiavelli certainly wanted his texts to be somewhat enigmatic. Like Cesare Borgia's assassination of Remiro d'Orco, or Junius Brutus's execution of his sons, they were intended to seize the attention, and to juxtapose contraries (justice and cruelty, benevolence and hardness of heart) in enigmatic symbols whose meaning was both plain and difficult to render in words. I do not think, though, that Machiavelli would have taken kindly to the claim that his texts had no purchase on the world and offered no practical advice. He had worked for long years as a civil servant and was used to having his instructions obeyed, not dismissed as incomprehensible. *The Prince* is intended to be a guide to action, and to dismiss its references to reality as mere rhetoric is to dismiss it as a failure.

Nevertheless, Machiavelli was acutely conscious of the gap between theory and action, and well knew his own enterprise might be impractical. He addresses both *The Prince* and the *Discourses* to people he hopes will be in a position to put his theories into practice, but since his theories stressed the need to adapt action to circumstances, he could scarcely advise on how to implement them. Machiavelli looked to the past and to contemporary events to find examples to imitate, like a cook collecting recipes. But why should one expect what had worked on one occasion to work on another? Machiavelli stressed that if the political culture of a community had changed—if it had become corrupt, or virtuous—then strategies that had once failed would now work, and vice versa. Often two quite different approaches to a problem might be equally successful, so there was no need to imitate slavishly a successful strategy. Often the same policies, even when pursued in similar circumstances, might have different outcomes, for everything might depend on the politician's personal style, his ability to carry conviction. There was little point, then, in trying to persuade people to act contrary to their own natures, to play a part rather than be themselves, and yet what was Machiavelli doing but trying to persuade politicians to imitate others, and in the process forget themselves? Imitate the Romans, above all, and yet, as Machiavelli keeps pointing out, they had imitated no one, and followed no blueprint. In any case, Machiavelli insists, only a wise man can distinguish good advice from bad, and a wise man hardly needs advice in the first place. Following Machiavelli's advice turns out to be far from straightforward after all.[90]

"What a mistake some people make when they cite the Romans at every turn! One would need to be in a city like theirs before one could be justified in following their example."[91] So Machiavelli was criticized by his friend Guicciardini, and to such criticism he offers no straightforward reply. *The Prince* begins with a painting, an illusion of reality. The *Discourses* begins with fragments of Roman statues, dug out of the ground, passed around among scholars and imitated by artists. Imitating fragments does not enable you to reconstruct the shattered statues; new statues made in the style of the old are not Roman, but modern. Like the artists of his day, Machiavelli understands this perfectly well, but he still believes the secret of success lies in the imitation of the ancients. Guicciardini complained that people who imitated the Romans were like donkeys pretending to be race horses; Machiavelli, for his part, was impatient with people who lacked ambition and were prepared to make do with second best. To accept fortune, not struggle against her, might be prudent, but could scarcely be glorious.

If what most strikes readers of our generation is the slipperiness of the distinctions on which Machiavelli's argument depends—between Borgia and Agathocles, rhetoric and reality, imitation and self-expression—sixteenth- and seventeenth-century readers found him straightforward, even when teaching how to be deceptive. "We are much beholden to Machiavelli and other writers of that class who openly and unfeignedly declare or describe what men do, and not what they ought to do," said Bacon.[92] But to describe what men do was to teach immorality. "Murdrous Machiavel" Shakespeare called him. "Am I politic, am I subtle, am I Machiavel?" one of his characters asks.[93] Since Machiavelli's works were placed on the Index in 1559, his name has been associated with evil. Yet few authors have been more widely read, more commented upon, and, indeed, have provoked such strong loyalty and admiration.

As soon as we begin to approach the study of Machiavelli we find ourselves facing a series of conflicting images out of which it is very difficult to resolve a coherent picture of a man or a consistent doctrine. In *The Prince* Machiavelli seems to advocate tyranny; yet in the *Discourses* he praises freedom. Even within these works we find in close combination arguments we would expect to be irreconcilable. In order to maximize his own power, the prince, it turns out, must serve the interests of his subjects. In order to build freedom, a society must conquer and enslave others. Machiavelli looks forward: He declares he has discovered a new continent of knowledge, and some think modernity begins with him. But at the same time he looks backward: His only recommendation is that we imitate the Romans, and some think he is best understood as reviving Roman values. Some, like Bacon, see him as the founder of a new, objective science of politics, concerned not with what should be, but with what is, not with hopes and fears, but with practical realities. Others insist he is an idealist, constantly striving for justice, freedom, and equality. Some believe he is a cynic, while others claim he is a moralist. He is, it seems, simultaneously open and unfeigning, yet politic and subtle.

When it comes to Machiavelli, every reader has to make up her or his own mind on how to reconcile the irreconcilable. In this introduction I have tried to outline the main orthodoxies that are entrenched in current scholarship, while pointing out a number of alternative views, some of which seem to me persuasive. Would Machiavelli have recognized himself in my portrait of him? He would at least have been gratified at the thought that we might sit down to discuss politics with him, as he discussed politics with Livy.

In the translations that follow, I have done my best to let him speak in his own voice. Others before me have produced translations that, taken word by word, are closer to Machiavelli's text. My primary concern has been to convey the sense and the style, which is aphoristic, lively, persuasive. Machiavelli was never the dull, worthy, pedantic author who appears in the pages of other translations.[94] But it is time to stop speaking about him, for I have done my best to let him speak for himself.

Notes

1.   Roberto Ridolfi, *The Life of Niccolò Machiavelli*, trans. C. Grayson (Chicago: University of Chicago Press, 1963), 133–38; Sebastian de Grazia, *Machiavelli in Hell* (Princeton, N.J.: Princeton University Press, 1989), 32–40; C. H. Clough, *Machiavelli Researches* (Naples: Publicazioni della Sezione romanza dell'Istituto universitario orientale, 1967), 33.

2.   John H. Langbein, *Torture and the Law of Proof* (Chicago: University of Chicago Press, 1977).

3.   E.g., Vettori to Machiavelli, 23 November 1513; Machiavelli to Vettori, 19 December 1513; Francesco Guicciardini to Machiavelli, 17 May 1521: Niccolò Machiavelli, *Lettere*, ed. F. Gaeta (Milan: Feltrinelli, 1961) [*Opere*, vol. 6], 298, 308–9, 401–2.

4.   Elizabeth L. Eisenstein, *The Printing Revolution in Early Modern Europe* (Cambridge: Cambridge University Press, 1983).

5.   S. Bertelli, "Noterelle Machiavelliane," *Rivista storica italiana* 73 (1961), 544–53. In his lifetime, Machiavelli published an amusing play, *Mandragola*, and a poem, the *Decennale primo*, but only one book in which he displayed his

professional skills: *The Art of War* (1521). Copies of his *The Prince* circulated in manuscript, and it was published only after his death.

6. Carlo M. Cipolla, *European Culture and Overseas Expansion* (Harmondsworth: Penguin Books, 1970), 38.

7. Arnaldo Momigliano, "Polybius' Reappearance in Western Europe," [1973] in his *Sesto contributo alla storia degli studi classici e del mondo antico* (2 vols., Rome: Edizioni di storia e letteratura, 1980), 103–23, at 114–15.

8. Nicolai Rubinstein, "Machiavelli and the World of Florentine Politics," in *Studies on Machiavelli*, ed. M. P. Gilmore (Florence: Sansoni, 1972), 5–28, at 7. Ridolfi, however, does not find the evidence convincing: *Life of Niccolò Machiavelli*, 257, n. 4.

9. Machiavelli to Guicciardini, 3 January 1526: "Always, as far back as I can remember, war has either been going on or has been talked about. . . ." *Opere*, 6:451; for a translation, see Niccolò Machiavelli, *The Chief Works and Others*, ed. and trans. Allan Gilbert (3 vols., Durham, N.C.: Duke University Press, 1965), 2:991.

10. Quoted in Garrett Mattingly, *Renaissance Diplomacy* [1955] (Harmondsworth: Penguin Books, 1965), 111.

11. Machiavelli, *Chief Works*, 2:895–97. This letter was once thought to have been written to Soderini shortly after his fall, but is now known to have been written as early as 1506, not to Piero Soderini but to his nephew, Giovan Battista: R. Ridolfi and P. Ghiglieri, "I *ghiribizzi* al Soderini," *La bibliofilia* 72 (1970), 53–74; M. Martelli, " 'I ghiribizzi' a Giovan Battista Soderini," *Rinascimento* 9 (1969), 147–80.

12. Carlo Dionisotti, "Machiavelli, Cesare Borgia e don Micheletto" [1967], in his *Machiavellerie* (Turin: Einaudi, 1980), 3–59. See Roslyn Pesman Cooper, "Machiavelli, Francesco Soderini and Don Michelotto," *Nuova rivista storica* 66 (1982), 342–57, and Robert Black, "Machiavelli, Servant of the Florentine Republic," in *Machiavelli and Republicanism*, ed. G. Bock, Q. Skinner, and M. Viroli (Cambridge: Cambridge University Press, 1990), 71–99.

13. Felix Gilbert, "Machiavelli: the Renaissance of the Art of War," in *Makers of Modern Strategy: From Machiavelli to the Nuclear Age*, ed. P. Paret (Princeton, N.J.: Princeton University Press, 1986), 11–31.

14. *Discourses*, bk. 3, ch. 3.

15. Machiavelli, *Chief Works*, 3:1463.

16. John M. Najemy, "The Controversy Surrounding Machiavelli's Service to the Republic," in *Machiavelli and Republicanism*, ed. Bock et al., 101–17.

17. Note Machiavelli's insistence in 1520 that Florence needed to have someone in charge: Niccolò Machiavelli, *Arte della guerra e scritti politici minori*, ed. S. Bertelli (Milan: Feltrinelli, 1961) [*Opere*, vol. 2], 265; *Chief Works*, 1:105; and the views attributed to him in 1512 by Giovanni Folchi: J. N. Stephens and H. C. Butters, "New Light on Machiavelli," *English Historical Review* 97 (1982), 54–69, at 67.

18. E.g., Q. Skinner, *Machiavelli* (Oxford: Oxford University Press, 1981), 24; idem, "Introduction" to N. Machiavelli, *The Prince*, ed. Q. Skinner and R. Price (Cambridge: Cambridge University Press, 1988), ix–xxiv, at xii–xiii.

19. The arguments involved are important, even if, in my view, wrong. See Garrett Mattingly, "Machiavelli's *Prince*: Political Science or Political Satire?" *American Scholar* 27 (1958), 482–91; Mary G. Dietz, "Trapping the Prince: Machiavelli and the Politics of Deception," *American Political Science Review* 80 (1986), 777–99; Stephen M. Fallon, "Hunting the Fox: Equivocation and Authorial Duplicity in *The Prince*," *PMLA* 107 (1992), 1181–95. On Machiavelli's attitude to deception, Wayne Rebhorn, *Foxes and Lions: Machiavelli's Confidence Men* (Ithaca: Cornell University Press, 1988). One of the merits of the Mattingly approach is that it is an interpretation that would have amused Machiavelli. Moreover, it would seem reasonable to argue that Machiavelli did not intend intelligent readers to take everything he says in *The Prince* literally: One is bound to suspect the religious language of the last chapter is, at least in part, a joke.

20. Clough, *Machiavelli Researches*, 27–79. Much of the evidence supporting this view is brought to the fore in Hans Baron's essays (below, n. 48), but he seems to have been unwilling to commit himself to it: See his review of Clough in *English Historical Review* 84 (1969), 579–82. For criticism of an earlier version of Clough's argument, see Gennaro Sasso, "Filosofia o 'scopo pratico' nel *Principe*?" in his *Studi su Machiavelli* (Naples: Morano, 1967), 81–110. For a differing view, which I find unconvincing, J. N. Stephens, "Machiavelli's *Prince* and the Florentine Revolution of 1512," *Italian Studies* 41 (1986), 45–61.

21. For the exception, see below, p. 65. Petrucci, like the Medici, was trying to hold on to power in a city used to political freedom.

22. J. J. Marchand, *Niccolò Machiavelli, i primi scritti politici (1499–1512)* (Padua: Antenore, 1975), 533–35; *Chief Works*, 1:101–15; *Opere*, 2:261–77.

23. Machiavelli, *Opere*, 6:331; *Chief Works*, 2:926–27. The date of this letter is uncertain. Redating it to September, as proposed in John M. Najemy, *Between Friends* (Princeton, N.J.: Princeton University Press, 1993), 277–78, would not significantly affect the argument.

24. J.G.A. Pocock, *The Machiavellian Moment: Florentine Political Thought and the Atlantic Republican Tradition* (Princeton, N.J.: Princeton University Press, 1975), 160.

25. See below, p. 4. Also Machiavelli to Vettori, 16 April 1513: *Opere*, 6:244; *Chief Works*, 2:902. Machiavelli expected Giuliano to assist him because they had an association that predated the fall of the Medici in 1494: M. Martelli, "Preistoria (medicea) di Machiavelli," *Studi di filologia italiana* 29 (1971), 377–405.

26. Vettori to Machiavelli, 24 December 1513: *Opere*, 6:312.

27. See the half dozen letters between Machiavelli and Vettori in December 1514: *Opere*, 6:348–70.

28. As Machiavelli himself feared: Second letter to Vettori, 20 December 1514: *Opere*, 6:366; *Chief Works*, 2:958.

29. See Vettori to Machiavelli, 12 July 1513: *Opere*, 6:267–70. In my view, this was in all probability the immediate inspiration of *The Prince*. Also Vettori to Machiavelli, 16 May 1514 (idem, 336–37).

30. Machiavelli to Vettori, 31 January 1515: *Opere*, 6:374–75; *Chief Works*, 2:962–63. I am not, I think, persuaded by the intriguing interpretation of the letter proposed by Najemy, *Between Friends*, 333–34. Machiavelli's appointment was vetoed by Cardinal Giulio de' Medici: Hans Baron, "The *Principe* and the Puzzle of the Date of Chapter Twenty-Six," *Journal of Medieval and Renaissance Studies* 21 (1991), 83–102, at 99.

31. As Vettori put it, 12 July 1513: "Non voglio entrare in consideratione quale stato disegni, perché in questo muterà proposito, secondo la occasione." Machiavelli, *Opere*, 6:268–69.

32. Baron, "The *Principe* and the Puzzle of the Date of Chapter Twenty-Six." For a discussion of Mario Martelli's view that chapter twenty-six was written in 1518 ("Da Poliziano a Machiavelli: sull'epigramma *dell'occasione* e sull'occasione," *Interpres* 2 (1979), 230–54), see Najemy, *Between Friends*, 177–85. I am persuaded by several of his arguments against Martelli, but by none of those against Baron.

33. Hans Baron, "Machiavelli the Republican Citizen and Author of *The Prince*" [1961], in his *In Search of Florentine Civic Humanism* (2 vols., Princeton, N.J.: Princeton University Press, 1988), 2:101–51, at 130–31.

34. Cf. Vettori to Machiavelli, 12 July 1513: *Opere*, 6:268.

35. R. Pesman Cooper, "Machiavelli, Pier Soderini and *Il Principe*," in *Altro Polo: A Volume of Italian Renaissance Studies*, ed. C. Condren and R. Pesman Cooper (Sydney: Fredrick May Foundation, University of Sydney, 1982), 119–44.

36. Cf. Machiavelli to Vettori, 31 January 1515: *Opere*, 6:375; *Chief Works*, 2:962.

37. *Discourses*, bk. 1, ch. 26.

38. Victoria Kahn, "*Virtù* and the example of Agathocles in Machiavelli's *Prince*," [1986] in *Machiavelli and the Discourse of Literature*, ed. A. R. Ascoli and V. Kahn (Ithaca: Cornell University Press, 1993), 195–217.

39. *Discourses*, bk. 1, ch. 10.

40. Machiavelli, *Opere*, 2:268; *Chief Works*, 1:107.

41. E.g., *Discourses*, bk. 3, ch. 40.

42. Cf. *Discourses*, bk. 1, ch. 9; bk. 3, ch. 41. In chapter eighteen of *The Prince* it is the common man, not Machiavelli, who always approves of success.

43. The first sentence of chapter eight of *The Prince* is sometimes taken to be a reference to the *Discourses* (e.g., surprisingly, Baron, "Machiavelli: Citizen and Author," 112), though it seems evident to me it is a reference to chapter nine.

44. J. H. Whitfield, *Machiavelli* (Oxford: Blackwell, 1947).

45. John Plamenatz, "In Search of Machiavellian *virtù*," in *The Political Calculus*, ed. A. Parel (Toronto: University of Toronto Press, 1972), 157–78.

46. Federico Chabod, *Machiavelli and the Renaissance* (New York: Harper and Row, 1965).

47. Mark Hulliung, *Citizen Machiavelli* (Princeton, N.J.: Princeton University Press, 1983).

48. Hans Baron, "The *Principe* and the Puzzle of the Date of the *Discorsi*," *Bibliothèque d'Humanisme et Renaissance* 18 (1956), 405–28; idem, "Machiavelli the Republican Citizen and Author of *The Prince*"; idem, "The *Principe* and the Puzzle of the Date of Chapter Twenty-Six."

49. There has been a good deal of discussion about when the *Discourses* were written and how Machiavelli's project may have changed over time. The most influential account is Felix Gilbert, "The Composition and Structure of Machiavelli's *Discorsi*" [1953], in his *History: Choice and Commitment* (Cambridge, Mass.: Harvard University Press, 1977), 115–33; most recent is F. Bausi, *I "Discorsi" di Niccolò Machiavelli. Genesi e strutture* (Florence: Sansoni, 1985).

50. In *Discourses*, bk. 1, ch. 55, Machiavelli insists it would be impossible to establish a republic in either Naples or the Romagna.

51. I owe this point to R. F. Tannenbaum.

52. Machiavelli, *Chief Works*, 2:1015. Also on thrush-hunting, see the letter to Vettori of 25 February 1514: *Opere*, 6:327–30; *Chief Works*, 2:938–41.

53. Machiavelli, *Opere*, 6:239; *Chief Works*, 2:900.

54. *Discourses*, bk. 1, ch. 10.

55. See Machiavelli's correspondence between April and November 1520: *Opere*, 6:386–97.

56. Louis Green, "Machiavelli's *Vita di Castruccio Castracani* and its Lucchese Model," *Italian Studies* 42 (1987), 37–55.

57. Cf. below pp. 71–72.

58. Niccolò Machiavelli, *Istorie fiorentine*, ed. F. Gaeta (Milan: Feltrinelli, 1962) [*Opere*, vol. 7], 36; *Chief Works*, 2:555.

59. Felix Gilbert, "Machiavelli's *Istorie fiorentine*," in his *History: Choice and Commitment*, 135–53, at 142–43.

60. E.g., Leo Strauss, *Thoughts on Machiavelli* (Glencoe, Ill.: The Free Press, 1958); Harvey C. Mansfield, *Machiavelli's New Modes and Orders: A Study of the "Discourses on Livy"* (Ithaca: Cornell University Press, 1979).

61. Russell Price, "Self-Love, 'Egoism' and *ambizione* in Machiavelli's Thought," *History of Political Thought* 9 (1988), 237–61.

62. Maurizio Viroli, "Machiavelli and the Republican Conception of Politics," in his *From Politics to Reason of State* (Cambridge: Cambridge University Press, 1992), 126–77. It would suit my own argument to stress, as Viroli does, "the

absence of any *politico*-rooted word in *The Prince*" (128), but it would be wrong to make too much of this as, for Machiavelli, *civile* is a synonym for *politico*.

63. Marcia L. Colish, "Cicero's *De officiis* and Machiavelli's *Prince*," *Sixteenth Century Journal* 9 (1978), 81–93.

64. John Freccero, "Medusa and the Madonna of Forlì: Political Sexuality in Machiavelli," in *Machiavelli and the Discourse of Literature*, ed. Ascoli and Kahn, 161–78, at 163–64.

65. A mistake, I should say, that the standard discussions do not make. See Hannah Pitkin, *Fortune is a Woman* (Berkeley, Cal.: University of California Press, 1984), and Wendy Brown, *Manhood and Politics* (Totowa, N.J.: Rowman and Littlefield, 1988), 71–123. On Renaissance views on gender, Ian Maclean, *The Renaissance Notion of Woman* (Cambridge: Cambridge University Press, 1980) and Constance Jordan, *Renaissance Feminism* (Ithaca: Cornell University Press, 1990) are helpful.

66. Giulio Ferroni, " 'Transformation' and 'Adaptation' in Machiavelli's *Mandragola*" [1972], in *Machiavelli and the Discourse of Literature*, ed. Ascoli and Kahn, 81–116, at 99.

67. Ronald L. Martinez, "Benefit of Absence: Machiavellian Valediction in *Clizia*," in *Machiavelli and the Discourse of Literature*, ed. Ascoli and Kahn, 117–44, at 139.

68. Freccero, "Medusa and the Madonna." Machiavelli even uses for the countess's genital organs a term usually used only for men (175–76).

69. Sheldon S. Wolin, *Politics and Vision* (Boston: Little, Brown, 1960), 220–24.

70. For fine analyses of Machiavelli's deliberate cultivation of contrasting attitudes, styles, and tones of voice see Ferroni, " 'Transformation' and 'Adaptation'," and idem, "Le 'cose vane' nelle *Lettere* di Machiavelli," *La rassegna della letteratura italiana* 76 (1972), 215–64.

71. Nicola Matteucci: "Il *vivere libero* . . . è usato esclusivamente per le repubbliche," "Machiavelli Politologo," in *Studies on Machiavelli*, ed. Gilmore, 209–48, at 222. Contrast Baron, "Machiavelli: Citizen and Author," 114. A helpful context for Machiavelli's views on liberty is provided by Patricia J. Osmond, "Sallust and Machiavelli: From Civic Humanism to Political Prudence," *Journal of Medieval and Renaissance Studies* 23 (1993), 407–38.

72. Quentin Skinner, "The Republican Ideal of Political Liberty," in *Machiavelli and Republicanism*, ed. Bock et al., 293–309, at 301–6, seems to me to provide an idealistic reading of Machiavelli, employing phrases such as "willingly to serve the common good" and "devote ourselves wholeheartedly to a life of public service." Compare his earlier discussion of the same question, *Machiavelli*, 64–67: "Although motivated entirely by their selfish interests, the factions will thus be guided, as if by an invisible hand, to promote the public interest. . . ."

73. John M. Najemy, "*Arti* and *ordini* in Machiavelli's *Istorie fiorentine*," in *Essays Presented to Myron Gilmore*, ed. S. Bertelli and G. Ramakus (Florence:

La nuova italia, 1978), 161–91. Mark Phillips, "Barefoot Boy Makes Good: A Study of Machiavelli's Historiography," *Speculum* 59 (1984), 585–605.

74. See Gisela Bock, "Civil Discord in Machiavelli's *Istorie fiorentine*" in *Machiavelli and Republicanism*, ed. Bock et al., 181–202.

75. Machiavelli does consider the possibility of a federation of cities, such as that of the ancient Tuscans, but the problem is only postponed: The freedom of such a federation depends on its conquering its neighbors.

76. See the excellent translation of the tercets "On Ambition" in de Grazia, *Machiavelli in Hell*, 165–66.

77. I am grateful to Matthew Carrington for discussing this question with me.

78. Michael Baxandall, *Painting and Experience in Fifteenth-Century Italy* (Oxford: Oxford University Press, 1972), 14–23.

79. Ludwig Heydenreich, "The Military Architect," in *Leonardo the Inventor*, ed. L. W. Heydenreich, B. Dibner, L. Reti (New York: McGraw-Hill, 1980), 11–71.

80. Machiavelli, *Opere*, 7:303–4; *Chief Works*, 3:1214. In *Discourses* bk. 1, ch. 1 he also mentions Deinocrates, a civil engineer like Brunelleschi, Leonardo, and Machiavelli himself.

81. Characteristically, in chapter fourteen of *The Prince*, he claims that Scipio imitated Cyrus, not that those writing about Scipio have imitated Xenophon.

82. Quentin Skinner, "Thomas Hobbes: Rhetoric and the Construction of Morality," *Proceedings of the British Academy* 76 (1990), 1–61, at 23–25.

83. Cf. Machiavelli, *Opere*, 2:518; *Chief Works*, 2:724.

84. Salvatore di Maria, "La struttura dialogica nel *Principe* di Machiavelli," *MLN* 99 (1984), 65–79.

85. Quentin Skinner, *The Foundations of Modern Political Thought* (2 vols., Cambridge: Cambridge University Press, 1978), 1:129–31.

86. A. R. Ascoli and V. Kahn, "Introduction" to *Machiavelli and the Discourse of Literature*, ed. Ascoli and Kahn, 1–15.

87. Robert Hariman, "Composing Modernity in Machiavelli's Prince" [1989], in *Renaissance Essays II*, ed. W. J. Connell (Rochester, N.Y.: University of Rochester Press, 1993), 224–50.

88. E.g., Eugene M. Garver, "Machiavelli's *The Prince*: A Neglected Rhetorical Classic," *Philosophy and Rhetoric* 13 (1980), 99–120; Michael McCanles, *The Discourse of "Il principe"* (Malibu: Undena, 1983); Thomas M. Greene, "The End of Discourse in Machiavelli's *Prince*," *Yale French Studies* 67 (1984), 57–71; Barbara Spackman, "Machiavelli and Maxims," *Yale French Studies* 77 (1990), 137–55; idem, "Politics on the Warpath: Machiavelli's *Art of War*," in *Machiavelli and the Discourse of Literature*, ed. Ascoli and Kahn, 179–93; Jeffrey T. Schnapp, "Machiavellian Foundlings: Castruccio Castracani and the Aphorism," *Renaissance Quarterly* 45 (1992), 653–76.

89. Machiavelli's own interest in diagrams is relevant: J. R. Hale, "A Humanistic Visual Aid. The Military Diagram in the Renaissance," *Renaissance Studies*

2 (1988), 281–98, stresses the novelty of the diagrams accompanying the *Art of War.*

90. John D. Lyons, "Machiavelli: Example and Origin," in his *Exemplum: the Rhetoric of Example in Early Modern France and Italy* (Princeton, N.J.: Princeton University Press, 1989), 35–71; Timothy Hampton, *Writing from History: The Rhetoric of Exemplarity in Renaissance Literature* (Ithaca, N.Y.: Cornell University Press, 1990), 62–79.

91. Francesco Guicciardini, *Ricordi*, ed. R. Spongano (Florence: Sansoni, 1951), 110; idem, *Maxims and Reflections of a Renaissance Statesman* (New York: Harper and Row, 1965), 69.

92. Francis Bacon, *Works*, ed. J. Spedding, R. L. Ellis, D. D. Heath (15 vols., Cambridge, Mass.: Riverside Press, 1863), 3:31; 6:327.

93. Shakespeare, *3 Henry 6*, 3.02.193; *Merry Wives of Windsor*, 3.01.101.

94. Nietzsche defined what a good translation would be like when he wrote: "But how could the German language, even in the prose of a Lessing, imitate the tempo of Machiavelli, who in his *Principe* lets us breathe the subtle dry air of Florence and cannot help presenting the most serious affairs in a boisterous *allegrissimo:* not perhaps without a malicious artist's sense of the contrast he is risking—thoughts protracted, difficult, hard, dangerous and the tempo of the gallop and the most wanton good humour." Friedrich Nietzsche, *Beyond Good and Evil*, trans. R. J. Hollingdale (Harmondsworth: Penguin Books, 1973), 41–42.

FURTHER READING

The standard edition of Machiavelli's *The Prince* and *Discourses* is that edited by S. Bertelli as vol. 1 of Niccolò Machiavelli, *Opere* ed. S. Bertelli and F. Gaeta (8 vols., Milan: Feltrinelli, 1960–65). I have followed this edition throughout, with the single exception of the penultimate sentence of chapter eighteen of *The Prince*, where I have followed the alternate reading of the Gotha manuscript. Although for convenience I have cited the edition of the letters in the same series, a better edition now is that edited by F. Gaeta (Turin: UTET, 1984). The most extensive selection of Machiavelli's works in English is *Chief Works, and Others*, ed. and trans. A. Gilbert (3 vols., Durham, N.C.: Duke University Press, 1965).

The best short introduction to Machiavelli's thought is Quentin Skinner, *Machiavelli* (Oxford: Oxford University Press, 1981). Two useful collections of articles are *Machiavelli and Republicanism*, ed. G. Bock, Q. Skinner and M. Viroli (Cambridge: Cambridge University Press, 1990) and *Machiavelli and the Discourse of Literature*, ed. A. R. Ascoli and V. Kahn (Ithaca: Cornell University Press, 1993). A valuable study of Machiavelli's life is Sebastian de Grazia, *Machiavelli in Hell* (Princeton, N.J.: Princeton University Press, 1989), although his account of Machiavelli's attitude to Christianity is unconvincing: Compare Alberto Tenenti, "La religione di Machiavelli," *Studi storici* 10 (1969), 709–48.

Two articles on Machiavelli are of outstanding importance: Hans Baron, "Machiavelli the Republican Citizen and Author of *The Prince*" [1961], rev. ed. in H. Baron, *In Search of Florentine Civic Humanism* (2 vols., Princeton, N.J.: Princeton University Press, 1988), 2:101–51, and Isaiah Berlin, "The Originality of Machiavelli," in *Studies on Machiavelli*, ed. M. P. Gilmore (Florence: Sansoni, 1972), 149–206. For a close reading of a famous text one may single out the discussion of the letter to Vettori of 10 December 1513 in John M. Najemy, "Machiavelli and Geta: Men of Letters," *Machiavelli and the Discourse of Literature*, ed. Ascoli and Kahn, 53–79.

Six essays on Machiavelli's vocabulary provide introductions to the key terms: Russell Price, "The Senses *of virtù* in Machiavelli," *European Studies Review* 3 (1973), 315–45; J. H. Hexter, "*Il principe* and *lo stato*" [1957], in *The Vision of Politics on the Eve of the Reformation* (London:

Allen Lane, 1973), 150–78; J. H. Whitfield, "On Machiavelli's Use of *ordini*" [1955], in his *Discourses on Machiavelli* (Cambridge: W. Heffer and Sons, 1969), 141–62, and "The Politics of Machiavelli," idem, 163–79; M. Colish, "The Idea of Liberty in Machiavelli" [1971], in *Renaissance Essays II*, ed. W. J. Connell (Rochester, N.Y.: University of Rochester Press, 1993), 180–207; Hannah Pitkin, "Fortune," in her *Fortune is a Woman* (Berkeley, Cal.: University of California Press, 1984), chapter six.

A recent study of the wider context of Machiavelli's political thought is Maurizio Viroli, *From Politics to Reason of State* (Cambridge: Cambridge University Press, 1992). For Florentine politics in Machiavelli's lifetime, H. C. Butters, *Governors and Government in Early Sixteenth-Century Florence, 1502–1519* (Oxford: Clarendon Press, 1985). For a survey of Machiavelli's influence, see Felix Gilbert, "Machiavellism" [1973], in his *History: Choice and Commitment* (Cambridge, Mass.: Harvard University Press, 1977), 155–76. Finally, the vast body of scholarship on Machiavelli that appeared between 1935 and 1985 is surveyed in Silvia R. Fiore, *Niccolò Machiavelli: An Annotated Bibliography of Modern Criticism and Scholarship* (Westport, Conn.: Greenwood, 1990).

Acknowledgments: I would like to thank William Connell, Alan Houston, Donald Kelley, John Najemy, Quentin Skinner, Robert Tannenbaum, Maurizio Viroli, and Blair Worden for their comments on a draft of the Introduction, and Jack Hexter and Paul Spade for their comments on sections of the translation. Kindness takes many forms, and criticizing a colleague's sloppy thinking and bad grammar is one of them. Matthew Carrington, John Kavcic, and Lesley Sutton have taught me more than I have taught them. The errors that remain are mine alone.

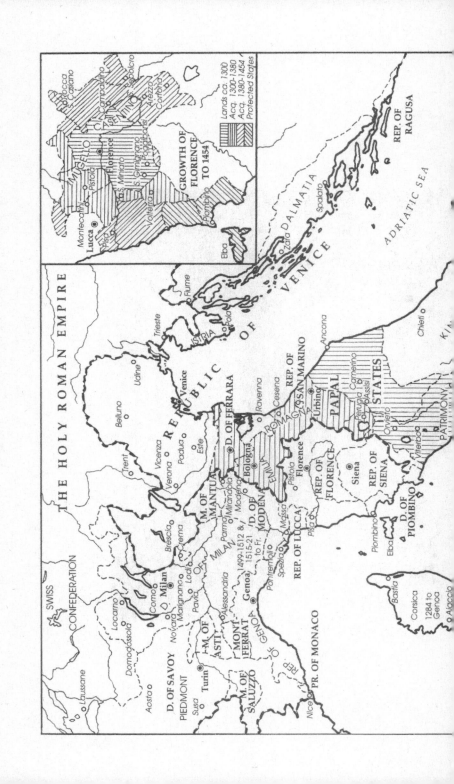

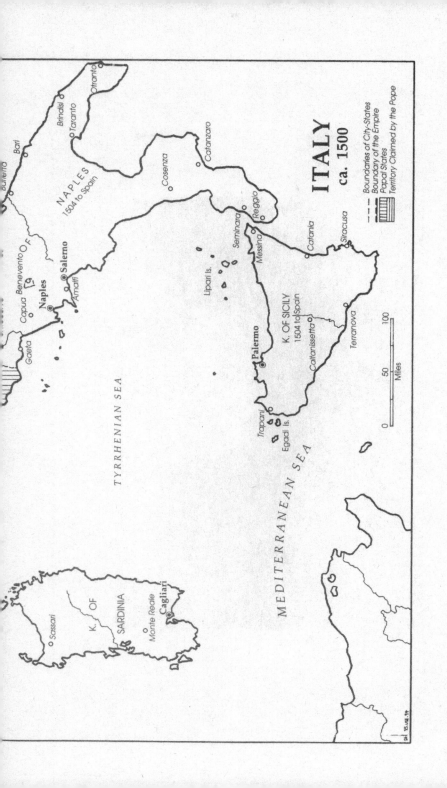

ITALY
ca. 1500

Boundaries of City-States
Boundary of the Empire
Papal States
Territory Claimed by the Pope

NAPLES
1504 to Spain

K. OF SICILY
1504 to Spain

K. OF
SARDINIA

TYRRHENIAN SEA

MEDITERRANEAN SEA

Otranto
Brindisi
Bari
Taranto
Catanzaro
Cosenza
Reggio
Seminara
Catania
Siracusa
Messina
Lipari Is.
Benevento
Capua
Salerno
Amalfi
Naples
Gaeta
Palermo
Caltanissetta
Teranova
Trapani
Egadi Is.
Sassari
Monte Reale
Cagliari

0   50   100
Miles

Letter to Francesco Vettori

To His Excellency the Florentine Ambassador to his Holiness the Pope, and my benefactor, Francesco Vettori, in Rome.

Your Excellency. "Favors from on high are always timely, never late."[1] I say this because I had begun to think I had, if not lost, then mislaid your goodwill, for you had allowed so long to go by without writing to me, and I was in some uncertainty as to what the reason could be. All the explanations I could think of seemed to me worthless, except for the possibility that occurred to me, that you might have stopped writing to me because someone had written to tell you I was not taking proper care of your letters to me; but I knew that I had not been responsible for their being shown to anyone else, with the exception of Filippo and Paolo.[2]

Anyway, I have now received your most recent letter of the 23rd of last month. I was delighted to learn you are fulfilling your official responsibilities without fussing and flapping. I encourage you to carry on like this, for anyone who sacrifices his own convenience in order to make others happy is bound to inconvenience himself, but can't be sure of receiving any thanks for it. And since fortune wants to control everything, she evidently wants to be left a free hand; meanwhile we should keep our own counsel and not get in her way, and wait until she allows human beings to have a say in the course of events. That will be the time for you to work harder, and keep a closer eye on events, and for me to leave my country house and say: "Here I am!"

Since I want to repay your kind gesture, I have no alternative but to describe to you in this letter of mine how I live my life. If you decide you'd like to swap my life for yours, I'll be happy to make a deal.

I am still in my country house: Since my recent difficulties began I have not been, adding them all together, more than twenty days in Florence. Until recently I have been setting bird snares with my own hands. I've been getting up before dawn, making the bird-lime, and setting out with a bundle of cages on my back, so I look like Geta

---

1. Petrarch, *Trionfo della Divinità*, 13.

2. Paolo is Francesco Vettori's brother; Filippo Casavecchia was a close mutual friend.

when he comes back from the harbor laden down with Amphitryo's books.[3] I always caught at least two thrushes, but never more than six. This is how I spent September;[4] since then I am sorry to say I have had to give up my rather nasty and peculiar hobby, so I will describe the life I lead now.

I get up in the morning at daybreak and go to a wood of mine where I am having some timber felled. I stay there two hours to check on the work done during the preceding day and to chat to the woodcutters, who are always involved in some conflict, either among themselves or with the neighbors. I could tell you a thousand fine stories about my dealings over this wood, both with Frosino da Panzano and with others who wanted some of the timber. Frosino in particular had them supply some cords without mentioning it to me, and when I asked for payment he wanted to knock off ten lire he said I had owed him for four years, ever since he beat me at cards at Antonio Guicciardini's. I began to cut up rough; I threatened to charge with theft the wagon driver who had fetched the wood. However, Giovanni Machiavelli intervened, and got us to settle our differences. Batista Guicciardini, Filippo Gino-ri, Tommaso del Bene, and a number of other citizens each bought a cord from me when the cold winds were blowing. I made promises to all of them, and supplied one to Tommaso. But in Florence it turned out to be only half a cord, because there were he, his wife, his servants, and his sons to stack it: They looked like Gabburra on a Thursday when, assisted by his workmen, he slaughters an ox.[5] Then, realizing I wasn't the one who was getting a good deal, I told the others I had run out of wood. They've all complained bitterly about it; especially Battista, who thinks this is as bad as anything else that has happened as a result of the battle of Prato.[6]

When I leave the wood I go to a spring, and from there to check my bird-nets. I carry a book with me: Dante, or Petrarch, or one of the minor poets, perhaps Tibullus, Ovid, or someone like that. I read about their infatuations and their love affairs, reminisce about my own,

---

3.   See John M. Najemy, "Machiavelli and Geta: Men of Letters," in *Machiavelli and the Discourse of Literature,* ed. Ascoli and Kahn, 53–79.

4.   Ridolfi points out that Machiavelli must have meant to write November, since this is the month for thrush hunting.

5.   In other words, just as the butcher turns a large ox into a small pile of steaks, so Tommaso and his family turned a large pile of wood into a small, neat, and cheap stack.

6.   The Battle of Prato (1512) had led to the downfall of Soderini, the return of the Medici, and Machiavelli's own dismissal from office.

and enjoy my reveries for a while. Then I set out on the road to the inn. I chat to those who pass by, asking them for news about the places they come from. I pick up bits and pieces of information, and study the differing tastes and various preoccupations of mankind. It's lunchtime before I know it. I sit down with my family to eat such food as I can grow on my wretched farm or pay for with the income from my tiny inheritance. Once I have eaten I go back to the inn. The landlord will be there, and, usually, the butcher, the miller, and a couple of kiln owners. With them I muck about all day, playing card games. We get into endless arguments and are constantly calling each other names. Usually we only wager a quarter, and yet you could hear us shouting if you were in San Casciano. So, in the company of these bumpkins, I keep my brain from turning moldy, and put up with the hostility fate has shown me. I am happy for fate to see to what depths I have sunk, for I want to know if she will be ashamed of herself for what she has done.

When evening comes, I go back home, and go to my study. On the threshold I take off my work clothes, covered in mud and filth, and put on the clothes an ambassador would wear. Decently dressed, I enter the ancient courts of rulers who have long since died. There I am warmly welcomed, and I feed on the only food I find nourishing, and was born to savor. I am not ashamed to talk to them, and to ask them to explain their actions. And they, out of kindness, answer me. Four hours go by without my feeling any anxiety. I forget every worry. I am no longer afraid of poverty, or frightened of death. I live entirely through them.

And because Dante says there is no point in studying unless you remember what you have learned, I have made notes of what seem to me the most important things I have learned in my dialogue with the dead, and written a little book *On princedoms*[7] in which I go as deeply as I can into the questions relevant to my subject. I discuss what a principality is, how many types of principality there are, how one acquires them, how one holds onto them, why one loses them. And if any of my little productions have ever pleased you, then this one ought not to displease you; and a ruler, especially a new ruler, ought to be delighted by it. Consequently, I have addressed it to His Highness Giuliano.[8] Filippo Casavecchia has seen it; he can give you a preliminary report, both on the text, and on the discussions I have had with him: though I am still adding to the text and polishing it.

---

7. *De principatibus*, Machiavelli calls it.

8. Giuliano de' Medici, the senior member of the Medici family after his brother, Pope Leo X.

You may well wish, Your Excellency, that I should give up this life, and come and enjoy yours with you. I will do so if I can; what holds me back at the moment is some business that won't take me more than six weeks to finish. Though I am a bit concerned the Soderini family is there,[9] and I will be obliged, if I come, to visit them and socialize with them. My concern is that I might intend my return journey to end at my own house, but find myself instead dismounting at the prison gates. For although this government is well established and solidly based, still it is new, and consequently suspicious, nor is there a shortage of clever fellows who, in order to get a reputation like Pagolo Bertini's, would put me in prison, and leave me to worry about how to get out. I beg you to persuade me this fear is irrational, and then I will make every effort to come and visit you before six weeks are up.

I have discussed my little book with Filippo, asking him whether it was a good idea to present it or not; and if I ought to present it, then whether I should deliver it in person, or whether I should send it through you. My concern is that if I do not deliver it in person Giuliano may not read it; even worse, that chap Ardinghelli[10] may claim the credit for my latest effort. In favor of presenting it is the fact that the wolf is at the door, for my funds are running down, and I cannot continue like this much longer without becoming so poor I lose face. In any case, I would like their lordships, the Medici, to start putting me to use, even if they only assign me some menial task, for if, once I was in their employment, I did not win their favor, I would have only myself to blame. As for my book, if they were to read it, they would see the fifteen years I have spent studying statecraft have not been wasted: I haven't been asleep at my desk or playing cards. Anyone should be keen to employ someone who has had plenty of experience and has learned from the mistakes he made at his previous employers' expense. As for my integrity, nobody should question it: For I have always kept my word, and I am not going to start breaking it now. Someone who has been honest and true for forty-three years, as I have been, isn't going to be able to change character. And that I am honest and true is evident from my poverty.

So: I would like you to write to me again and let me have your opinion on this matter. I give you my regards. Best wishes.

Niccolò Machiavegli in Florence
10 December 1513.

9.   Piero and his brother Cardinal Francesco were in Rome.
10.   Secretary to Pope Leo X.

THE PRINCE[1]

Niccolò Machiavelli to His Magnificence Lorenzo de' Medici[2]

Those who wish to acquire favor with a ruler most often approach him
with those among their possessions that are most valuable in their eyes,
or that they are confident will give him pleasure. So rulers are often
given horses, armor, cloth of gold, precious stones, and similar orna-
ments that are thought worthy of their social eminence. Since I want
to offer myself to your Magnificence, along with something that will
symbolize my desire to give you obedient service, I have found nothing
among my possessions I value more, or would put a higher price upon,
than an understanding of the deeds of great men, acquired through a
lengthy experience of contemporary politics and through an uninter-
rupted study of the classics. Since I have long thought about and studied
the question of what makes for greatness, and have now summarized
my conclusions on the subject in a little book, it is this I send your
Magnificence.

And although I recognize this book is unworthy to be given to
Yourself, yet I trust that out of kindness you will accept it, taking
account of the fact there is no greater gift I can present to you than
the opportunity to understand, after a few hours of reading, everything
I have learned over the course of so many years, and have undergone
so many discomforts and dangers to discover. I have not ornamented
this book with rhetorical turns of phrase, or stuffed it with pretentious
and magnificent words, or made use of allurements and embellishments
that are irrelevant to my purpose, as many authors do. For my intention
has been that my book should be without pretensions, and should rely

1. For an edition of *The Prince* which provides extensive notes and apparatus
see *Il Principe*, ed. L. Arthur Burd (Oxford: Clarendon Press, 1891, repr.
1968): The text is in Italian, but the notes and apparatus are in English.
2. Lorenzo (1492–1519) was the grandson of Lorenzo the Magnificent
(1449–92), son of Piero de' Medici (1471–1503, ruler of Florence, 1492–94),
and nephew of Giovanni de' Medici (1475–1521), who became Pope Leo X
in 1513. Lorenzo became Duke of Urbino in 1516. We know Machiavelli
originally intended to give *The Prince* to Lorenzo's uncle and Leo's brother,
Giuliano de' Medici (1479–1516).

entirely on the variety of the examples and the importance of the subject to win approval.

I hope it will not be thought presumptuous for someone of humble and lowly status to dare to discuss the behavior of rulers and to make recommendations regarding policy. Just as those who paint landscapes set up their easels down in the valley in order to portray the nature of the mountains and the peaks, and climb up into the mountains in order to draw the valleys, similarly in order to properly understand the behavior of the lower classes one needs to be a ruler, and in order to properly understand the behavior of rulers one needs to be a member of the lower classes.

I therefore beg your Magnificence to accept this little gift in the spirit in which it is sent. If you read it carefully and think over what it contains, you will recognize it is an expression of my dearest wish, which is that you achieve the greatness your good fortune and your other fine qualities seem to hold out to you. And if your Magnificence, high up at the summit as you are, should occasionally glance down into these deep valleys, you will see I have to put up with the unrelenting malevolence of undeserved ill fortune.

Chapter One: How many types of principality are there? And how are they acquired?

All states, all forms of government that have had and continue to have authority over men, have been and are either republics or principalities. And principalities are either hereditary, when their rulers' ancestors have long been their rulers, or they are new. And if they are new, they are either entirely new, as was Milan for Francesco Sforza,[3] or they are like limbs added on to the hereditary state of the ruler who acquires them, as the kingdom of Naples has been added on to the kingdom of Spain.[4] Those dominions that are acquired by a ruler are either used to living under the rule of one man, or accustomed to being free; and they are either acquired with soldiers belonging to others, or with one's own; either through fortune or through strength [*virtù*].

Chapter Two: On hereditary principalities.

I will leave behind me the discussion of republics, for I have discussed them at length elsewhere. I will concern myself only with principalities.

---

3. Sforza acquired Milan in 1450. See below, chapter twelve.
4. Ferdinand the Catholic (1452–1516) acquired Naples in 1504. See below, chapters three and twenty-one.

The different types of principality I have mentioned will be the threads from which I will weave my account. I will debate how these different types of principality should be governed and defended.

I maintain, then, it is much easier to hold on to hereditary states, which are accustomed to being governed by the family that now rules them, than it is to hold on to new acquisitions. All one has to do is preserve the structures established by one's forebears, and play for time if things go badly. For, indeed, an hereditary ruler, if he is of no more than normal resourcefulness, will never lose his state unless some extraordinary and overwhelming force appears that can take it away from him; and even then, the occupier has only to have a minor setback, and the original ruler will get back to power.

Let us take a contemporary Italian example: The Duke of Ferrara was able to resist the assaults of the Venetians in '84, and of Pope Julius in 1510, only because his family was long established as rulers of that state. For a ruler who inherits power has few reasons and less cause to give offense; as a consequence he is more popular; and, as long as he does not have exceptional vices that make him hateful, it is to be expected he will naturally have the goodwill of his people. Because the state has belonged to his family from one generation to another, memories of how they came to power, and motives to overthrow them, have worn away. For every change in government creates grievances that those who wish to bring about further change can exploit.

Chapter Three: On mixed principalities.

New principalities are the ones that present problems. And first of all, if the whole of the principality is not new, but rather a new part has been added on to the old, creating a whole one may term "mixed," instability derives first of all from a natural difficulty that is to be found in all new principalities. The problem is that people willingly change their ruler, believing the change will be for the better; and this belief leads them to take up arms against him. But they are mistaken, and they soon find out in practice they have only made things worse. The reason for this, too, is natural and typical: You always have to give offense to those over whom you acquire power when you become a new ruler, both by imposing troops upon them, and by countless other injuries that follow as necessary consequences of the acquisition of power. Thus, you make enemies of all those to whom you have given offense in acquiring power, and in addition you cannot keep the good-will of those who have put you in power, for you cannot satisfy their aspirations as they thought you would. At the same time you cannot use heavy-handed methods against them, for you are obliged to them. Even if you have an overwhelmingly powerful army, you will have needed the support of the locals to take control of the province. This is why Louis XII of France lost Milan as quickly as he gained it.[5] All that was needed to take it from him the first time were Ludovico's own troops. For those who had opened the gates to him, finding themselves mistaken in their expectations and disappointed in their hopes of future benefit, could not put up with the burdensome rule of a new sovereign.

Of course it is true that, after a ruler has regained power in rebel territories, he is much more likely to hang on to it. For the rebellion gives him an excuse, and he is able to take firmer measures to secure his position, punishing delinquents, checking up on suspects, and taking precautions where needed. So, if the first time the King of France lost Milan all that was needed to throw him out was Duke Ludovico growling on his borders, to throw him out a second time it took the whole world united against him, and the destruction or expulsion from Italy of his armies.[6] We have seen why this was so.

Nevertheless, he lost Milan both times. We have discussed why he was almost bound to lose it the first time; now we must discuss why he managed to lose it the second. What remedies should he have adopted? What can someone in the King of France's position do to hold on to an acquisition more effectively than he did?

Let me start by saying these territories that are newly added on to a state that is already securely in the possession of a ruler are either in the same geographical region as his existing possessions and speak the same language, or they are not. When they are, it is quite straightforward to hold on to them, especially if they are not used to governing themselves. In order to get a secure hold on them one need merely eliminate the surviving members of the family of their previous rulers. In other respects one should keep things as they were, respecting established traditions. If the old territories and the new have similar customs, the new subjects will live quietly. Thus, Burgundy, Brittany, Gascony, and Normandy have for long quietly submitted to France. Although they do not all speak exactly the same language, nevertheless their customs are similar, and they can easily put up with each other.

5.   Louis XII (1462–1515) became King of France in 1498 and invaded Italy in 1499. He gained Milan in February 1500 and lost it in April.

6.   Louis regained Milan after the battle of Novara (April 1500), and lost it again after the Battle of Ravenna (April 1512). Ludovico Sforza (1451–1510), younger son of Francesco Sforza, ruled Milan from 1494 to 1500.

He who acquires neighboring territories in this way, intending to hold on to them, needs to see to two things: First, he must ensure their previous ruler has no heirs; and second, he must not alter their old laws or impose new taxes. If he follows these principles they will quickly become inseparable from his hereditary domains.

But when you acquire territories in a region that has a different language, different customs, and different institutions, then you really have problems, and you need to have great good fortune and great resourcefulness if you are going to hold on to them. One of the best policies, and one of the most effective, is for the new ruler to go and live in his new territories. This will make his grasp on them more secure and more lasting. This is what the Sultan of Turkey has done in Greece.[7] All the other measures he has taken to hold on to that territory would have been worthless if he had not settled there. For if you are on the spot, you can identify difficulties as they arise, and can quickly take appropriate action. If you are at a distance, you only learn of them when they have become serious, and when it is too late to put matters right. Moreover, if you are there in person, the territory will not be plundered by your officials. The subjects can appeal against their exactions to you, their ruler. As a consequence they have more reason to love you, if they behave themselves, and, if they do not, more reason to fear you. Anyone who wants to attack the territory from without will have to think twice, so that, if you live there, you will be unlucky indeed to lose it.

The second excellent policy is to send colonies to settle in one or two places; they will serve to tie your new subjects down. For it is necessary either to do this, or to garrison your new territory with a substantial army. Colonies do not cost much to run. You will have to lay out little or nothing to establish and maintain them. You will only offend those from whom you seize fields and houses to give to your settlers, and they will be only a tiny minority within the territory. Those whom you offend will be scattered and become poor, so they will be unable to do you any harm. All the rest will remain uninjured, and so ought to remain quiet; at the same time they will be afraid to make a false move, for they will have before them the fate of their neighbors as an example of what may happen to them. I conclude such colonies are economical, reliable, and do not give excessive grounds for resistance; those who suffer by their establishment are in no position to resist, being poor and scattered, as I have said. There is a general rule to be noted here: People should either be caressed or crushed. If you

7.   Constantinople became capital of the Turkish empire in 1453.

do them minor damage they will get their revenge; but if you cripple them there is nothing they can do. If you need to injure someone, do it in such a way that you do not have to fear their vengeance.

But if, instead of establishing colonies, you rely on an occupying army, it costs a good deal more, for your army will eat up all your revenues from your new territory. As a result, your acquisition will be a loss, not a gain. Moreover, your army will make more enemies than colonies would, for the whole territory will suffer from it, the burden moving from one place to another as the troops are billeted first here, then there. Everybody suffers as a result, and everyone becomes your enemy. And these are enemies who can hurt you, for they remain, even if beaten, in their own homes. In every respect, then, an occupying army is a liability, while colonies are an asset.

In addition, anyone who finds himself with territory in a region with different customs from those of his hereditary possessions should make himself the leader and protector of neighboring powers who are weaker than he is, and should set out to weaken his powerful neighbors. He should also take care no outsider as powerful as himself has any occasion to intervene. Outside powers will always be urged to intervene by those in the region who are discontented, either because their ambitions are unsatisfied, or because they are afraid of the dominant powers. So, long ago, the Aetolians invited the Romans into Greece;[8] and, indeed, in every other region the Romans occupied they were invited by local people. It is in the nature of things that, as soon as a foreign power enters into a region, all the local states that are weak rally to it, for they are driven by the envy they have felt for the state that has exercised predominance over them. As a result, the invader does not have to make any effort at all to win over these lesser states, because they all immediately ally themselves to the territory he has acquired there. He only has to take care they do not become too strong and exercise too much influence. He can easily, with his own troops and his new allies' support, strike down the powerful states, and make himself the arbiter of all the affairs of the region. Anyone who does not see how to play this role successfully will quickly lose what he has gained, and, while he holds it, will have innumerable difficulties and vexations.

The Romans, in the regions they seized, obeyed these principles admirably. They settled colonies; were friendly towards the weaker rulers, without building up their strength; broke the powerful; and did not allow foreign powers to build up support. Let me take just the

8.   211 B.C. See Livy, bk. 26, ch. 24.

region of Greece as an example.[9] The Romans favored the Acheans and the Aetolians; they crushed the Kingdom of Macedon; they expelled Antiochus[10] from the region. Despite the credit the Acheans and the Aetolians had earned with them, they never allowed them to build up any independent power; nor did the blandishments of Philip[11] ever persuade them to treat him as a friend before they had destroyed his power; nor did Antiochus's strength intimidate them into permitting him to retain any territory in that region.

The Romans did in such matters what all wise rulers ought to do. It is necessary not only to pay attention to immediate crises, but to foresee those that will come, and to make every effort to prevent them. For if you see them coming well in advance, then you can easily take the appropriate action to remedy them, but if you wait until they are right on top of you, then the prescription will no longer take effect, because the disease is too far advanced. In this matter it is as doctors say of consumption: In the beginning the disease is easy to cure, difficult to diagnose; but, after a while, if it has not been diagnosed and treated early, it becomes easy to diagnose and hard to cure. So, too, in politics, for if you foresee problems while they are far off (which only a prudent man is able to do) they can easily be dealt with; but when, because you have failed to see them coming, you allow them to grow to the point that anyone can recognize them, then it is too late to do anything.

The Romans always looked ahead and took action to remedy problems before they developed. They never postponed action in order to avoid a war, for they understood you cannot escape wars, and when you put them off only your opponents benefit. Thus, they wanted to have a war with Philip and Antiochus in Greece, so as not to have one with them in Italy. At the time they could have avoided having a war at all, but this they did not want. They never approved the saying that nowadays is repeated *ad nauseam* by the wise: "Take advantage of the passage of time." Rather they relied on their strength [*virtù*] and prudence, for in time anything can happen, and the passage of time brings good mixed with evil, and evil mixed with good.

But let us return to the kings of France, and let us see whether they followed any of the principles I have outlined. I will discuss Louis, not Charles, for, since Louis held territory in Italy for a longer time, we

---

9.   The events to which Machiavelli refers occurred in 192 B.C. to 189 B.C. See Livy, bk. 37.

10.   Antiochus III, King of Syria.

11.   Philip V of Macedon.

can have a better understanding of the policies he was following.[12] We will see he did the opposite of what one ought to do in order to hold on to territory in a region unlike one's hereditary lands.

King Louis was brought into Italy by the ambition of the Venetians, who hoped to gain half of the territory of Lombardy as a result of his invasion. I do not want to criticize the king's decision to ally with the Venetians. Since he wanted to get a foothold in Italy, and since he had no friends in that region (rather the opposite, for all the gateways to Italy were closed against him as a result of the actions of King Charles), he was obliged to take what allies he could get. His decision would have been a good one, if he had done everything else right. Now when the king had conquered Lombardy, he at once recovered the reputation Charles had lost for him. Genoa gave itself up and the Florentines became his friends. Everybody came forward to meet him as he advanced and sought his friendship: the Marquis of Mantua, the Duke of Ferrara, Bentivoglio, the Countess of Forlì, the rulers of Faenza, Pesaro, Rimini, Camerino, Piombino, the citizens of Lucca, Pisa, and Siena. Then the Venetians were able to see the risk they had chosen to run; in order to acquire a couple of fortresses in Lombardy, they had made the King of France master of two-thirds of Italy.

Now consider how easy it would have been for the king to preserve his authority in Italy if he had followed the principles I have laid out, and if he had protected and defended all his new friends. They were numerous, weak, and fearful, some afraid of the Church, some of the Venetians, and so had no choice but to remain loyal to him; and with their help he could easily have overwhelmed the surviving great powers. But he had no sooner got to Milan than he did the opposite, coming to the assistance of Pope Alexander so he could occupy the Romagna.[13] He did not realize that by this decision he weakened himself, alienating his friends and those who had flung themselves into his arms; and at the same time strengthened the Church, adding to its already extensive spiritual authority an increased temporal power. And having made one error he was forced to make another, for, in order to put a stop to Alexander's ambitions, and to prevent his gaining control of Tuscany, he was obliged to march into Italy once more. Nor was he satisfied with having strengthened the Church and thrown away his alliances,

12.   Charles VIII (1470–98) ruled France from 1492 and invaded Italy in 1494. He was crowned King of Naples in 1494, but was forced out of Italy in 1495. Louis invaded Italy in 1499. His forces were decisively defeated at the Second Battle of Novara, 1512.

13.   See below, chapter seven.

but in addition, because he wanted the Kingdom of Naples, he agreed to divide it with the King of Spain.[14] Where he had been all-powerful in Italy, he now shared his power with another, giving ambitious rulers in the region and those who were discontented with him someone to whom they could turn. Where he could have left in the Kingdom of Naples a king who was on his payroll, he threw him out, and replaced him with someone who might aspire to kick out the French.

It is perfectly natural and normal to want to acquire new territory; and whenever men do what will succeed towards this end, they will be praised, or at least not condemned. But when they are not in a position to make gains, and try nevertheless, then they are making a mistake, and deserve condemnation. If the King of France had the military capacity to attack Naples, he should have done so; if he did not have it, he should not have proposed to partition the territory. The division of Lombardy between France and Venice was justified because it gave the French a foothold in Italy; the division of Naples was blameworthy, for it was not justifiable on the same grounds.

Thus, Louis had made the following five mistakes: He wasted his alliance with the lesser states; he increased the strength of one of the more powerful Italian states; he invited an extremely powerful foreign state to intervene in Italy; he did not go and live in Italy; he did not establish settlements there. Even these mistakes might have had no evil consequences while he lived, had he not made a sixth, attacking the Venetians. Had he not strengthened the Church and brought the Spanish into Italy, then it would have been reasonable and appropriate to attack them; but having done what he had done, he should never have given his consent to a policy aimed at their destruction. For as long as they remained powerful, the others would never have been prepared to undertake an attack upon Lombardy. For the Venetians would not have consented to Lombardy's falling into the hands of others, and not themselves; while the others would not have wanted to take Lombardy from the King of France only to give it to the Venetians, and would not have had the courage to try to take it away from both of them.

And if someone were to reply that King Louis allowed Alexander to take the Romagna, and the King of Spain to have the Kingdom of Naples, in order to avoid a war, I would answer as I did above: One should never allow a problem to develop in order to avoid a war, for you end up not avoiding the war, but deferring it to a time that will

---

14.   Louis agreed to divide the Kingdom of Naples with Ferdinand the Catholic in 1500, but lost the whole state to him in 1504.

be less favorable. And if others were to appeal to the promise the king
had given to the pope, to help him seize the Romagna in return for
the pope's giving him a divorce and making the Bishop of Rouen a
cardinal, I would reply with what I will say later on the subject of
whether and to what extent rulers should keep their word.

Thus, King Louis lost Lombardy because he did not follow any of the
policies others have adopted when they have established predominance
within a region and have wanted to hold on to it. There is nothing
remarkable about what happened: It is entirely natural and predictable.
I spoke about these matters with the Cardinal of Rouen in Nantes,
when Valentino (as Cesare Borgia, son of Pope Alexander, was com-
monly called) was taking possession of the Romagna. The cardinal
said to me that the Italians did not understand war; so I told him that
the French did not understand politics, for if they did, they would not
allow the church to acquire so much power. And in practice we have
seen that the strength of the papacy and of the King of Spain within
Italy has been brought about by the King of France, and they in turn
have been the cause of his own ruin. From this one can draw a general
conclusion that will never (or hardly ever) be proved wrong: He who
is the cause of someone else's becoming powerful is the agent of his
own destruction; for he makes his protegé powerful either through his
own skill or through his own strength, and either of these must provoke
his protegé's mistrust once he has become powerful.

Chapter Four: Why the kingdom of Darius, which Alexander
occupied, did not rebel against his successors after
Alexander's death.

When you think of the difficulties associated with trying to hold on
to a newly acquired state, you might well be puzzled: Since Alexander
the Great had conquered Asia in the space of a few years, and then
died when he had scarcely had time to take possession of it, at that point
you would expect the whole state to rebel.[15] Nevertheless, Alexander's
successors maintained possession of it and had no difficulty in keeping
hold of it, beyond the conflicts that sprung up between themselves as
a result of their own ambitions. My explanation is that the principalities
recorded in history have been governed in two different ways: either
by a single individual, and everyone else has been his servant, and they
have helped to govern his kingdom as ministers, appointed by his grace

---

15. Alexander conquered Asia between 334 and 327 B.C., and died in 323 B.C.

and benevolence; or by a monarch together with barons, who, not by concession of the ruler, but by virtue of their noble lineage, hold that rank. Such barons have their own territories and their own subjects: subjects who recognize them as their lords and feel a natural affection for them. In those states that are governed by a single individual and his servants, the sovereign has more authority in his own hands; for in all his territories there is no one recognized as having a right to rule except him alone; and if his subjects obey anyone else, they do so because he is the ruler's minister and representative, and they do not feel any particular loyalty to these subordinate authorities.

In our own day the obvious examples of these two types of ruler are the Sultan of Turkey and the King of France. All the kingdom of Turkey is ruled by a single monarch, and everyone else is his servant. He divides his kingdom into sanjaks,[16] sending administrators, whom he replaces and transfers as he thinks best, to rule them. But the King of France is placed among a multitude of long-established nobles, whose rights are recognized by their subjects and who are loved by them. They have their own inherited privileges, and the king cannot take them away without endangering himself. If you compare these two states, you will realize it would be difficult to seize the sultan's kingdom, but, once you had got control of it, it would be very easy to hold on to it.

It would be difficult to occupy the lands of the sultan for two reasons: The local authorities of that kingdom will not invite you to invade, nor can you hope those around the ruler will rebel, making your task easier. And this for the reasons I have explained. For, since they are all his slaves, and indebted to him, it is harder to corrupt them; and even if you can corrupt them, they are not going to be much use to you, for they cannot command the obedience of the people, as I have explained. Consequently, anyone attacking the sultan must expect to find the Turks united in his defense and must rely more on his own strength than on the disorder of his opponents. But once he has defeated them and has destroyed their forces on the field of battle so completely they cannot muster an army, then he has no one to worry about except the sultan's close relatives. Once he has got rid of them, then there is no one left for him to fear, for there is no one else with influence over the people. Just as the invader, before his victory, had no reason to hope for support, so, after his victory, he has no reason to fear opposition.

The opposite is true in kingdoms governed like that of France. For

16.   An administrative region.

it is easy to invade them, once one has gained the support of some local noble. For in such kingdoms one can always find malcontents who hope to benefit from innovation. These, as we have seen, can ease your entrance into the state and help you win victory. But then, when you try to hold on to power, you will find the nobility, both those who have been your allies and those you have defeated, present you with an infinity of problems. It simply is not sufficient to kill the ruler and his close relatives, for the rest of the nobility will survive to provide leadership for new insurrections. You cannot win their loyalty or wipe them out, so you will always be in danger of losing your kingdom should anything go wrong.

Now if you ask yourself what sort of state it was Darius ruled, you will see it was similar to that of the sultan. So it was necessary for Alexander, first to take on his forces and seize control of the territory. Once he was victorious, and Darius was dead, Alexander had a firm grip on his new lands, for the reasons I have given. And his successors, if they had stayed united, could have enjoyed them at their leisure; nor was there any resistance to them in that kingdom, apart from their own conflicts with one another. But states that are organized after the French model cannot be held onto, once seized, with such ease. This is why there were frequent rebellions in Spain, France,[17] and Greece against the Romans. For there were many rulers in those territories, and as long as people remembered them, the Romans were always unsure of their grip. Once the memory of these rulers had faded completely away, thanks to the long duration of Roman rule, they became secure in their possession. Even after that, each faction among the Romans, when they fought among themselves, could call on the support of a section of those provinces, depending on the influence they had built up within them. The subjects of these territories, because their former rulers had no heirs, had no loyalties except to Roman eaders. Once you have considered all these matters, you will not be at all surprised at the ease with which Alexander held on to Asia or at the difficulties other conquerors (one might take Pyrrhus as one example among many) have had in keeping control of their acquisitions. The crucial factor in these differing outcomes is not the strength [*virtù*] or weakness of the conqueror but the contrasting character of the societies that have been conquered.

17.   Machiavelli uses "France" to refer both to modern France and the ancient province of Gaul. Because one of his beliefs is that the French have not changed, I have kept his terminology as a reminder of his conviction that there is a real continuity between the ancient world and the present.

Chapter Five: How you should govern cities or kingdoms that,
before you acquired them, lived under their own laws.

When the states one acquires by conquest are accustomed to living
under their own laws and in freedom, there are three policies one can
follow in order to hold on to them: The first is to lay them waste; the
second is to go and live there in person; the third is to let them continue
to live under their own laws, make them pay you, and create there an
administrative and political elite who will remain loyal to you. For since
the elite are the creation of the head of state, its members know they
cannot survive without both his friendship and his power, and they
know it is in their interest to do everything to sustain it. It is easier to
rule a city that is used to being self-governing by employing its own
citizens than by other means, assuming you do not wish to destroy it.

Examples are provided by the Spartans and the Romans. The Spartans took Athens and Thebes, establishing oligarchies there. However,
they lost them again.[18] The Romans, in order to hold on to Capua,
Carthage, and Numantia razed them and never lost them.[19] They
sought to govern Greece according to more or less the same policies
as those used by Sparta, letting the Greek cities rule themselves and
enforce their own laws, but the policy failed, so in the end they were
obliged to demolish many cities in that territory in order to hold on
to them. The simple truth is there is no reliable way of holding on to
a city and the territory around it, short of demolishing the city itself.
He who becomes the ruler of a city that is used to living under its own
laws and does not knock it down, must expect to be knocked down by
it. Whenever it rebels, it will find strength in the language of liberty
and will seek to restore its ancient constitution. Neither the passage
of time nor good treatment will make its citizens forget their previous
liberty. No matter what one does, and what precautions one takes, if
one does not scatter and drive away the original inhabitants, one will
not destroy the memory of liberty or the attraction of the old institutions.
As soon as there is a crisis, they will seek to restore them. This is what
happened in Pisa after it had been enslaved by the Florentines for a
hundred years.[20]

But when cities or provinces are used to being ruled by a monarch,

18. The Spartan-sponsored oligarchies controlled Athens from 404 to 403 B.C.
and Thebes from 382 to 379 B.C.

19. Capua in 211 B.C., Carthage in 146 B.C., Numantia in 133 B.C.

20. Pisa was controlled by Florence from 1406 to 1494, and recaptured in 1509.

and one has wiped out his relatives and descendants, then matters are
very different. They are used to being obedient. Their old ruler is
gone, and they cannot agree among themselves as to who should replace
him. They do not know how to rule themselves. The result is that they
are slower to take up arms, and it is easier for a new ruler to win them
over and establish himself securely in power. But in former republics there is more vitality, more hatred, more desire for revenge. The
memory of their former freedom gives them no rest, no peace. So the
best thing to do is to demolish them or to go and live there oneself.

Chapter Six: About new kingdoms acquired with one's own armies
and one's own skill [*virtù*].

No one should be surprised if, in talking about completely new kingdoms (that is, states that are governed by someone who was not a ruler
before, and were themselves not previously principalities), I point to
the greatest of men as examples to follow. For men almost always walk
along the beaten path, and what they do is almost always an imitation
of what others have done before. But you cannot walk exactly in the
footsteps of those who have gone before, nor is it easy to match the
skill [*virtù*] of those you have chosen to imitate. Consequently, a prudent
man will always try to follow in the footsteps of great men and imitate
those who have been truly outstanding, so that, if he is not quite as
skillful [*virtù*] as they, at least some of their ability may rub off on him.
One should be like an experienced archer, who, trying to hit someone
at a distance and knowing the range [*virtù*] of his bow, aims at a point
above his target, not so his arrow will strike the point he is aiming at,
but so, by aiming high, he can reach his objective.

I maintain that, in completely new kingdoms, the new ruler has more
or less difficulty in keeping hold of power depending on whether he
is more or less skillful [*virtuoso*]. Now you only find yourself in this
situation, a private individual only becomes a ruler, if you are either
lucky, or skillful [*virtù*]. Both luck and skill enable you to overcome
difficulties. Nevertheless, he who relies least on luck has the best
prospect of success. One advantage is common to any completely new
sovereign: Because he has no other territories, he has no choice but
to come in person and live in his new kingdom. Let us look at those
who through their own skill [*virtù*], and not merely through chance,
have become rulers. In my view, the greatest have been Moses, Cyrus,
Romulus, Theseus, and others like them.[21]

21. Cyrus overcame the Medes around 550 B.C. and founded the Persian
Empire. Romulus is the mythical founder of Rome, and Theseus the slayer

Obviously, we should not discuss Moses' skill, for he was a mere agent, following the instructions given him by God. So he should be admired, not for his own skill, but for that grace that made him worthy to talk with God. But let us discuss Cyrus and the others who have acquired existing kingdoms or founded new ones. You will find them all admirable. And if you look at the actions and strategies of each one of them, you will find they do not significantly differ from those of Moses, who could not have had a better teacher. If you look at their deeds and their lives, you will find they were dependent on chance only for their first opportunity. They seized their chance to make of it what they wanted. Without that first opportunity their strength [*virtù*] of purpose would never have been revealed. Without their strength [*virtù*] of purpose, the opportunity they were offered would not have amounted to anything.

Thus, it was necessary for Moses to find the people of Israel in Egypt, enslaved and oppressed by the Egyptians, so they, in order to escape from slavery, would be prepared to follow him. It was essential for Romulus to have no future in Alba, it was appropriate he should have been exposed at birth, otherwise he would not have formed the ambition of becoming King of Rome and succeeded in founding that nation. It was necessary that Cyrus should find the Persians hostile to the rule of the Medes, and the Medes weak and effeminate from too much peace. Theseus could not have demonstrated his strength of purpose [*virtù*] if he had not found the Athenians scattered. These opportunities made these men lucky; but it was their remarkable political skill [*virtù*] that enabled them to recognize these opportunities for what they were. Thanks to them their nations were ennobled and blessed with good fortune.

Those who become rulers through strength of purpose [*vie virtuose*], as they did, acquire their kingdoms with difficulty, but they hold on to them with ease. And much of the difficulty they have in getting to power derives from the new institutions and customs they are obliged to establish in order to found their governments and make them secure. One ought to pause and consider the fact that there is nothing harder to undertake, nothing more likely of failure, nothing more risky to pull off, than to set oneself up as a leader who plans to found a new system of government. For the founder makes enemies of all those who are doing well under the old system, and has only lukewarm support from those who hope to do well under the new one. The weakness of their

---

of the Minotaur and founder of Athens (1234 B.C.): Machiavelli took them to be genuine historical persons.

support springs partly from their fear of their adversaries, who have the law on their side, partly from their own want of faith. For men do not truly believe in new things until they have had practical experience of them. So it is that, whenever those who are enemies of the new order have a chance to attack it, they do so ferociously, while the others defend it half-heartedly. So the new ruler is in danger, along with his supporters.

It is necessary, however, if we are going to make sense of his situation, to find out if our innovator stands on his own feet, or depends on others to prop him up. That is, we need to know if he is obliged to try to obtain his objectives by pleading, or whether he can resort to force. In the first case, he is bound to come to a bad end, and won't achieve anything. But when he can stand on his own feet, and can resort to force, then he can usually overcome the dangers he faces. Thus it is that all armed prophets are victorious, and disarmed ones are crushed. For there is another problem: People are by nature inconstant. It is easy to persuade them of something, but it is difficult to stop them from changing their minds. So you have to be prepared for the moment when they no longer believe: Then you have to force them to believe. Moses, Cyrus, Theseus, and Romulus would not have been able to make their peoples obey their new structures of authority for long if they had been unarmed. This is what happened, in our own day, to Friar Girolamo Savonarola.[22] He and his new constitution were destroyed as soon as the multitude began to stop believing in him. He had no way of stiffening the resolution of those who had been believers or of forcing disbelievers to obey.

Thus the founders of new states have immense difficulties to overcome, and dangers beset their path, dangers they must overcome by skill and strength of purpose [*virtù*]. But, once they have overcome them, and they have begun to be idolized, having got rid of those who were jealous of their superior qualities, they are established, they are powerful, secure, honored, happy.

We have looked at some noble examples, and to them I want to add one less remarkable. Nevertheless, it has some points of similarity to them, and I want it to stand for all the other lesser examples I could have chosen. My example is Hiero of Syracuse.[23] He was a private

22.   Girolamo Savonarola (b. 1452) was a Dominican friar and prophetic preacher. He dominated Florentine politics from the expulsion of the Medici in 1494 until 1498, when he was executed as a heretic.

23.   Hiero II became King of Syracuse in 269 B.C. Machiavelli's sources are Polybius, bk. 7, ch. 8, and Justin, bk. 23, ch. 4.

individual who became ruler of Syracuse. He, too, did not depend on luck once he had been given his opportunity. The people of Syracuse were oppressed and elected him as their military commander; so he deserved to be made their ruler. He was so remarkable [*di tanta virtù*], even before he became a ruler, history records "that he had everything one would look for in a king, except a kingdom." He disbanded the old militia and instituted a new one. Dropped his old friends and chose new ones. Since both his friends and his soldiers were his creatures, he had laid the foundations for constructing any political system he chose. He, too, had difficulties enough to overcome in acquiring power, and few in holding on to it.

Chapter Seven: About new principalities that are acquired with the
forces of others and with good luck.

Those who, having started as private individuals, become rulers merely out of good luck, acquire power with little trouble but have a hard time holding on to it. They have no problems on the road to power, because they leap over all the obstacles; but dangers crowd around them once they are in power. I am talking about people who are given a state, either in return for money, or out of the goodwill of him who hands it over to them. This happened to many individuals in Greece, in the cities of Ionia and the Hellespont, who were made rulers by Darius, who wanted them to hold their cities for his own greater safety and glory.[24] So, too, with those who, having been private citizens, were made emperors of Rome because they had corrupted the soldiers.[25] Such rulers are entirely dependent on the goodwill and good fortune of whoever has given them power. Good will and good fortune are totally unreliable and capricious. Such rulers do not know how to hold on to their position and cannot do so. They do not know how, because they have always been private citizens, and only a brilliant and immensely skillful [*di grande virtù*] man is likely to know how to command without having had training and experience. They cannot because they have no troops of their own on whose loyalty and commitment they can count.

Moreover, states that spring up overnight, like all other things in nature that are born and grow in a hurry, cannot have their roots deep in the soil, so they shrivel up in the first drought, blow over in the first

24. Machiavelli is referring to Greek-speaking cities in Asia and the Hellespont in the sixth century B.C.

25. See below, chapter nineteen.

storm. Unless, as I have said, those who are suddenly made into rulers are of such extraordinary capacity [*virtù*] they can work out on the spot how to hold on to the gift fortune has unexpectedly handed them; and those preparations the others made before they became rulers, they must find a way of making after the event.

I want to add to the one and the other of these two ways of becoming a ruler, by skill [*virtù*] or by luck, two examples drawn from the events that have occurred in our own lifetimes: the examples of Francesco Sforza and Cesare Borgia. Francesco, by using the right methods and consummate skill [*virtù*], started out as a private citizen and ended up as Duke of Milan. And what he had acquired with painstaking effort, he held on to without trouble.[26] On the other hand Cesare Borgia, who was called Duke Valentino by the common people, acquired his state thanks to the good fortune of his father, and when that came to an end he lost it.[27] This despite the fact he used every technique and did all the things a prudent and skillful [*virtuoso*] man ought to do, to entrench himself in those territories that the arms and fortune of others had acquired for him. For, as I said above, he who does not prepare the foundations first can (in principle), if he is immensely skillful [*virtù*], make up for it later, although the architect will find catching up a painful process, and there is a real danger the building will collapse. So, if we look at all the things Borgia did, we will see he had laid solid foundations for future power. I do not think it irrelevant to discuss his policies, because I cannot think of any better example I could offer a new ruler than that of his actions. And if his strategy did not lead to success, this was not his fault; his failure was due to extraordinary and exceptional hostility on the part of fortune.

Pope Alexander VI, in setting out to make his son the duke into a ruler, was faced with considerable immediate and long-term difficulties. In the first place, he could find no way of making him the lord of any territory, except territory that belonged to the church. And he knew if he took land from the church to give to Cesare, he would have to overcome the opposition of the Duke of Milan, and also of the Venetians, for both Faenza and Rimini were already under Venetian protection. Secondly, he saw the armed forces of Italy, and particularly those he could hope to employ, were under the control of individuals who had reason to fear any increase in papal power. Consequently, he could

26. See below, chapter twelve.

27. Cesare Borgia (1475–1507) was the natural son of Rodrigo Borgia (1431–1503), who became Pope Alexander VI in 1492. He began the conquest of the Romagna in 1499.

not regard them as reliable. He could not trust the Orsini, the Colonna, or their associates, but there was no one else to whom he could turn.[28] So it was necessary to break out of this framework, and to bring disorder to the territories of his opponents, so he could safely seize a part of them. This proved easy, for he found the Venetians, for reasons of their own, had decided to invite the French to invade Italy. He not only did not oppose this, but he facilitated it by dissolving the previous marriage of King Louis. So the king marched into Italy, with the help of the Venetians and the consent of Alexander. No sooner was he in Milan than the pope had borrowed forces from him for the attack on the Romagna, which was ceded to him out of fear of the King of France.

So, once Cesare had been made Duke of the Romagna, and the Colonnesi had been beaten, wanting to hang on to his new territories and make further conquests, he was faced with two obstacles. In the first place, his military forces did not appear reliable. In the second, the King of France might oppose him. He had made use of the troops of the Orsini, but they were likely to abandon him, and not only prevent him from making further acquisitions, but take from him what he had already acquired. And the same was true of the king. He had an indication of how far he could trust the Orsini when, after Faenza had been taken by storm, he attacked Bologna, for he discovered they had no appetite for that battle.[29] And as for the king, he discovered his attitude when, having seized the Duchy of Urbino, he attacked Tuscany, for Louis made him abandon that enterprise.[30] So the duke decided he must no longer depend on the troops and the good fortune of others.

The first thing he did was to weaken the factions of the Orsini and the Colonna in Rome. All the nobles who were allied to these families he won over to himself, making them members of his court, and giving them substantial pensions. He favored them with civil and military appointments appropriate to their standing. Thus, in the course of a few months, their attachment to their factions was dissolved, and they became committed to the duke. Next, he looked for a chance to crush the Orsini, having already defeated the forces of the Colonna family. He soon had his chance and he made the most of it. For the Orsini, having realized late in the day that the growing strength of the duke and the pope would be their ruin, called a meeting at Magione, near

---

28. On the Orsini and the Colonna, see below, chapter eleven.

29. In the spring of 1501.

30. In the summer of 1502.

Perugia. From that meeting sprang the rebellion of Urbino and the
uprisings in the Romagna that almost destroyed the duke; but he
overcame all resistance with the help of the French.[31] And, having got
back his authority and realizing he could trust neither the French nor
other external forces, he decided that, in order to prevent their allying against him, he must deceive them. He so successfully concealed
his intentions that the Orsini, represented by Signor Paolo, made peace
with him. The duke took every opportunity to ingratiate himself with
Paolo, giving him money, clothes, and horses. So the leaders of the
Orsini were brought, unsuspecting, to Sinigallia, where they were at
his mercy.[32] Having got rid of the leaders and won the allegiance of
their followers, the duke could feel he had laid decent foundations for
his future power. He had control of all the Romagna and the Duchy
of Urbino, and it looked as though he had won over the Romagna and
acquired the support of its population, who were beginning to enjoy
a new prosperity.

   Now, since it is worth paying attention to this question, and since
it would be sensible to imitate Cesare's actions, I want to amplify what
I have just said. Once the duke had subdued the Romagna, he found
it had been under the control of weak nobles, who had rather exploited
than governed their subjects and had rather been the source of conflict
than of order, with the result the whole province was full of robbers,
bandits, and every other type of criminal. So he decided it was necessary, if he was going to make the province peaceful and obedient to
his commands, to give it good government. He put Mr. Remiro d'Orco,
a man both cruel and efficient, in charge, and gave him absolute
power. D'Orco in short order established peace and unity, and acquired
immense authority. At that point, the duke decided such unchecked
power was no longer necessary, for he feared people might come to
hate it. So he established a civil court in the center of the province,
placing an excellent judge in charge of it, and requiring every city to
appoint a lawyer to represent it before the court. Since he knew the
harsh measures of the past had given rise to some enmity towards him,
in order to purge the ill-will of the people and win them completely
over to him, he wanted to make clear that, if there had been any cruelty,
he was not responsible for it, and that his hard-hearted minister should
be blamed. He saw his opportunity and exploited it. One morning, in
the town square of Cesena, he had Remiro d'Orco's corpse laid out

31. October 1502.

32. They were captured on 31 December 1502. Some were killed at once; others
a few weeks later.

in two pieces, with a chopping board and a bloody knife beside it.[33] This ferocious sight made the people of the Romagna simultaneously happy and dumbfounded.

But let us get back to where we were. I was saying the duke found himself rather powerful and had taken precautions against immediate dangers, for he had built up a military force that he had planned himself and had in large part destroyed neighboring forces that could be a threat to him. So what remained, if he wanted to make further acquisitions, was the problem of the King of France; for he knew the king had, late in the day, realized his policy towards Borgia had been misconceived and would not allow him to make further conquests. So Borgia began to look for new alliances and to prevaricate with the French when they dispatched a force towards the Kingdom of Naples to attack the Spanish who were laying siege to Gaeta.[34] His intention was to protect himself against them, which he would soon have succeeded in doing, if Alexander had gone on living.

These were the policies he pursued with regard to his immediate concerns. But there were future problems he also had to consider. In the first place, he had to worry that a new pope would be hostile to him and would try to take from him what Alexander had given him. He had four ways of trying to deal with this threat. In the first place, he set out to eliminate all the relatives of those rulers whose lands he had seized, to make it difficult for the pope to restore their previous rulers. Second, he sought to acquire the allegiance of the nobility of Rome, as I have explained, so he could use them to restrict the pope's freedom of action. Third, to make as many as possible of the members of the College of Cardinals his allies. Fourth, to acquire so much power, before the pope died, that he would be able on his own to resist a first attack. Of these four policies he had successfully carried out three by the time Alexander died; the fourth he had almost accomplished. Of the rulers he had dispossessed, he murdered as many as he could get his hands on, and only a very few survived. The Roman nobility were his supporters, and he had built up a very large faction in the College of Cardinals. As far as new acquisitions were concerned, he had plans for conquering Tuscany; he already held Perugia and Piombino; and he had taken Pisa under his protection. And, as soon as he would no longer have to worry about the King of France (which was already the case, for the French had already lost the Kingdom of Naples to the Spanish, with the result that both France and Spain were now obliged

33.   26 December 1502.
34.   1503.

to try to buy his friendship), he would be free to seize Pisa. After which, Lucca and Siena would quickly give in, partly because they hated the Florentines, and partly because they would have been terrified. The Florentines could have done nothing.

If he had succeeded in all this (and he was on the point of succeeding in the very year Alexander died) he would have acquired so much strength and so much authority he would have become his own master. He would no longer have depended on events outside his control and on the policies of others, but would have been able to rely on his own power and strength [*virtù*]. But Alexander died only five years after Cesare Borgia had unsheathed his sword.[35] He found himself with only his control over the Romagna firmly established, with everything else up in the air, caught between two powerful hostile armies, and dangerously ill. But the duke was so pugnacious and so strong [*virtù*], he so well understood what determines whether one wins or loses, and he had laid such sound foundations within such a short time, that, if he had not had these enemy armies breathing down his neck, or if he had been in good health, he could have overcome every difficulty.

I am justified in claiming he had laid sound foundations, for the Romagna remained loyal to him in his absence for more than a month; in Rome, although he was half dead, he was quite safe, and although the Ballioni, the Vitelli, and the Orsini congregated in Rome, they could not muster a following to attack him; and, if he was not in a position to choose who should be pope, he could at least veto anyone he did not trust. So, if he had been well when Alexander died he would have been able to deal with his problems without difficulty. He told me himself, on the day Julius II was elected,[36] that he had asked himself what he would do if his father died and had been confident he could handle the situation, but that it had never occurred to him that when his father died he himself would be at death's door.

So, now I have surveyed all the actions of the duke, I still cannot find anything to criticize. It seems to me I have been right to present him as an example to be imitated by all those who come to power through good luck and thanks to someone else's military might. For, since he was great-hearted and ambitious, he had no choice as to what to do; and he only failed to achieve his goals because Alexander died

---

35.   18 August 1503.

36.   28 October 1503. Giuliano della Rovere (1443–1513) had been appointed Cardinal of San Piero ad Vincula in 1471, when his uncle became Pope Sixtus IV. For Machiavelli's assessment of his papacy, see below, chapters eleven and twenty-five.

too soon, and he himself fell ill. So anyone who decides that the policy to follow when one has newly acquired power is to destroy one's enemies, to secure some allies, to win wars, whether by force or by fraud, to make oneself both loved and feared by one's subjects, to make one's soldiers loyal and respectful, to wipe out those who can or would want to hurt one, to innovate, replacing old institutions with new practices, to be both harsh and generous, magnanimous and open-handed, to disband disloyal troops and form new armies, to build alliances with other powers, so kings and princes either have to win your favor or else think twice before going against your wishes—anyone who thinks in these terms cannot hope to find, in the recent past, a better model to imitate than Cesare Borgia.

His only mistake was to allow Julius to be elected pope, for there he made a bad choice. The choice was his to make, for as I have said, if he could not choose who should be pope, he could veto anyone he did not like, and he should never have agreed to any cardinal's being elected with whom he had been in conflict in the past, or who, once he had been elected, would have been likely to be afraid of him. For men attack either out of fear or out of hatred. Those who had scores to settle with him included San Piero ad Vincula, Colonna, San Giorgio, Ascanio; all the others, if elected pope, would have had good reason to fear him, with the exception of Rouen and of the Spanish cardinals. The Spanish were his relatives and allies; Rouen was powerful, having the support of the King of France. So the duke's first objective should have been to ensure a Spaniard was elected pope; failing that, he should have agreed to the election of Rouen and vetoed that of San Piero ad Vincula. If he imagined recent gestures of goodwill make the powerful forget old injuries, he was much mistaken. So the duke made a mistake during the election of the pope, and this mistake was, in the end, the cause of his destruction.

Chapter Eight: Of those who come to power through wicked
actions.

But since there are two other ways a private citizen can become a ruler, two ways that do not simply involve the acquisition of power either through fortune or strength [*virtù*], I feel I cannot omit discussion of them, although one of them can be more fully treated elsewhere, where I discuss republics. These are, first, when one acquires power through some wicked or nefarious action, and second when a private citizen becomes ruler of his own country because he has the support of his fellow citizens. Here I will talk about the first of these two routes to

power, and will use two examples, one ancient, one modern, to show
how it is done. These will be sufficient, I trust, to provide a model for
anyone who has no alternative options. I do not intend to discuss in
detail the rights and wrongs of such a policy.

Agathocles of Sicily became King of Syracuse, although he was not
merely a private citizen, but of humble and poverty-stricken origins.[37]
He was the son of a potter, and from start to finish lived a wicked life;
nevertheless, his wicked behavior testified to so much strength [*virtù*]
of mind and of body that, when he joined the army, he was promoted
through the ranks to the supreme command. Having risen so high, he
decided to become the sole ruler and to hold on to power, which he
had originally been granted by the consent of his fellow citizens, by
violence and without being dependent on anyone else. Having entered
into a conspiracy with a Carthaginian called Hamilcar, who was commander of a hostile army serving in Sicily, one morning he called
together the people and the senate of Syracuse, as if he wanted to
discuss matters of government policy, and, at a prearranged signal,
had his soldiers kill all the senators and the richest citizens. With
them out of the way, he made himself ruler of the city and held power
without any resistance. Although the Carthaginians twice defeated his
armies and even advanced to the walls of the city, he was not only able
to defend his city, but, leaving part of his army behind to withstand
the siege, he was able to attack the Carthaginians in Africa with the
remainder of his forces. Within a short time he had forced them to
lift the siege and was threatening to conquer Carthage. In the end they
were obliged to come to terms with him, leaving Sicily to Agathocles
in return for security in Africa.

If you consider Agathocles' bold achievements [*azioni e virtù*], you
will not find much that can be attributed to luck; for, as I have said,
he did not come to power because he had help from above, but because
he worked his way up from below, climbing from rank to rank by
undergoing infinite dangers and discomforts until in the end he
obtained a monopoly of power, and then holding on to his position by
bold and risky tactics.

One ought not, of course, to call it *virtù* [virtue or manliness] to
massacre one's fellow citizens, to betray one's friends, to break one's
word, to be without mercy and without religion. By such means one
can acquire power but not glory. If one considers the manly qualities
[*virtù*] Agathocles demonstrated in braving and facing down danger,

---

37. Agathocles (361–289 B.C.) seized control of Syracuse in 317 B.C. Machiavelli's source is Justin, bk. 22.

and the strength of character he showed in surviving and overcoming adversity, then there seems to be no reason why he should be judged less admirable than any of the finest generals. But on the other hand, his inhuman cruelty and brutality, and his innumerable wicked actions, mean it would be wrong to praise him as one of the finest of men. It is clear, at any rate, that one can attribute neither to luck nor to virtue [*virtù*] his accomplishments, which owed nothing to either.

In our own day, when Alexander VI was pope, Oliverotto of Fermo, whose father had died a few years before, was raised by his maternal uncle, Giovanni Fogliani.[38] As soon as he was old enough he joined the forces of Paolo Vitelli, so that, with a good military training, he could pursue a career in the army.[39] When Paolo died, he signed up with his brother, Vitellozzo. In a very short time, because he was bright and had both a strong body and a lively spirit, he became Vitellozzo's second-in-command. Soon he thought it to be beneath his dignity to serve under another, and so he conspired to occupy Fermo, relying on the help of some citizens of that city who preferred to see their fatherland enslaved than free, and on the support of Vitellozzo. He wrote to his uncle, saying that, since he had been away from home for many years, he wanted to come to visit him and to see his city, and so, in a manner of speaking, reacquaint himself with his inheritance. He said he had only gone to war in order to acquire honor. So his fellow citizens would be able to see he had not been wasting his time, he wanted to arrive in state, accompanied by a hundred men on horseback, some of them his friends, and others his servants. He asked his uncle to ensure that the inhabitants of Fermo received him with respect: This would enhance not only his reputation, but that of his uncle, who raised him.

Giovanni did everything he could for his nephew. He ensured he was greeted by the people of Fermo with every honor, and he put him up in his own house. After a few days had gone by, and he had had time to make the arrangements necessary for the carrying out of his wicked plans, he held a lavish banquet at his uncle's, to which he invited his uncle and the most powerful citizens of Fermo. After the food had been eaten, and the guests had been entertained in all the ways that are customary upon such occasions, Oliverotto deliberately began discussing serious questions, talking about the greatness of Pope

38. Oliverotto Euffreducci (b. ca. 1475) seized Fermo in 1501. Borgia had him killed at Sinigallia in December 1502.

39. The Florentines made Vitelli commander of their forces in 1498 and executed him in 1499. See below, chapter twelve.

Alexander and his son Cesare, and about their undertakings. When his uncle Giovanni and the others picked up the subject, he sprang to his feet, saying such matters should be discussed in a more private place. He withdrew into another room, where Giovanni and all the other leading citizens followed. No sooner had they sat down than soldiers emerged from their hiding places and killed Giovanni along with all the rest. Once the killing was over, Oliverotto got on his horse and took possession of the city, laying siege to the government building. Those in authority were so terrified they agreed to obey him and to establish a new regime of which he was the head. With all those who had something to lose and would have been able to resist him dead, he was able to entrench himself by establishing new civilian and military institutions. Within a year of coming to power, he was not only securely in control of Fermo, but had become a threat to all the cities round about. It would soon have been as difficult to get rid of him as to get rid of Agathocles, had he not allowed himself to be taken in by Cesare Borgia, when, as I have already explained, he got rid of the Orsini and the Vitelli at Sinigallia. Oliverotto was seized at the same time, and, a year after he had killed his uncle, he was strangled along with Vitellozzo from whom he had learned how to be bold [*virtù*] and how to be wicked.

Perhaps you are wondering how Agathocles and others like him, despite their habitual faithlessness and cruelty, have been able to live safely in their homelands year after year, and to defend themselves against their enemies abroad. Why did their fellow subjects not conspire against them? After all, mere cruelty has not been enough to enable many other rulers to hang on to power even in time of peace, let alone during the turmoil of war. I think here we have to distinguish between cruelty well used and cruelty abused. Well-used cruelty (if one can speak well of evil) one may call those atrocities that are committed at a stroke, in order to secure one's power, and are then not repeated, rather every effort is made to ensure one's subjects benefit in the long run. An abuse of cruelty one may call those policies that, even if in the beginning they involve little bloodshed, lead to more rather than less as time goes by. Those who use cruelty well may indeed find both God and their subjects are prepared to let bygones be bygones, as was the case with Agathocles. Those who abuse it cannot hope to retain power indefinitely.

So the conclusion is: If you take control of a state, you should make a list of all the crimes you have to commit and do them all at once. That way you will not have to commit new atrocities every day, and you will be able, by not repeating your evil deeds, to reassure your subjects and to win their support by treating them well. He who acts otherwise, either out of squeamishness or out of bad judgment, has to hold a bloody knife in his hand all the time. He can never rely on his subjects, for they can never trust him, for he is always making new attacks upon them. Do all the harm you must at one and the same time, that way the full extent of it will not be noticed, and it will give least offense. One should do good, on the other hand, little by little, so people can fully appreciate it.

A ruler should, above all, behave towards his subjects in such a way that, whatever happens, whether for good or ill, he has no need to change his policies. For if you fall on evil times and are obliged to change course, you will not have time to benefit from the harm you do, and the good you do will do you no good, because people will think you have been forced to do it, and they will not be in the slightest bit grateful to you.

Chapter Nine: Of the citizen-ruler.

But, coming to the alternative possibility, when a private citizen becomes the ruler of his homeland, not through wickedness or some act of atrocity, but through the support of his fellow citizens, so that we may call him a citizen-ruler (remember we are discussing power acquired neither by pure strength [*virtù*] nor mere luck—in this case one needs a lucky cunning), I would point out there are two ways to such power: the support of the populace or the favor of the elite. For in every city one finds these two opposed classes. They are at odds because the populace do not want to be ordered about or oppressed by the elite; and the elite want to order about and oppress the populace. The conflict between these two irreconcilable ambitions has in each city one of three possible consequences: rule by one man, liberty, or anarchy.

Rule by one man can be brought about either by the populace or the elite, depending on whether one or the other of these factions hopes to benefit from it. For if the elite fear they will be unable to control the populace, they begin to build up the reputation of one of their own, and they make him sole ruler in order to be able, under his protection, to achieve their objectives. The populace on the other hand, if they fear they are going to be crushed by the elite, build up the reputation of one of their number and make him sole ruler, in order that his authority may be employed in their defense. He who comes to power with the help of the elite has more difficulty in holding on to power than he who comes to power with the help of the populace, for in the former case he is surrounded by many who think of themselves as his equals, and whom he consequently cannot order about or manipulate as he might wish. He who comes to power with the support of the populace, on the other hand, has it all to himself: There is no one, or hardly anyone, around him who is not prepared to obey. In addition, one cannot honorably give the elite what they want, and one cannot do it without harming others; but this is not true with the populace, for the objectives of the populace are less immoral than those of the elite, for the latter want to oppress, and the former not to be oppressed. Thirdly, if the masses are opposed to you, you can never be secure, for there are too many of them; but the elite, since there are few of them, can be neutralized.

The worst a ruler who is opposed by the populace has to fear is that they will give him no support; but from the elite he has to fear not only lack of support, but worse, that they will attack him. For the elite have more foresight and more cunning; they act in time to protect themselves, and seek to ingratiate themselves with rivals for power. Finally, the ruler cannot get rid of the populace but must live with them; he can, however, get by perfectly well without the members of the elite, being able to make and unmake them each day, and being in a position to give them status or take it away, as he chooses.

In order to clarify the issues, let me point out there are two principal points of view from which one should consider the elite. Either they behave in a way that ties their fortunes to yours, or they do not. Those who tie themselves to you and are not rapacious, you should honor and love; those who do not tie themselves to you are to be divided into two categories. If they retain their independence through pusillanimity and because they are lacking in courage, then you should employ them, especially if they have good judgment, for you can be sure they will help you achieve success so long as things are going well for you, and you can also be confident you have nothing to fear from them if things go badly. But if they retain their independence from you out of calculation and ambition, then you can tell they are more interested in their own welfare than yours. A ruler must protect himself against such people and fear them as much as if they were publicly declared enemies, for you can be sure that, in adversity, they will help to overthrow you.

Anyone who becomes a ruler with the support of the populace ought to ensure he keeps their support; which will not be difficult, for all they ask is not to be oppressed. But anyone who becomes a ruler with the support of the elite and against the wishes of the populace must above all else seek to win the populace over to his side, which will be easy to do if he protects their interests. And since people, when they are well-treated by someone whom they expected to treat them badly, feel all the more obliged to their benefactor, he will find that the populace will quickly become better inclined towards him than if he had come to power with their support. There are numerous ways the ruler can win the support of the populace. They vary so much depending on the circumstances they cannot be reduced to a formula, and, consequently, I will not go into them here. I will simply conclude by saying a ruler needs to have the support of the populace, for otherwise he has nothing to fall back on in times of adversity.

Nabis, ruler of the Spartans, survived an attack by the confederate forces of all Greece, together with an almost invincible Roman army, and successfully defended both his homeland and his own hold on power. All he needed to do, when faced with danger, was neutralize a few; but if he had had the populace opposed to him, this would have been insufficient.[40] Do not think you can rebut my argument by citing the well-worn proverb, "Relying on the people is like building on the sand." This is quite true when a private citizen depends upon them and gives the impression he expects the populace to free him if he is seized by his enemies or by the magistrates. In such a case one can easily find oneself disappointed, as happened to the Gracchi in Rome and to Mr. Giorgio Scali in Florence.[41] But if you are a ruler and you put your trust in the populace, if you can give commands and are capable of bold action, if you are not nonplused by adversity, if you take other necessary precautions, and if through your own courage and your policies you keep up the morale of the populace, then you will never be let down by them, and you will discover you have built on a sound foundation.

The type of one-man rule we are discussing tends to be at risk at the moment of transition from constitutional to dictatorial government. Such rulers either give commands in their own name, or act through the officers of state. In the second case, their situation is more dangerous and less secure. For they are entirely dependent on the cooperation of those citizens who have been appointed to the offices of state, who can, particularly at times of crisis, easily deprive them of their power, either by directly opposing them or by simply failing to carry out their instructions. It is too late for the ruler once a crisis is upon him to seize dictatorial authority, for the citizens and the subjects, who are

40. Nabis (ca. 240–192 B.C.) became ruler of Sparta in 207 B.C. Livy (bk. 34) puts the number assassinated at eighty.

41. The Gracchi brothers (Tiberius Sempronius [163–133 B.C.] and Gaius Sempronius [153–121 B.C.]) were advocates of agrarian reform who both died in riots. Scali was a populist leader in Florence during the Ciompi rising of 1378 but was executed for an attack on the authorities in 1382.

used to obeying the constituted authorities, will not, in such circumstances, obey him, and he will always have, in difficult circumstances, a shortage of people on whom he can rely. For such a ruler cannot expect things to continue as they were when there were no difficulties, when all the citizens are conscious of what the government can do for them. Then everyone flocked round, everyone promised support, everyone was willing to die for him, when there was no prospect of having to do so. But when times are tough, when the government is dependent on its citizens, then there will be few who are prepared to stand by it. One does not learn the danger of such an erosion of support from experience, as the first experience proves fatal. So a wise ruler will seek to ensure that his citizens always, no matter what the circumstances, have an interest in preserving both him and his authority. If he can do this, they will always be faithful to him.

Chapter Ten: How one should measure the strength of a ruler.

There is another factor one should take into account when categorizing rulers: One should ask if a ruler has enough resources to be able, if necessary, to look after himself, or whether he will always be dependent on having alliances with other rulers. In order to clarify this question, I would maintain those rulers can look after themselves who have sufficient reserves, whether of troops or of money, to be able to put together a sound army and face battle against any opponent. On the other hand, I judge those rulers to be dependent on the support of others who could not take the field against any potential enemy, but would be obliged to take shelter behind the walls of their cities and castles, and stay there. We have talked already about those who can look after themselves, and we will have more to say in due course; to those who are in the second situation, all one can do is advise them to build defenseworks and stockpile arms, and to give up all thought of holding the open ground. He who has well fortified his city and who has followed the policies towards his own subjects that I have outlined above and will describe below, can be sure his enemies will think twice before they attack him, for people are always reluctant to undertake enterprises that look as if they will be difficult, and no one thinks it will be easy to attack someone who is well-fortified and has the support of the populace.

The cities of Germany are free to do as they please. They have little surrounding territory, and obey the emperor only when they want. They fear neither him nor any other ruler in their region, for they are so well-fortified everyone thinks it will be tedious and difficult to take them. They all have appropriate moats and ramparts, and more than enough artillery. They always keep in the public stores enough food and drink, and enough firewood, to be able to hold out for a year. Moreover, in order to be able to keep the populace quiet and to guarantee tax revenues, they always keep in stock enough supplies to keep their subjects occupied for a year in those crafts that are the basis of the city's prosperity and provide employment for the bulk of the people. They also emphasize military preparedness and have numerous ordinances designed to ensure this.

A ruler, therefore, who has a well-fortified city, and who does not set out to make enemies, is not going to be attacked; and, suppose someone does attack him, his adversary will have to give up in disgrace. For political circumstances change so fast it is impossible for anyone to keep an army in the field for a year doing nothing but maintaining a siege. And if you are tempted to reply that if the people have property outside the city walls and see it burning, then they will not be able patiently to withstand a siege, and that as time goes by, and their own interests are damaged, they will forget their loyalty to their ruler; then I reply that a ruler who is strong and bold will always be able to overcome such difficulties, sometimes encouraging his subjects to think relief is at hand, sometimes terrifying them with stories of what the enemy will do to them if they concede defeat, sometimes taking appropriate action to neutralize those who seem to him to be agitators. Moreover, it is in the nature of things that the enemy will burn and pillage the countryside when they first arrive, at which time the subjects will still be feeling brave and prepared to undertake their own defense. So the ruler has little to fear, for after a few days, when the subjects are feeling less courageous, the damage will already have been done, and it will be too late to prevent it. Then they will be all the more ready to rally to their ruler, believing him to be in their debt, since they have had their houses burnt and their possessions looted for defending him. It is in men's nature to feel as obliged by the good they do to others, as by the good others do to them. So if you consider all the factors, you will see it is not difficult for a wise ruler to keep his subjects loyal during a siege, both at the beginning and as it continues, providing they are not short of food and of arms.

Chapter Eleven: About ecclesiastical states.

All that remains for us to discuss, at this point, is the ecclesiastical states. As far as they are concerned, all the problems are encountered before one gets possession of them. One acquires them either through strength [*virtù*] or through luck, but one can hold on to them without either. For they are maintained by their long-established institutions that are rooted in religion. These have developed to such a pitch of strength they can support their rulers in power no matter how they live and behave. Only ecclesiastical rulers have states, but no need to defend them; subjects, but no need to govern them. Their states, though they do not defend them, are not taken from them; their subjects, though they do not govern them, do not resent them, and they neither think of replacing their rulers nor are they in a position to do so. So these are the only rulers who are secure and happy. But because they are ruled by a higher power, which human intelligence cannot grasp, I will say no more about them; for, since they have been built up and maintained by God, only a presumptuous and rash person would debate about them. Nevertheless, if someone were to ask me how it comes about that the church has acquired so much temporal power, given that, until the papacy of Alexander [VI], the rulers of Italy, and indeed not only those who called themselves rulers, but every baron and lord, no matter how small, regarded the papacy's temporal power as of little significance, while now a King of France trembles at its power, for a pope has kicked him out of Italy and been the ruin of the Venetians: Though the answer to this question is well known, I think it will not be a waste of time to remind you of the main principles.

Before Charles, King of France, invaded Italy, control over this geographical region was divided between the pope, the Republic of Venice, the King of Naples, the Duke of Milan, and the Republic of Florence.[42] These rulers were obliged to have two principal preoccupations: In the first place, they had to make sure no foreign power brought an army into Italy; in the second, they had to make sure none of the Italian powers increased its territory. The powers they were most concerned about were the pope and the Venetians. In order to prevent the Venetians from expanding all the rest had to cooperate, as happened when the Venetians tried to take Ferrara.[43] In order to keep the pope in his place they relied on the nobles of Rome. These were divided into two factions, the Orsini and the Colonna, and so there was always occasion for friction between them. Because both factions were constantly in arms within sight of the pope, their strength kept the pope weak and sickly. Although there was occasionally a pope who had ambitions, Sixtus [IV] for example, yet neither luck nor skill enabled him to free himself of that handicap.

42.   Charles VIII invaded Italy in 1494.
43.   In 1482–84.

The real cause was the shortness of the popes' lives. On average, a pope lived ten years, which was scarcely enough time to crush one of the factions. Suppose a pope had almost destroyed the Colonna; his successor would prove to be an enemy of the Orsini, would rebuild the power of the Colonna, and would not have time to crush the Orsini. The result was the temporal power of the pope was not thought by the Italians to be of much importance. Then along came Alexander VI, who, more than all the other popes there have been, demonstrated how much a pope, using both money and arms, could get his own way. It was Alexander who, by making use of Duke Valentino and by taking advantage of the invasion of Italy by the French, brought about all those things I have mentioned above, when discussing the achievements of the duke.[44] Although his objective was not to make the church, but rather the duke, powerful, nevertheless, he did make the church a power to be reckoned with. It was the church that, after he had died and the duke had been destroyed, inherited the results of his labors.

After him came Julius [II]. The church was already powerful, for it had control of the whole of the Romagna, and the barons of Rome had been crushed, and the two factions of Orsini and Colonna had, as a result of the hiding given them by Alexander, been eliminated. Moreover, Julius had opportunities to accumulate money of a sort that had not existed before Alexander. Julius not only took over where Alexander had left off, but made further advances. He planned to acquire Bologna, to destroy the power of the Venetians, and to throw the French out of Italy. He not only laid plans, but he succeeded in everything he undertook. His achievements were all the more admirable in that his goal was to build up the power of the Church, not of any private individual. He kept the factions of the Orsini and the Colonna in the feeble condition in which he had found them. Although they made some efforts to rise again, two things kept them down: in the first place, the new power of the church, which intimidated them; and in the second, the fact none of their number were cardinals, for it is the cardinals who have been at the origin of the conflicts between the factions. These two factions have never behaved themselves at times when they have had cardinals, for the cardinals, both in Rome and outside Rome, foster the factions, and the barons are obliged to come to their support. Thus the ambition of the prelates is the cause of the conflicts and tumults among the nobility.

Now His Holiness Pope Leo [X] has acquired the papacy, along with all its immense temporal power. We may hope, if his predecessors

---

44. See chapter seven.

made it a military power to be reckoned with, he, who is so good and has so many virtues [*virtù*], will not only increase its power, but also make it worthy of respect.

Chapter Twelve: How many types of army are there, and what
opinion should one have of mercenary soldiers?

So far I have discussed one by one the various types of one-man rule I listed at the beginning, and I have to some extent described the policies that make each type succeed or fail. I have shown the various techniques employed by numerous individuals who have sought to acquire and to hold on to power. Now my task is to outline the various strategies for offense and defense that are common to all these principalities. I said above it was necessary for a ruler to lay good foundations; otherwise, he is likely to be destroyed. The principal foundations on which the power of all governments is based (whether they be new, long-established, or mixed) are good laws and good armies. And, since there cannot be good laws where there are not good armies, and since where there are good armies, there must be good laws, I will omit any discussion of laws, and will talk about armies.

Let me begin by saying, then, that a ruler defends his state with armies that are made up of his own subjects, or of mercenaries, or of auxiliary forces, or of some combination of these three types. Mercenaries and auxiliaries are both useless and dangerous. Anyone who relies on mercenary troops to keep himself in power will never be safe or secure, for they are factious, ambitious, ill-disciplined, treacherous. They show off to your allies and run away from your enemies. They do not fear God and do not keep faith with mankind. A mercenary army puts off defeat for only so long as it postpones going into battle. In peacetime they pillage you, in wartime they let the enemy do it. This is why: They have no motive or principle for joining up beyond the desire to collect their pay. And what you pay them is not enough to make them want to die for you. They are delighted to be your soldiers when you are not at war; when you are at war, they walk away when they do not run. It should not be difficult to convince you of this, because the sole cause of the present ruin of Italy has been the fact that for many years now the Italians have been willing to rely on mercenaries. It is true that occasionally a ruler seems to benefit from their use, and they boast of their own prowess, but as soon as they face foreign troops their true worth becomes apparent. This is why Charles, King of France, was able to conquer Italy with a piece of chalk; and the person who said we were being punished for our sins spoke the truth.[45] But our sins were not the ones of which he was thinking, but those I have been discussing. Because these were the sins of our rulers, our rulers as well as the common people had to pay the price for them.

I want now to make crystal clear the worthlessness of mercenary armies. Mercenary commanders are either excellent or not. If they are excellent, you cannot trust them, for they will always be looking for ways of increasing their own power, either by turning on you, their employer, or by turning on others whom you want them to leave alone. On the other hand, if they are not first rate [*virtuoso*], then they will be the ruin of you in the normal course of events. And if you want to reply the same problems will arise whoever makes up the army, whether they are mercenaries or not, I will argue it depends on whether they take their orders from a sovereign or from a republic. A sovereign ought to go to war himself, and be his own general. A republic has to send one of its citizens. If it chooses someone who turns out not to be a successful soldier, it must replace him; if it chooses someone who is successful, it must tie his hands with laws, to ensure he keeps within the limits assigned to him. Experience shows individual sovereigns and republics that arm the masses are capable of making vast conquests; but mercenary troops are always a liability. Moreover, it is harder for a treacherous citizen to suborn an army consisting of his own fellow subjects than one made up of foreigners.

Rome and Sparta were armed and free for many centuries. The Swiss are armed to the teeth and do not have to take orders from anyone. In ancient history, we can take the Carthaginians as an example of the consequences of relying on mercenaries. They were in danger of being oppressed by their mercenary soldiers when the first war with Rome was over,[46] despite the fact they employed their own citizens as commanders. Philip of Macedon was made general of the Theban armies after the death of Epaminondas; and, after he had won the war, he enslaved the Thebans.[47] In modern times, Milan, after Duke Filippo died, employed Francesco Sforza to fight the Venetians. Once he had defeated the enemy at Caravaggio, he joined forces with them to attack the Milanese, his employers.[48] Sforza his father, who was employed

---

45. The chalk was used by Charles's quartermasters to mark the soldiers' billets. Savonarola attributed Charles's victory to sins such as fornication and usury.

46. In 346 B.C.

47. In 338 B.C.

48. In 1448.

by Queen Giovanna of Naples, abandoned her without warning and without defenses.[49] As a consequence, she was obliged to throw herself into the embrace of the King of Aragon in order to hold on to her kingdom. If the Venetians and the Florentines have in the past succeeded in acquiring new territory with mercenary armies, and if their commanders have not seized the conquests for themselves, but have held onto them for their employers, this, I would argue, is because the Florentines have had more than their share of luck. For of the first-rate [*virtuosi*] commanders, whom they would have had reason to fear, some have not been victorious, some have not been in sole command, and some have turned their ambitions elsewhere. It was John Hawkwood who did not win: We cannot know if he would have proved reliable had he been victorious, but no one can deny that if he had won Florence would have been his for the taking.[50] Sforza always had to share command with the Braccheschi, and neither could act for fear of the other. Francesco turned his ambitions to Lombardy; Braccio[51] turned his against the church and the Kingdom of Naples.

But let us look at what happened only a short time ago. The Florentines made Paolo Vitelli their commander.[52] He was a very astute man, and, despite being of modest origin, he had acquired a tremendous reputation. If he had succeeded in taking Pisa, no one can deny the Florentines would have needed his goodwill, for, if he had transferred his support to their enemies, they would have been without defenses; and if they had managed to keep his support, they would have had no choice but to do as he told them.

Consider next the conquests made by the Venetians. You will see they ran no risks and won magnificent victories as long as they relied on their own troops, which was until they tried to conquer territory on the mainland. When they armed both the nobility and the populace they had a magnificent fighting force [*operorono virtuosissimamente*], but when they began to fight on the mainland they abandoned this sound policy [*questa virtù*], and began to copy the other Italian states. When they began their conquests on the mainland, because they had little territory there, and because their own reputation was fearsome, they had little to fear from their mercenary commanders. But as their conquests extended, as they did under Carmagnola, they began to discover

49.   In 1420.

50.   Hawkwood (ca. 1320–94) began to be employed by Florence in 1380.

51.   Andrea Fortebraccio (1368–1424).

52.   In 1498.

their mistake.[53] They recognized he was a first-rate [*virtuosissimo*] general, and that they had, under his command, defeated the Duke of Milan, but they realized he had lost his taste for war, and concluded they could no longer win with him, because he no longer wanted victory; but they could not dismiss him, or the land they had acquired would go with him. So, in order to neutralize him, they had to kill him. Since then they have employed as commanders of their forces Bartolemeo of Bergamo, Roberto of San Severino, the Count of Pitigliano, and others like them. With such commanders they had reason to fear defeat, not the consequences of victory. And indeed they were defeated at Vailà, where, in one day, they lost all they had acquired with so much effort in eight hundred years.[54] For with mercenary troops one acquires new territory slowly, feebly, after many attempts; but one loses so much so quickly that it seems an act of God.

And, since these examples have been drawn from recent Italian experience, and since Italy has been entirely dependent on mercenary forces for many years, I want to trace the present state of affairs back to its source, so that, having seen the origin and development of the problem, it will be easier to see how to correct it. You need to understand, then, that in modern times, as soon as the authority of the Holy Roman Empire began to be rejected in Italy, and the pope began to acquire greater authority in temporal affairs, Italy began to be divided into a number of different states. Many of the larger cities went to war against the nobility of the surrounding countryside, who had been oppressing them, and who were, at first, supported by the emperor. The Church, on the other hand, favored the cities in order to build up its temporal authority. In many other cities individual citizens established princedoms. So Italy came to be more or less divided up between those who owed allegiance to the papacy and a number of independent republican city states. Since neither the priests nor the citizens of the republics were accustomed to fighting wars, they began to employ foreigners in their armies.

The first to win a reputation for these mercenary troops was Alberigo of Conio in the Romagna.[55] Among those who were trained by him were Braccio and Sforza, who were, at the height of their powers, the

---

53. Francesco Bussone, Count of Carmagnola (b. ca. 1390), hired by the Venetians in 1425, executed in 1432.

54. The Battle of Vailà, generally known as Agnadello, 4 May 1509.

55. Really the first Italian: He had been preceded, for example, by Hawkwood. He was victor at Marino (1379) and died in 1409.

arbiters of Italian affairs. After them came all the others who have commanded mercenary forces down to the present time. The outcome of all their prowess [*virtù*] has been that Italy has, in quick succession, been overrun by Charles, plundered by Louis, raped by Ferdinand, and humiliated by the Swiss.

The first objective these mercenary commanders have pursued has been to destroy the reputation of the infantry in order to build up that of their own forces. They did this because they have had no resources of their own, but have been dependent on their contracts. A few infantry would have done little for their reputation, while they could not afford to feed a large number. So they specialized in cavalry, for they could feed a reasonably large number, and with them win respect. It came to the point that in an army of twenty thousand soldiers there would not even be two thousand infantry. In addition, they have done everything they could to free themselves and their troops from trouble and from danger. During skirmishes between opposing forces they did not kill each other: Indeed, they not only took prisoners, but released them without demanding a ransom. They were in no hurry to assault fortifications under cover of darkness, while the defending troops were far from eager to mount sorties against their assailants. When they made camp they did not protect themselves with trenches or palisades. They passed the winters in barracks. And all these practices were permitted by their standing orders and were invented, as I said, so they could avoid effort and risk: so much so that they have reduced Italy to a despicable slavery.

Chapter Thirteen: About auxiliary troops, native troops, and
composite armies.

Auxiliaries are the other sort of useless troops. You rely on auxiliaries when you appeal to another ruler to come with his own armies to assist or defend you. This is what Pope Julius did in recent times, when, having discovered the incompetence of his mercenary troops during the siege of Ferrara, he decided to rely on auxiliaries, and reached an agreement with King Ferdinand of Spain that he would come to his assistance with his men and arms.[56] Auxiliary troops can be useful and good when fighting on their own behalf, but they are almost always a liability for anyone relying on their assistance. For if they lose, it is you who are defeated; if they win, you are their prisoner. There are plenty of examples of this in ancient history, but I do not want to stray

56. In 1510.

from the contemporary case of Pope Julius II; he can have had no idea what he was doing when, in the hope of acquiring Ferrara, he placed himself entirely into the hands of a foreigner. But he was lucky: The outcome was neither defeat nor imprisonment, so he did not have to pay the price for his foolish decision. His auxiliaries were routed at Ravenna,[57] but then the Swiss came along and drove out the victors, so that, contrary to everyone's expectation, including his own, he did not end up either a prisoner of his enemies, who had fled, or of his auxiliaries, for it was not they who had been victorious. Another example: The Florentines, having no troops of their own, brought ten thousand French soldiers to take Pisa.[58] This decision placed them in more danger than at any other time during their troubles. Again, the Emperor of Constantinople, in order to attack his neighbors, brought ten thousand Turks into Greece. They, when the war was over, had no intention of leaving: This was the beginning of Greece's enslavement to the infidels.[59]

He, then, who has no desire to be the victor should use these troops, for they are much more dangerous than mercenaries. If your auxiliaries win you are ruined, for they are united in their obedience to someone else. If your mercenaries win it takes them more time and more favorable circumstances to turn against you, for they are not united among themselves, and it is you who recruited and paid them. If you appoint an outsider to command them, it takes him time to establish sufficient authority to be able to attack you. In short, where mercenaries are concerned the main risk is cowardice; with auxiliaries it is valor [*virtù*].

A wise ruler, therefore, will always avoid using mercenary and auxiliary troops, and will rely on his own forces. He would rather lose with his own troops than win with someone else's, for he will not regard it a true victory if it is won with troops that do not belong to him. I never hesitate to cite Cesare Borgia as a model to be imitated. This duke entered the Romagna with an auxiliary army, for his troops were all Frenchmen, and he used it to take Imola and Forlì.[60] But since he did not feel such troops were reliable, he then switched over to mercenaries, believing that using them involved fewer risks, and so he hired the Orsini and the Vitelli. But in practice he found them unreliable, treacherous, and dangerous, and so he got rid of them and formed his own

57.   11 April 1512.

58.   In 1500.

59.   The war lasted from 1341 to 1347; Constantinople did not finally fall to the Turks until 1453.

60.   In the winter of 1499–1500.

army. And it is easy to see the differences among these three types of army, for you only have to consider how the duke's reputation changed, depending on whether he was relying on the French alone, on the Orsini and the Vitelli, or on his own troops and his own resources. With each change of policy it increased, but he was only taken seriously when everyone could see he was in complete command of his own forces.

I wanted to stick to examples that are both recent and Italian, but I cannot resist mentioning Hiero of Syracuse, since I have already discussed him above. He, when he was made commander-in-chief by the Syracusans, as I have described, quickly realized their mercenary army was worthless, for it was made up of condottieri like our own Italian armies. He decided he could not risk either keeping them on, or letting them go, so he had them massacred. Thereafter, he went to war with troops of his own, not with other people's soldiers. I also want to remind you of an Old Testament story that is relevant. When David proposed to Saul that he should go and fight with Goliath, the Philistine champion, Saul, in order to give him confidence, dressed him in his own armor. David, having tried it on, rejected it, saying he could not give a good account of himself if he relied on Saul's weapons. He wanted to confront the enemy armed with his sling and his knife.[61]

In short, someone else's armor either falls off, or it weighs you down, or it trips you up. Charles VII, father of King Louis XI, having through good luck and valor [*virtù*] driven the English out of France,[62] recognized that it was essential to have one's own weapons and, so, issued instructions for the establishment of a standing army of cavalry and infantry. Later, his son King Louis abolished the infantry[63] and began to recruit Swiss troops. It was this mistake, imitated by his successors, that was, as we can see from recent events, the cause of the dangers faced by that kingdom.[64] For he built up the reputation of the Swiss while undermining his own military capacity, for he destroyed his own infantry and made his own cavalry dependent on the support of foreign troops, for they, having become accustomed to fighting alongside the Swiss, no longer think they can win without them. The result is the French dare not fight against the Swiss, and without the Swiss they are ineffective against anyone else. So the French armies have been

61.   I Kings 17.
62.   In 1453.
63.   In 1474.
64.   Machiavelli is thinking of the defeats of 1512, which had virtually forced the French out of Italy.

mixed, partly mercenary and partly native. Such a mixed army is much preferable to one made up only of auxiliaries or only of mercenaries, but it is much inferior to one made up entirely of one's own troops. The French example is sufficient to make the point, for the Kingdom of France would be able to overcome any enemy if the foundations laid by Charles VII had been built upon, or even if his instructions had merely been kept in force. But men are foolish, and they embark on something that is attractive in its outward appearance, without recognizing the evil consequences that will follow from it: a point I have already made when talking about consumption.

A ruler who cannot foresee evil consequences before they have time to develop is not truly wise; but few have such wisdom. And if one studies the first destruction of the Roman Empire one discovers it came about as a result of the first recruitment of Gothic soldiers,[65] for from that moment the armies of the Roman Empire began to grow feeble. And all the strength [*virtù*] that ebbed from the Romans accrued to the Goths. I conclude, therefore, that no ruler is secure unless he has his own troops. Without them he is entirely dependent on fortune, having no strength [*virtù*] with which to defend himself in adversity. Wise men have always believed and said that, "Nothing is so fragile as a reputation for strength that does not correspond to one's real capacities." Now one's own troops can be made up out of one's subjects, or one's citizens, or one's dependents: All others are either mercenaries or auxiliaries. And the correct way of organizing one's own troops is easy to find out by looking over the instructions given by the four rulers whose conduct I have approved, or by finding out how Philip, the father of Alexander the Great, and how many other republics and sovereigns levied and trained troops: I have complete confidence in their methods.

Chapter Fourteen: What a ruler should do as regards the militia.

A ruler, then, should have no other concern, no other thought, should pay attention to nothing aside from war, military institutions, and the training of his soldiers. For this is the only field in which a ruler has to excel. It is of such importance [*virtù*] that military prowess not only keeps those who have been born rulers in power, but also often enables men who have been born private citizens to come to power. On the other hand, one sees that when rulers think more about luxuries than about weapons, they fall from power. The prime reason for losing

---

65. In 376.

power is neglect of military matters; while being an expert soldier opens the way to the acquisition of power.

Francesco Sforza, because he had troops, became Duke of Milan,[66] having begun life as a private citizen. His descendants, who had no taste for the sweat and dust of a soldier's life, started out as dukes and ended up as private citizens. For, among the other deleterious consequences of not having one's own troops, one comes to be regarded with contempt. There are several types of disgrace a ruler should avoid, as I will explain below. This is one of them. For there is no comparison between a ruler who has his own troops and one who has not. It is not to be expected that someone who is armed should cheerfully obey someone who is defenseless, or that someone who has no weapon should be safe when his employees are armed. For the armed man has contempt for the man without weapons; the defenseless man does not trust someone who can overpower him. The two cannot get on together. So, too, a ruler who does not know how to organize a militia, beyond the other dangers he faces, which I have already described, must recognize that he will not be respected by his troops, and that he cannot trust them.

So a ruler must think only of military matters, and in time of peace he should be even more occupied with them than in time of war. There are two ways he can prepare for war: by thinking and by doing. As far as actions are concerned, he should not only keep his troops in good order and see they are well-trained; he should be always out hunting, thereby accustoming his body to fatigue. He should take the opportunity to study the lie of the land, climbing the mountains, descending into the valleys, crossing the plains, fording rivers, and wading through marshes. He should spare no effort to become acquainted with his own land, and this for two reasons. First, the knowledge will stand him in good stead if he has to defend his state against invasion; second, his knowledge and experience on his own terrain will make it easy for him to understand any other landscape with which he has to become acquainted from scratch. The hills, the valleys, the plains, the rivers, the marshes of, for example, Tuscany have a good deal in common with those of the other regions of Italy. A knowledge of the terrain in one region will make it easy for him to learn about the others. A ruler who lacks this sort of skill does not satisfy the first requirement in a military commander, for it is knowledge of the terrain that enables you to locate the enemy and to get the edge over him when deciding where

66. In 1450.

to camp, in what order to march, how to draw up the troops on the field of battle, and where to build fortifications.

Philopoemon,[67] ruler of the Achaeans, is much praised by the historians,[68] but in particular he is admired because during peacetime he thought about nothing but warfare. When he was out riding in the countryside with his friends, he would often halt and ask: "If the enemy were up on those hills, and we were down here with our army, who would have the better position? How should we advance, following the rule book, to attack him? If we wanted to retreat, how would we set about it? If they were retreating, how would we pursue them?" And so he would invite them to discuss, as they rode along, all the possible eventualities an army may have to face. He listened to their views, he explained his own and backed them up with arguments. Thanks to this continual theorizing he ensured that, if he was at the head of an army, he would be perfectly prepared for anything that might happen.

Such theorizing is not enough. Every ruler should read history books, and in them he should study the actions of admirable men. He should see how they conducted themselves when at war, study why they won some battles and lost others, so he will know what to imitate and what to avoid. Above all he should set himself to imitate the actions of some admirable historical character, as great men have always imitated their glorious predecessors, constantly bearing in mind their actions and their ways of behaving. So, it is said, Alexander the Great took Achilles as his model; Caesar took Alexander; Scipio took Cyrus. If you read the life of Cyrus that was written by Xenophon and then study the life of Scipio you will realize to what extent those qualities that are admired in Scipio derive from Cyrus: His chastity, his affability, his kindness, his generosity, all are modelled upon Cyrus as Xenophon portrays him. A wise ruler will follow these examples. He will never relax during peacetime, but will always be working to take advantage of the opportunities peace presents, so he will be fully prepared when adversity comes. When his luck changes, he must be ready to fight back.

Chapter Fifteen: About those factors that cause men, and especially rulers, to be praised or censured.

Our next task is to consider the policies and principles a ruler ought to follow in dealing with his subjects or with his friends. Since I know

67. 253–184 B.C.
68. Livy, bk. 25, ch. 28. Machiavelli would also have known the accounts in Plutarch and Polybius.

many people have written on this subject, I am concerned it may be thought presumptuous for me to write on it as well, especially since what I have to say, as regards this question in particular, will differ greatly from the recommendations of others.[69] But my hope is to write a book that will be useful, at least to those who read it intelligently, and so I thought it sensible to go straight to a discussion of how things are in real life and not waste time with a discussion of an imaginary world. For many authors have constructed imaginary republics and principalities that have never existed in practice and never could; for the gap between how people actually behave and how they ought to behave is so great that anyone who ignores everyday reality in order to live up to an ideal will soon discover he has been taught how to destroy himself, not how to preserve himself. For anyone who wants to act the part of a good man in all circumstances will bring about his own ruin, for those he has to deal with will not all be good. So it is necessary for a ruler, if he wants to hold on to power, to learn how not to be good, and to know when it is and when it is not necessary to use this knowledge.

Let us leave to one side, then, all discussion of imaginary rulers and talk about practical realities. I maintain that all men, when people talk about them, and especially rulers, because they hold positions of authority, are described in terms of qualities that are inextricably linked to censure or to praise. So one man is described as generous, another as a miser [*misero*] (to use the Tuscan term; for "avaricious," in our language, is used of someone who has a rapacious desire to acquire wealth, while we call someone a "miser" when he is unduly reluctant to spend the money he has); one is called open-handed, another tight-fisted; one man is cruel, another gentle; one untrustworthy, another reliable; one effeminate and cowardly, another bold and violent; one sympathetic, another self-important; one promiscuous, another monogamous; one straightforward, another duplicitous; one tough, another easy-going; one serious, another cheerful; one religious, another atheistical; and so on. Now I know everyone will agree that if a ruler could have all the good qualities I have listed and none of the bad ones, then this would be an excellent state of affairs. But one cannot have all the good qualities, nor always act in a praiseworthy fashion, for we do not live in an ideal world. You have to be astute enough to avoid being thought to have those evil qualities that would make it impossible for you to retain power; as for those that are compatible

69.   Machiavelli is thinking in particular of Cicero, *De officiis*, and Seneca, *De clementia*.

with holding on to power, you should avoid them if you can; but if you cannot, then you should not worry too much if people say you have them. Above all, do not be upset if you are supposed to have those vices a ruler needs if he is going to stay securely in power, for, if you think about it, you will realize there are some ways of behaving that are supposed to be virtuous [*che parrà virtù*], but would lead to your downfall, and others that are supposed to be wicked, but will lead to your welfare and peace of mind.

Chapter Sixteen: On generosity and parsimony.

Let me begin, then, with the qualities I mentioned first. I argue it would be good to be thought generous; nevertheless, if you act in the way that will get you a reputation for generosity, you will do yourself damage. For generosity used skillfully [*virtuosamente*] and practiced as it ought to be, is hidden from sight, and being truly generous will not protect you from acquiring a reputation for parsimony. So, if you want to have a reputation for generosity, you must throw yourself into lavish and ostentatious expenditure. Consequently, a ruler who pursues a reputation for generosity will always end up wasting all his resources; and he will be obliged in the end, if he wants to preserve his reputation, to impose crushing taxes upon the people, to pursue every possible source of income, and to be preoccupied with maximizing his revenues. This will begin to make him hateful to his subjects, and will ensure no one thinks well of him, for no one admires poverty. The result is his supposed generosity will have caused him to offend the vast majority and to have won favor with few. Anything that goes wrong will destabilize him, and the slightest danger will imperil him. Recognizing the problem, and trying to economize, he will quickly find he has acquired a reputation as a miser.

So we see a ruler cannot seek to benefit from a reputation as generous [*questa virtù del liberale*] without harming himself. Recognizing this, he ought, if he is wise, not to mind being called miserly. For, as time goes by, he will be thought of as growing ever more generous, for people will recognize that as a result of his parsimony he is able to live on his income, maintain an adequate army, and undertake new initiatives without imposing new taxes. The result is he will be thought to be generous towards all those whose income he does not tax, which is almost everybody, and stingy towards those who miss out on handouts, who are only a few. In modern times nobody has succeeded on a large scale except those who have been thought miserly; the others came to nothing. Pope Julius II took advantage of a reputation for generosity

in order to win election, but once elected he made no effort to keep
his reputation, for he wanted to go to war. The present King of France[70]
has fought many wars without having to impose additional taxes on
his people, because his occasional additional expenditures are offset
by his long-term parsimony. The present King of Spain[71] could not
have aspired to, or achieved, so many conquests if he had had a
reputation for generosity.

So a ruler should not care about being thought miserly, for it means
he will be able to avoid robbing his subjects; he will be able to defend
himself; he will not become poor and despicable, and he will not be
forced to become rapacious. This is one of those vices that make
successful government possible. And if you say: But Caesar rose to
power thanks to his generosity, and many others have made their way
to the highest positions of authority because they have both been
and have been thought to be generous. I reply, either you are already a
ruler, or you are on your way to becoming one. If you are already a
ruler, generosity is a mistake; if you are trying to become one then
you do, indeed, need to be thought of as generous. Caesar was one of
those competing to become the ruler of Rome; but if, having acquired
power, he had lived longer and had not learned to reduce his expenditures, he would have destroyed his own position. You may be tempted to
reply: Many established rulers who have been thought to be immensely
generous have been successful in war. But my answer is: Rulers either
spend their own wealth and that of their subjects, or that of other
people. Those who spend their own and their subjects' wealth should
be abstemious; those who spend the wealth of others should seize every
opportunity to be generous. Rulers who march with their armies, living
off plunder, pillage, and confiscations are spending other people's
money, and it is essential they should seem generous, for otherwise
their soldiers will not follow them. With goods that belong neither
to you nor to your subjects, you can afford to be generous, as Cyrus,
Caesar, and Alexander were. Squandering other people's money does
not do your reputation any harm, quite the reverse. The problem is
with squandering your own. There is nothing so self-defeating as
generosity, for the more generous you are, the less you are able to be
generous. Generosity leads to poverty and disgrace, or, if you try to
escape that, to rapacity and hostility. Among all the things a ruler
should try to avoid, he must avoid above all being hated and despised.
Generosity leads to your being both. So it is wiser to accept a reputa-

70. Louis XII.
71. Ferdinand the Catholic.

tion as miserly, which people despise but do not hate, than to aspire to a reputation as generous, and as a consequence, be obliged to face criticism for rapacity, which people both despise and hate.

Chapter Seventeen: About cruelty and compassion; and about
whether it is better to be loved than feared, or
the reverse.

Going further down our list of qualities, I recognize every ruler should want to be thought of as compassionate and not cruel. Nevertheless, I have to warn you to be careful about being compassionate. Cesare Borgia was thought of as cruel; but this supposed cruelty of his restored order to the Romagna, united it, rendered it peaceful and law-abiding. If you think about it, you will realize he was, in fact, much more compassionate than the people of Florence, who, in order to avoid being thought cruel, allowed Pistoia to tear itself apart.[72] So a ruler ought not to mind the disgrace of being called cruel, if he keeps his subjects peaceful and law-abiding, for it is more compassionate to impose harsh punishments on a few than, out of excessive compassion, to allow disorder to spread, which leads to murders or looting. The whole community suffers if there are riots, while to maintain order the ruler only has to execute one or two individuals. Of all rulers, he who is new to power cannot escape a reputation for cruelty, for he is surrounded by dangers. Virgil has Dido say:

> Harsh necessity, and the fact my kingdom is new, oblige me to do
> these things,
> And to mass my armies on the frontiers.[73]

Nevertheless, you should be careful how you assess the situation and should think twice before you act. Do not be afraid of your own shadow. Employ policies that are moderated by prudence and sympathy. Avoid excessive self-confidence, which leads to carelessness, and avoid excessive timidity, which will make you insupportable.

This leads us to a question that is in dispute: Is it better to be loved than feared, or vice versa?[74] My reply is one ought to be both loved and feared; but, since it is difficult to accomplish both at the same time, I maintain it is much safer to be feared than loved, if you have

72. In 1501.
73. Virgil, *Aeneid*, I, 563–4.
74. Cicero, *De officiis*, bk. 2, ch. 7, § 23–24.

to do without one of the two. For of men one can, in general, say this: They are ungrateful, fickle, deceptive and deceiving, avoiders of danger, eager to gain. As long as you serve their interests, they are devoted to you. They promise you their blood, their possessions, their lives, and their children, as I said before, so long as you seem to have no need of them. But as soon as you need help, they turn against you. Any ruler who relies simply on their promises and makes no other preparations, will be destroyed. For you will find that those whose support you buy, who do not rally to you because they admire your strength of character and nobility of soul, these are people you pay for, but they are never yours, and in the end you cannot get the benefit of your investment. Men are less nervous of offending someone who makes himself lovable, than someone who makes himself frightening. For love attaches men by ties of obligation, which, since men are wicked, they break whenever their interests are at stake. But fear restrains men because they are afraid of punishment, and this fear never leaves them. Still, a ruler should make himself feared in such a way that, if he does not inspire love, at least he does not provoke hatred. For it is perfectly possible to be feared and not hated. You will only be hated if you seize the property or the women of your subjects and citizens. Whenever you have to kill someone, make sure you have a suitable excuse and an obvious reason; but, above all else, keep your hands off other people's property; for men are quicker to forget the death of their father than the loss of their inheritance. Moreover, there are always reasons why you might want to seize people's property; and he who begins to live by plundering others will always find an excuse for seizing other people's possessions; but there are fewer reasons for killing people, and one killing need not lead to another.

When a ruler is at the head of his army and has a vast number of soldiers under his command, then it is absolutely essential to be prepared to be thought cruel; for it is impossible to keep an army united and ready for action without acquiring a reputation for cruelty. Among the extraordinary accomplishments of Hannibal, we may note one in particular: He commanded a vast army, made up of men of many different nations, who were fighting far from home, yet they never mutinied and they never fell out with one another, either when things were going badly, or when things were going well.[75] The only possible explanation for this is that he was known to be harsh and cruel. This, together with his numerous virtues [*virtù*], meant his soldiers always

---

75. Hannibal (247–ca. 183 B.C.) campaigned in Italy from 218 to 203 B.C. Machiavelli's source is Polybius, bk. 11, ch. 19.

regarded him with admiration and fear. Without cruelty, his other virtues [*virtù*] would not have done the job. Those who write about Hannibal without thinking things through both admire the loyalty of his troops and criticize the cruelty that was its principal cause. If you doubt my claim that his other virtues [*virtù*] would have been insufficient, take the case of Scipio.[76] He was not only unique in his own day, but history does not record anyone his equal. But his army rebelled against him in Spain.[77] The sole cause of this was his excessive leniency, which meant his soldiers had more freedom than is compatible with good military discipline. Fabius Maximus criticized him for this in the senate and accused him of corrupting the Roman armies. When Locri was destroyed by one of his commanders,[78] he did not avenge the deaths of the inhabitants, and he did not punish his officer's insubordination. He was too easygoing. This was so apparent that one of his supporters in the senate was obliged to excuse him by saying he was no different from many other men, who were better at doing their own jobs than at making other people do theirs. In course of time, had he remained in command without learning from his mistakes, this aspect of Scipio's character would have destroyed his glorious reputation. But, because his authority was subordinate to that of the senate, not only were the consequences of this defect mitigated, but it even enhanced his reputation.

I conclude, then, that, as far as being feared and loved is concerned, since men decide for themselves whom they love, and rulers decide whom they fear, a wise ruler should rely on the emotion he can control, not on the one he cannot. But he must take care to avoid being hated, as I have said.

Chapter Eighteen: How far rulers are to keep their word.

Everybody recognizes how praiseworthy it is for a ruler to keep his word and to live a life of integrity, without relying on craftiness. Nevertheless, we see that in practice, in these days, those rulers who have not thought it important to keep their word have achieved great things, and have known how to employ cunning to confuse and disorientate other men. In the end, they have been able to overcome those who have placed store in integrity.

76. Scipio (ca. 236–183 B.C.) defeated Hannibal at Zama in North Africa (202 B.C.).
77. In 206 B.C. Livy, bk. 28, chs. 24–29.
78. In 205 B.C.

You should therefore know there are two ways to fight: one while respecting the rules, the other with no holds barred. Men alone fight in the first fashion, and animals fight in the second.[79] But because you cannot always win if you respect the rules, you must be prepared to break them. A ruler, in particular, needs to know how to be both an animal and a man. The classical writers, without saying it explicitly, taught rulers to behave like this. They described how Achilles, and many other rulers in ancient times, were given to Chiron the centaur to be raised, so he could bring them up as he thought best. What they intended to convey, with this story of rulers' being educated by someone who was half beast and half man, was that it is necessary for a ruler to know when to act like an animal and when like a man; and if he relies on just one or the other mode of behavior he cannot hope to survive.

Since a ruler, then, needs to know how to make good use of beastly qualities, he should take as his models among the animals both the fox and the lion, for the lion does not know how to avoid traps, and the fox is easily overpowered by wolves.[80] So you must be a fox when it comes to suspecting a trap, and a lion when it comes to making the wolves turn tail. Those who simply act like a lion all the time do not understand their business. So you see a wise ruler cannot, and should not, keep his word when doing so is to his disadvantage, and when the reasons that led him to promise to do so no longer apply. Of course, if all men were good, this advice would be bad; but since men are wicked and will not keep faith with you, you need not keep faith with them. Nor is a ruler ever short of legitimate reasons to justify breaking his word. I could give an infinite number of contemporary examples to support my argument and to show how treaties and promises have been rendered null and void by the dishonesty of rulers; and he who has known best how to act the fox has come out of it the best. But it is essential to know how to conceal how crafty one is, to know how to be a clever counterfeit and hypocrite. You will find people are so simple-minded and so preoccupied with their immediate concerns, that if you set out to deceive them, you will always find plenty of them who will let themselves be deceived.

Among the numerous recent cases one could mention, there is one of particular interest. Alexander VI had only one purpose, only one thought, which was to take people in, and he always found people who were willing victims. There never has been anyone who was more convincing when he swore an oath, nor has there been anybody who

79.   Cicero, *De officiis*, bk. 1, ch. 11, § 34.
80.   The fox and the lion are from Cicero, *De officiis*, bk. 1, ch. 13, § 41.

has ever formulated more eloquent oaths and has at the same time been quicker to break them. Nevertheless, he was able to find gulls one after another, whenever he wanted them, for he was a master of this particular skill.

So a ruler need not have all the positive qualities I listed earlier, but he must seem to have them. Indeed, I would go so far as to say that if you have them and never make any exceptions, then you will suffer for it; while if you merely appear to have them, they will benefit you. So you should seem to be compassionate, trustworthy, sympathetic, honest, religious, and, indeed, be all these things; but at the same time you should be constantly prepared, so that, if these become liabilities, you are trained and ready to become their opposites. You need to understand this: A ruler, and particularly a ruler who is new to power, cannot conform to all those rules that men who are thought good are expected to respect, for he is often obliged, in order to hold on to power, to break his word, to be uncharitable, inhumane, and irreligious. So he must be mentally prepared to act as circumstances and changes in fortune require. As I have said, he should do what is right if he can; but he must be prepared to do wrong if necessary.

A ruler must, therefore, take great care that he never carelessly says anything that is not imbued with the five qualities I listed above. He must seem, to those who listen to him and watch him, entirely pious, truthful, reliable, sympathetic, and religious. There is no quality that it is more important he should seem to have than this last one. In general, men judge more by sight than by touch. Everyone sees what is happening, but not everyone feels the consequences. Everyone sees what you seem to be; few have direct experience of who you really are. Those few will not dare speak out in the face of public opinion when that opinion is reinforced by the authority of the state. In the behavior of all men, and particularly of rulers, against whom there is no recourse at law, people judge by the outcome. So if a ruler wins wars and holds on to power, the means he has employed will always be judged honorable, and everyone will praise them. The common man accepts external appearances and judges by the outcome; and when it comes down to it only the masses count; for the elite are powerless if the masses have someone to provide them with leadership. One contemporary ruler,[81] whom it would be unwise to name, is always preaching peace and good faith, and he has not a shred of respect for either; if he had respected either one or the other, he would have lost either his state or his reputation several times by now.

81. Ferdinand the Catholic.

56   *The Prince*

Chapter Nineteen: How one should avoid hatred and contempt.

Because I have spoken of the more important of the qualities I mentioned earlier, I want now to discuss the rest of them briefly under this general heading, that a ruler must take care (I have already referred to this in passing) to avoid those things that will make him an object of hatred or contempt. As long as he avoids these he will have done what is required of him, and he will find having a reputation for any of the other vices will do him no harm at all. You become hateful, above all, as I have said, if you prey on the possessions and the women of your subjects. You should leave both alone. The vast majority of men, so long as their goods and their honor are not taken from them, will live contentedly, so you will only have to contend with the small minority who are ambitious, and there are lots of straightforward ways of keeping them under control. You become contemptible if you are thought to be erratic, capricious, effeminate, pusillanimous, irresolute. You should avoid acquiring such a reputation as a pilot steers clear of the rocks. Make every effort to ensure your actions suggest greatness and endurance, strength of character and of purpose. When it comes to the private business of your subjects, you should aim to ensure you never have to change your decisions once they have been taken, and that you acquire a reputation that will discourage people from even considering tricking or deceiving you.

A ruler who is thought of in these terms has the sort of reputation he needs; and it is difficult to conspire against someone who is respected in this way, difficult to attack him, because people realize he is on top of his job and has the loyalty of his employees. For rulers ought to be afraid of two things: Within the state, they should fear their subjects; abroad, they should fear other rulers. Against foreign powers, a good army and reliable allies are the only defense; and, if you have a good army, you will always find your allies reliable. And you will find it easy to maintain order at home if you are secure from external threats, provided, that is, conspiracies against you have not undermined your authority. Even if foreign powers do attack, if you have followed my advice and lived according to the principles I have outlined, then, as long as you keep a grip on yourself, you will be able to resist any attack, just as I said Nabis of Sparta was able to. But where your subjects are concerned, when you are not being attacked by foreign powers, you have to be wary of secret conspiracies.[82] The best protection against

---

82.   Influential in Machiavelli's discussion of conspiracies is Aristotle, *Politics*, bk. 8.

these is to ensure you are not hated or despised, and the people are satisfied with your rule. It is essential to accomplish this, as I have already explained at length.

Indeed, one of the most effective defenses a ruler has against conspiracies is to make sure he is not generally hated. For conspirators always believe the assassination of the ruler will be approved by the people. If they believe the people will be angered, then they cannot screw up the courage to embark on such an enterprise, for conspirators have to overcome endless difficulties to achieve success. Experience shows the vast majority of conspiracies fail. For a conspirator cannot act alone, and he can only find associates among those whom he believes are discontented. As soon as you tell someone who is discontented what you are planning, you give him the means to satisfy his ambitions, because it is obvious he can expect to be richly rewarded if he betrays you. If he betrays you, his reward is certain; if he keeps faith with you, he faces danger, with little prospect of reward. So, you see, he needs either to be an exceptionally loyal friend or to be a completely intransigent enemy of the ruler, if he is to keep faith with you. So we can sum up as follows: The conspirators face nothing but fear, mutual distrust, and the prospect of punishment, so they lose heart; while the ruler is supported by the authority of his office and by the laws, and protected both by his supporters and by the forces of government. So, if you add to this inbuilt advantage the goodwill of the populace, then it is impossible to find anyone who is so foolhardy as to conspire against you. For in most situations a conspirator has to fear capture before he does the deed; but if the ruler has the goodwill of the people, he has to fear it afterwards as well, for the people will turn on him when the deed is done, and he will have nowhere to hide.

I could give an infinite number of examples to illustrate this, but I will confine myself to one only, a conspiracy that took place during the lifetime of our parents. Mr. Annibale Bentivoglio, grandfather of the present Mr. Annibale, was at the time ruler of Bologna. The Canneschi conspired against him and assassinated him.[83] His only surviving relative was Mr. Giovanni, who was still in the cradle. But as soon as he was killed the people rose up and killed all the Canneschi. This happened because the family of Bentivoglio had, in those days, the goodwill of the people. Their loyalty was such that, there being no surviving member of the family in Bologna who could, now Annibale was dead, take over the government, and they having heard that in Florence there was a member of the family, someone who so far had

83. In 1445.

been nothing more than the son of a blacksmith, the citizens of Bologna came to Florence to fetch him and made him the ruler of their city. He ruled it until Mr. Giovanni was old enough to take office.

I conclude, then, that a ruler need not worry much about conspiracies as long as the people wish him well; but if the people are hostile to him and hate him, then he should fear everything and everyone. States that are well-governed and rulers who are wise make every effort to ensure the elite are not driven to despair, and to satisfy the masses and keep them content; for this is one of the most important tasks a ruler must set himself.

Among the states that are well-ordered and well-ruled at the present time is France. There you will find innumerable good institutions that ensure the freedom of action and security of the king. First among them is the *parlement* and its authority.[84] For whoever set up the government of that country understood the powerful are ambitious and insolent, and judged it necessary they should be bridled so they could be controlled, but on the other hand he recognized the hatred most people have for the powerful, whom they have reason to fear, and the consequent need to reassure and protect the great. So he did not want this to be the responsibility of the king, in order to avoid his alienating the powerful by favoring the people or alienating the people by favoring the powerful, and he established an independent tribunal, whose task it is, without incurring blame for the king, to crush the powerful and defend the weak. This arrangement is as intelligent and prudent as could be, and makes a substantial contribution to the security of the king and the stability of the kingdom. This institution enables us to recognize a significant general principle: Rulers should delegate responsibility for unpopular actions, while taking personal responsibility for those that will win favor. And once again I conclude a ruler should treat the powerful with respect, but at all costs he should avoid being hated by the people.

Many perhaps will think, if they consider the lives and deaths of some of the Roman emperors, that these provide examples contrary to the opinion I have expressed. For it would seem some of them lived exemplary lives and demonstrated great strength [*virtù*] of character, yet they fell from power, or rather they were killed by their retainers, who had conspired against them. Since I want to reply to this objection, I will discuss the characters of some of the emperors, explaining the reasons why they were destroyed, and show they do not tell against

---

84. The *parlement* was the highest court of appeal. Its members belonged to a distinct social caste, the *noblesse de robe*.

my argument. This will primarily involve pointing out factors that would seem significant to anyone who read the history of those times. I will confine myself to discussing all those emperors who came after Marcus Aurelius, up to and including Maximilian:[85] that is, Marcus, his son Commodus, Pertinax, Julian, Severus, his son Antoninus Caracalla, Macrinus, Heliogabulus, Alexander, and Maximilian.

The first thing to be remarked is that, where in most states one only has to contend with the ambition of the great and the effrontery of the populace, the emperors of Rome had to face a third problem: They had to put up with the cruelty and greed of their soldiers. This was so difficult to do that it caused the downfall of many of the emperors, for it was almost impossible to satisfy both the soldiers and the populace. The people loved peace and quiet and, for this reason, liked their rulers to be unassuming; but the soldiers wanted the emperor to be a man of war and liked him to be arrogant, cruel, and rapacious. They wanted him to direct his aggression against the populace, so they could double their income and give free rein to their greed and cruelty. The result was those emperors who did not have a sufficiently intimidating reputation to keep both populace and soldiers in check (either because they did not think such a reputation desirable, or because they were incapable of acquiring it) were always destroyed. Most of them, especially those who acquired power without inheriting it, recognizing the difficulty of pleasing both soldiers and people, concentrated on pleasing the soldiers, thinking it could do little harm to alienate the populace. They had no choice, for, since rulers are bound to be hated by someone, their first concern must be to ensure they are not hated by any significant group; and, if they cannot achieve this, then they must make every possible effort to avoid the hatred of those groups that are most powerful. And so those emperors who had not inherited power and, thus, were in need of particularly strong support, attached themselves to the soldiers rather than to the people; a policy that proved successful or not, depending on whether the particular ruler in question knew how to establish his reputation with the army. For these reasons, then, Marcus, Pertinax, and Alexander, all of whom were unassuming, lovers of justice, haters of cruelty, sympathetic and kind, all came, apart from Marcus, to a tragic end. Marcus alone lived honorably and died peaceably, for he inherited power, and did not have to repay a debt to either the soldiers or the populace. Moreover, since he had many virtues [*virtù*] that made him widely respected, he was able, during

85. In other words, the period from 161 to 238. Machiavelli follows Herodian closely, probably relying on Poliziano's Latin translation.

his own lifetime, to keep both groups in their place, and he was never hated or despised. But Pertinax was made emperor against the wishes of the soldiers, who, being accustomed to an unbridled life under Commodus, were unable to tolerate the disciplined way of life Pertinax wanted to impose on them. So he made himself hated, and to this hatred was added contempt, for he was an old man, and so his rule had scarcely begun before he fell from power.

Here we should note one can become hated for the good things one does, as much as for the bad. That is why, as I said above, a ruler who wants to hold on to power is often obliged not to be good, for when some powerful group—whether the populace, the soldiers, or the elite—whose support you feel it is essential to have if you are to survive, is corrupt, then you have to adapt to its tastes in order to satisfy it, in which case doing good will do you harm. But let us turn to Alexander. He was so good that among the other things for which he is praised is the fact that during the fourteen years he retained power, nobody was ever executed at his orders without due trial. Nevertheless, he was thought effeminate, and blamed for being under the influence of his mother, and so he came to be despised, the army conspired against him and killed him.

By contrast, let us consider the qualities of Commodus, of Severus, Antoninus Caracalla, and Maximinus. They were, you will find, in the highest degree bloodthirsty and rapacious. In order to satisfy the soldiery, they did not fail to commit every possible type of crime against the populace; and all of them, with the exception of Severus, came to a bad end. For Severus was such a strong ruler [*in Severo fu tanta virtù*] that, with the support of the army, even though the populace were oppressed by him, he could always rule successfully; for his strength [*virtù*] inspired awe in the minds of both soldiers and people: The people were always to a considerable degree stupefied and astonished by him, while the soldiers were admiring and satisfied. Because his deeds were commendable in a new ruler, I want to pause to point out how well he understood how to play the part both of the fox and of the lion: These are the two styles of action I have maintained a ruler must know how to imitate. Severus, because he knew what a coward Julian the new emperor was, persuaded the army he had under his command in Slavonia that it was a good idea to march on Rome to revenge the death of Pertinax, who had been killed by his praetorian guard. With this excuse, and without displaying any ambition to seize the throne, he set out for Rome; and his army was in Italy before anyone knew it had left its station. When he reached Rome, the senate, out of fear, elected him emperor and had Julian put to death. Severus, having begun like this, faced two problems if he wanted to gain effective control of the whole empire: In Asia there was Niger, commander of the Asiatic armies, who had had himself proclaimed emperor; in the West there was Albinus, who also aspired to power. Because he thought it would be dangerous to take on both of them at once, he decided to attack Niger and deceive Albinus. So he wrote to Albinus saying now that he had been elected emperor by the senate, he wanted to share his authority with him. He offered him the title of Caesar and had the senate appoint him co-ruler. Albinus accepted these proposals at face value. But as soon as Severus had defeated and killed Niger and pacified the eastern empire, he returned to Rome and attacked Albinus in the senate, complaining that he, far from being grateful for the generosity he had been shown, had wickedly sought to assassinate him. Severus claimed to have no choice but to go and punish this ingrate. So he attacked him in France and deprived him of his offices and of his life.

Anyone who examines Severus's actions with care will find he was both a ferocious lion and a cunning fox. He will find he was feared and respected by all, and he was not hated by the armies. So it is no surprise Severus, who had not inherited power, was able to hold on to a vast empire, for his immense reputation was a constant defense against the hatred the populace might otherwise have felt for his exactions. Antoninus his son was also a man whose remarkable abilities inspired awe in the populace and gratitude in the soldiers. For he was a man of war, able to make light of the most arduous task and contemptuous of delicate food and all other luxuries. This made all his soldiers love him. Nevertheless, his ferocity and cruelty were without parallel. He did not only kill vast numbers of individuals, but, on one occasion, a large part of the population of Rome, and, on another, the whole of Alexandria. So he came to be loathed by everyone, and even his close associates began to fear him, with the result he was killed by a centurion while he was surrounded by his own troops. One should note rulers have no protection against an assassination like this, carried out by a truly determined individual, for anyone who is prepared to die can attack them. But, nevertheless, rulers should not worry unduly about such assassins because they are extremely rare. You should try merely to avoid giving grave injury to anyone you employ who comes close to you in the course of business. Antoninus had done just this, for he had outrageously put to death a brother of the centurion who killed him, and had repeatedly threatened the centurion's own life; yet he employed him as a bodyguard. This was foolhardy, and the disastrous outcome could have been predicted.

Now we come to Commodus, who had no difficulty in holding on

62 *The Prince*

to power, because he had inherited it, being the son of Marcus. All
he had to do was follow in his father's footsteps, and he would have
been satisfactory to both soldiers and populace. But, because he was
by nature cruel and brutal, he began to ingratiate himself with the
soldiers and to encourage them to be undisciplined, so he would be
able to give his own rapacity free rein against the people. On the other hand, he did not maintain his own dignity. Often, when he went to
the amphitheater, he came down and fought with the gladiators, and
he did other things that were despicable and incompatible with imperial majesty. So he became contemptible in the eyes of his soldiers. He
was hated by the people and despised by the soldiers, so there was
soon a conspiracy against him and he was killed.

There remains for us to discuss the character of Maximinus. He
was a most warlike individual. The armies had been irritated by the
feebleness of Alexander, whom I have already discussed, and so, with
him out of the way, they elected Maximinus emperor. But he did not
hold on to power for long, for there were two things that made him
hateful and contemptible. In the first place, he was of the lowest
social status, having once been a shepherd in Thrace (a fact known to
everyone, and one that made them all regard him with disdain); in the
second, when he was elected emperor he had delayed going to Rome
and taking possession of the throne, but had acquired a reputation for
terrible cruelty because his representatives, in Rome and throughout
the empire, had acted with great ferocity. So everybody was worked
up with disdain for his humble origins and agitated with hatred arising
from their fear of his ferocity. First Africa rebelled, and then the senate
and the whole population of Rome; soon all Italy was conspiring against
him. His own army turned against him. They were laying siege to
Aquileia, but were finding it hard to take the city, to which was added
their distaste for his cruelty. Seeing so many united against him, they
lost their fear of him and killed him.

I do not want to discuss Heliogabulus, Macrinus, and Julian, for
they were entirely contemptible and fell from power quickly. We can
now come to the end of this discussion. I would have you note the
rulers of our own day do not face in such an acute form the problem
of having to adopt policies that involve breaking the law in order to
satisfy their soldiers' appetites; for, although you cannot afford entirely
to ignore contemporary soldiers, you can handle them easily. Modern
rulers do not face standing armies with long experience of ruling and
administering provinces, such as the Roman armies had. But if in those
days it was more important to give satisfaction to the soldiers than to
the populace, that was because the soldiers were more to be feared
than the populace. Now all rulers, with the exception of the sultans of

Turkey and of Egypt, need to be more concerned to satisfy the populace than the soldiers, for the populace are the greater threat. I make an exception of the ruler of Turkey, for at all times he is surrounded by twelve thousand infantry and fifteen thousand cavalry, on whom depends the security and strength of his government. It is essential for him, more than anything else, to retain their loyalty. Similarly, the Sultan of Egypt is entirely at the mercy of his soldiers, so that he, too, must keep their loyalty, no matter what the consequences for the populace may be. And one should note the Sultan of Egypt is in a different position from all other rulers; for he is comparable to the Christian pope, who also cannot be described as either a hereditary or a new ruler. For the sons of the old ruler do not inherit his office and remain in power, but the new ruler is elected by a group who have the authority to appoint him. Since this arrangement has long been in existence, you cannot call the sultan a new ruler, for he faces none of the difficulties faced by those who are new to power. Even though he himself is new to power, the principle of succession is long-established, and ensures his authority is acknowledged as unquestioningly as would be the case if he were an hereditary ruler.

Let us return to our subject. I believe everyone should agree in the light of this discussion that hatred and contempt caused the fall of the emperors we have been considering, and will also understand how it comes about that, with one group of them following one line of policy and the other its opposite, in both groups one ruler was successful and the rest were killed. For it was pointless and dangerous for Pertinax and Alexander, who were new rulers, to try to imitate Marcus, who had inherited power; similarly it was a bad mistake for Caracalla, Commodus, and Maximinus to imitate Severus, for they lacked the strength [*virtù*] that would have been necessary for anyone following in his footsteps. Thus, a new ruler, who has not inherited power, should not follow the example of Marcus, but need not follow that of Severus. He ought to imitate in Severus those features that are essential for him to establish himself securely in power, and in Marcus those features that are effective and win glory for someone who is seeking to preserve a government that has already entrenched itself.

Chapter Twenty: Whether the building of fortresses (and many other things rulers regularly do) is useful or not.

Some rulers, in order to ensure they have a firm grip on power, have disarmed their subjects. Others have divided up the territories over which they rule. Some have positively encouraged opposition to their own authority. Others have set out to win over those who were hostile to them when they first came to power. Some have built fortresses. Others have destroyed them. It is impossible to pass definitive judgment on any of these policies until one considers the particular circumstances that existed in the state where the policy was adopted. Nevertheless, I will talk in general terms in so far as the subject itself permits.

No new ruler, let me point out, has ever disarmed his subjects; on the contrary, when he has found them disarmed, he has always armed them. For, when you arm them, their arms become yours, those who have been hostile to you become loyal, while those who have been loyal remain so, and progress from being your obedient subjects to being your active supporters. Because not every subject can be armed, provided you ensure those who receive arms stand to benefit, you will be more secure in your dealings with the others. When they recognize this diversity of treatment, it will make them all the more obliged to you; while the unarmed will forgive you, for they will recognize it is necessary that those who face more dangers and have more onerous obligations should be better rewarded. But if you take their arms away from those who have been armed, you begin to alienate them. You make it clear you do not trust them, either because you think they are poor soldiers or disloyal. Whichever view they attribute to you, they will begin to hate you. And, since you cannot remain undefended, you will be obliged to rely on mercenary troops, with the consequences we have already discussed. No matter how good they are, they will be unable to defend you against a combination of powerful foreign powers and hostile subjects. So, as I have said, a new ruler who has not inherited power has always formed his own army. There are innumerable examples in history. But when a ruler acquires a new state, which is simply added on to his existing territories, then it is essential to disarm the people, with the sole exception of those who have actively supported you in taking power. And they too, over time, and as opportunity occurs, should be encouraged to become weak and effeminate. You should arrange things so that all the weapons in your new state are in the hands of those of your own troops who were closely associated with you in your old territories.

Our ancestors, particularly those who were thought wise, used to say it was necessary to hold Pistoia by encouraging factional divisions, and Pisa by building fortresses. So, in some of the territory they occupied, they encouraged divisions in order to have better control. This was a sound policy in the days when Italy experienced a balance of power;[86] but I do not think it can be recommended now. For I do not

86.   From 1454 to 1494.

believe any good ever comes of internal conflicts. It is certain that when enemy forces approach you run the risk that divided cities will go over to the other side, for the weaker of the two internal factions will attach itself to the invaders, and the stronger will not be able to retain power against enemies within and without the walls.

The Venetians, following, I believe, the same line of thought as our ancestors, encouraged the division of the cities under their control into the two factions of Guelfs and Ghibellines.[87] Although they never allowed the conflicts between them to go so far as bloodshed, they encouraged these tensions so the inhabitants of these cities would be fully occupied with their own internal disagreements and would not unite against their masters. But history shows this policy did not pay off. For, when they were defeated at Vailà,[88] one of the factions quickly plucked up courage and deprived them of all their territories. Such policies, indeed, imply the ruler is weak, for a robust government would never allow such divisions, since you only benefit from them in time of peace, when they enable you to manage your subjects more easily; when war comes, such a policy proves to be misconceived.

There is no doubt rulers become powerful as they overcome the difficulties they face and the opposition they encounter. So fortune, especially when she wants to make a new ruler powerful (for new rulers have more need of acquiring a reputation than ones who have inherited power), makes him start out surrounded by enemies and endangered by threats, so he can overcome these obstacles and can climb higher on a ladder supplied by his enemies. Therefore, many conclude a wise ruler will, when he has the opportunity, secretly foster opposition to his rule, so that, when he has put down his opponents, he will be in a more powerful position.

Rulers, and especially those who are new to power, have sometimes found there is more loyalty and support to be had from those who were initially believed to be opposed to their rule, than from those whom from the start they could count on. Pandolfo Petrucci, ruler of Siena, governed his state by relying more on those who were supposed to be hostile to him than on his supporters.[89] But we cannot discuss this policy in general terms, because its success depends upon circumstances. I will only say those men who have been hostile when a ruler

87. These factions were present in many Italian cities. The Guelfs supported the papacy (and later the French), the Ghibellines the Holy Roman Emperor.

88. In 1509.

89. Petrucci (1450–1512) was effective ruler of Siena from 1487 until his death.

first acquires power, but who belong to those social groups that need to rely on government support in order to maintain their position, can always be won over by the new ruler with the greatest of ease. And they are all the more obliged to serve him faithfully because they know it is essential for them to undo by their actions the negative assessment that was initially made of them. Thus, the ruler can always get more out of them than out of those who, being all too confident of his goodwill, pay little attention to his interests.

And, since it is relevant to our subject, I do not want to fail to point out to rulers who have recently acquired a state through the support of people living within it, that they should give careful consideration to the motives of those who supported them. If they did not give their support out of natural affection for you, but gave it only because they were not happy with their previous government, you will find you can only retain their loyalty with much trouble and effort, for there is no way in which you will be able to keep them happy. If you think about it and consider the record of ancient and modern history, you will realize it will be much easier for you to win the loyalty of those men who were happy with the previous government and were therefore opposed to your seizure of power, than of those who, because they were unhappy with it, became your allies and encouraged you to take power from it.

Rulers have been accustomed, in order to have a more secure grip on their territories, to build fortresses. They are intended to be a bridle and bit for those who plan to rebel against you, and to provide you with a secure refuge in the event of an unexpected attack. I approve of this policy, for it was used by the Romans. Nevertheless, Mr. Niccolò Vitelli, in our own day, had two fortresses in Città di Castello destroyed so he could hold on to that state.[90] Guido Ubaldo, the Duke of Urbino, when he returned to power, having previously been driven into exile by Cesare Borgia, completely destroyed all the fortresses in his territory.[91] He believed that without them it would be harder to deprive him once again of power. The Bentivogli, when they recovered power in Bologna, adopted the same policy.[92]

We must conclude that fortresses are useful or not, depending on circumstances, and that, if they are useful at one time, they may also do you harm at another. We can identify the relevant factors as follows: A ruler who is more afraid of his subjects than of foreign powers should

90.   In 1482.
91.   In 1503.
92.   In 1511.

build fortresses; but a ruler who is more afraid of foreign powers than of his subjects should do without them. The castle of Milan, which was built by Francesco Sforza,[93] has done and will do more damage to the house of Sforza than any other defect in that state. For the best fortress one can have is not being hated by one's subjects; for if you have fortresses, but your subjects hate you, they will not save you, for your subjects, once they have risen in arms, will never be short of foreign allies who will come to their support.

In recent times, there is no evidence that fortresses have been useful to any ruler, except for the Contessa of Forlì, when her husband Count Girolamo died:[94] Because she could take refuge in one she was able to escape the popular uprising, hold out until assistance came from Milan, and retake her state. Circumstances at the time were such that the populace could not get assistance from abroad; but later, even she gained little benefit from her fortresses when Cesare Borgia attacked her, and the populace, still hostile to her, joined forces with the invaders.[95] So, both at first and later, it would have been safer for her not to have been hated by her people than to have fortresses. Consequently, having considered all these factors, I would praise both those who build fortresses and those who do not, but I would criticize anyone who, relying on his fortresses, thought it unimportant that his people hated him.

Chapter Twenty-One: What a ruler should do in order to acquire
a reputation.

Nothing does more to give a ruler a reputation than embarking on great undertakings and doing remarkable things. In our own day, there is Ferdinand of Aragon, the present King of Spain. He may be called, more or less, a new ruler, because having started out as a weak ruler he has become the most famous and most glorious of all the kings of Christendom. If you think about his deeds, you will find them all noble, and some of them extraordinary. At the beginning of his reign he attacked Granada, and this undertaking was the basis of his increased power.[96] In the first place, he undertook the reconquest when he had no other problems to face, so he could concentrate upon it. He used

---

93. In 1450.
94. In 1488.
95. In December 1499.
96. The muslim state of Granada was conquered between 1480 and 1492.

it to channel the ambitions of his Castilian barons, who, because they were thinking of the war, were no threat to him at home. Meanwhile, he acquired influence and authority over them without their even being aware of it. He was able to raise money from the church and from his subjects to build up his armies. Thus, this lengthy war enabled him to build up his military strength, which has paid off since. Next, in order to be able to engage in more ambitious undertakings, still exploiting religion, he practiced a pious cruelty, expropriating and expelling from his kingdom the Marranos:[97] an act without parallel and truly despicable. He used religion once more as an excuse to justify an attack on Africa.[98] He then attacked Italy and has recently[99] invaded France. He is always plotting and carrying out great enterprises, which have always kept his subjects bewildered and astonished, waiting to see what their outcome would be. And his deeds have followed one another so closely that he has never left space between one and the next for people to plot uninterruptedly against him.

It is also of considerable help to a ruler if he does remarkable things when it comes to domestic policy, such as those that are reported of Mr. Bernabò of Milan.[100] It is a good idea to be widely talked about, as he was, because, whenever anyone happened to do anything extraordinary, whether good or bad, in civil life, he found an imaginative way to reward or to punish them. Above all a ruler should make every effort to ensure that whatever he does it gains him a reputation as a great man, a person who excels.

Rulers are also admired when they know how to be true allies and genuine enemies: That is, when, without any reservations, they demonstrate themselves to be loyal supporters or opponents of others. Such a policy is always better than one of neutrality. For if two rulers who are your neighbors are at war with each other, they are either so powerful that, if one of them wins, you will have to fear the victor, or they are not. Either way, it will be better for you to take sides and fight a good fight; for, if they are powerful, and you do not take sides, you will still be preyed on by the victor, much to the pleasure and satisfaction of his defeated opponent. You will have no excuse, no defense, no

---

97.   The Marranos were Jews who had been forced to convert to Catholicism. On misinterpretations of this term, see Edward Andrew, "The Foxy Prophet: Machiavelli Versus Machiavelli on Ferdinand the Catholic," *History of Political Thought* 11 (1990), 409–22.

98.   In 1509.

99.   In 1512.

100.   Bernabò Visconti ruled Milan from 1354 to 1385.

refuge. For whoever wins will not want allies who are unreliable and who do not stand by him in adversity; while he who loses will not offer you refuge, since you were not willing, sword in hand, to share his fate.

The Aetolians invited Antiochus to Greece to drive out the Romans.[101] Antiochus sent an ambassador to the Achaeans, who were allies of the Romans, to encourage them to remain neutral; while the Romans urged them to fight on their side. The ruling council of the Achaeans met to decide what to do, and Antiochus's ambassador spoke in favor of neutrality. The Roman ambassador replied: "As for what they say to you, that it would be sensible to keep out of the war, there is nothing further from your true interests. If you are without credit, without dignity, the victor will claim you as his prize."

It will always happen that he who is not your ally will urge neutrality upon you, while he who is your ally will urge you to take sides. Rulers who are unsure what to do, but want to avoid immediate dangers, generally end up staying neutral and usually destroy themselves by doing so. But when a ruler boldly takes sides, if your ally wins, even if he is powerful, and has the ability to overpower you, he is in your debt and fond of you. Nobody is so shameless as to turn on you in so ungrateful a fashion. Moreover, victories are never so overwhelming that the victor can act without any constraint: Above all, victors still need to appear just. But if, on the other hand, your ally is defeated, he will offer you refuge, will help you as long as he is able, and will share your ill-fortune, in the hope of one day sharing good fortune with you. In the second case, when those at war with each other are insufficiently powerful to give you grounds to fear the outcome, there is all the more reason to take sides, for you will be able to destroy one of them with the help of the other, when, if they were wise, they would be helping each other. The one who wins is at your mercy; and victory is certain for him whom you support.

Here it is worth noting a ruler should never take the side of someone who is more powerful than himself against other rulers, unless necessity compels him to, as I have already implied. For if you win, you are your ally's prisoner; and rulers should do everything they can to avoid being at the mercy of others. The Venetians allied with the King of France against the Duke of Milan, when they could have avoided taking sides; they brought about their own destruction.[102] But when you cannot help but take sides (which is the situation the Florentines found themselves

101.   192 B.C. The source is Livy, bk. 35, chs. 48, 49.
102.   In 1499.

in when the pope and the King of Spain were advancing with their armies to attack Lombardy)[103] then you should take sides decisively, as I have explained. Do not for a moment think any state can always take safe decisions, but rather think every decision you take involves risks, for it is in the nature of things that you cannot take precautions against one danger without opening yourself to another. Prudence consists in knowing how to assess risks and in accepting the lesser evil as a good.

A ruler should also show himself to be an admirer of skill [*virtù*] and should honor those who are excellent in any type of work. He should encourage his citizens by making it possible for them to pursue their occupations peacefully, whether they are businessmen, farmers, or are engaged in any other activity, making sure they do not hesitate to improve what they own for fear it may be confiscated from them, and they are not discouraged from investing in business for fear of losing their profits in taxes; instead, he should ensure that those who improve and invest are rewarded, as should be anyone whose actions will benefit his city or his government. He should, in addition, at appropriate times of the year, amuse the populace with festivals and public spectacles. Since every city is divided into guilds or neighborhoods, he ought to take account of these collectivities, meeting with them on occasion, showing himself to be generous and understanding in his dealings with them, but at the same time always retaining his authority and dignity, for this he should never let slip in any circumstances.

Chapter Twenty-Two: About those whom rulers employ as
advisers.

A ruler's choice as to whom to employ as his advisers is of foremost importance. Rulers get the advisers they deserve, for good rulers choose good ones, bad rulers choose bad. The easiest way of assessing a ruler's ability is to look at those who are members of his inner circle. If they are competent and reliable, then you can be sure he is wise, for he has known both how to recognize their ability and to keep them faithful. But if they are not, you can always make a negative assessment of the ruler; for he has already proved his inadequacy by making a poor choice of adviser.

Nobody who knew Mr. Antonio of Venafro[104] when he was adviser

103.   In 1512.
104.   Machiavelli did, indeed, know Antonio Giordani of Venafro.

to Pandolfo Petrucci, ruler of Siena, could fail to conclude that Pandolfo was a brilliant man, for how else would he come by such an adviser? For there are three types of brains: One understands matters for itself, one follows the explanations of others, and one neither understands nor follows. The first is best, the second excellent, the third useless. It followed logically that if Pandolfo was not in the first rank, then he was at least in the second. For anyone who can judge the good or evil someone says and does, even if he does not have an original mind, will recognize what his adviser does well and what he does ill, and will encourage the first and correct the second. An adviser cannot hope to deceive such an employer, and will do his best.

But there is one infallible way for a ruler to judge his adviser. When you see your adviser give more thought to his own interests than yours, and recognize everything he does is aimed at his own benefit, then you can be sure such a person will never be a good adviser. You will never be able to trust him, for he who runs a government should never think of his own interests, but always of his ruler's, and should never suggest anything to his ruler that is not in the ruler's interests. On the other hand the ruler, in order to get the best out of his adviser, should consider his adviser's interests, heaping honors on him, enriching him, placing him in his debt, ensuring he receives public recognition, so that he sees that he cannot do better without him, that he has so many honors he desires no more, so much wealth he desires no more, so much status he fears the consequences of political upheaval. When a ruler has good advisers and knows how to treat them, then they can rely on each other; when it is otherwise, either ruler or adviser will suffer.

Chapter Twenty-Three: How sycophants are to be avoided.

I do not want to omit an important subject that concerns a mistake it is difficult for rulers to avoid making, unless they are very wise and good judges of men. My subject is sycophants, who pullulate at court. For men are so easily flattered and are so easily taken in by praise, that it is difficult for them to defend themselves against this plague, and in defending themselves they run the risk of making themselves despicable. For there is no way of protecting oneself against flattery other than by making it clear you do not mind being told the truth; but, when anyone can tell you the truth, then you are not treated with sufficient respect. So a wise ruler ought to find an alternative to flattery and excessive frankness. He ought to choose wise men from among his subjects, and give to them alone freedom to tell him the truth, but

only in reply to specific questions he puts to them, not on any subject
of their choice. But he ought to ask them about everything, and listen
to their replies; then think matters over on his own, in his own way.
His response to each of his advisers and their advice should make
it apparent that the more freely they talk, the happier he will be. But
he should listen to no one who has not been designated as an adviser,
he should act resolutely once he has made up his mind, and he should
cling stubbornly to his decisions once they have been taken. He who
acts otherwise either is rushed into decisions by flatterers or changes
his mind often in response to differing advice. Either way, people will
form a poor opinion of him.

I want, on this subject, to refer to an example from recent history.
The cleric Luca,[105] an adviser to Maximilian, the present emperor,
speaking of his sovereign, said that he did not ask for anyone's advice,
and that he never did anything the way he wanted to: which was because
he did not follow the principles I have just outlined. For the emperor
is a secretive man, he keeps things to himself and never asks anyone's
advice. But, when his decisions begin to be discovered, which is when
they begin to be put into effect, he begins to be criticized by those
who are close to him, and, as one might expect, he is persuaded to
change his mind. The result is that he undoes each day what he did
the day before; that nobody ever knows what he really wants or intends
to do; and that one cannot rely upon his decisions.

A ruler, therefore, should always take advice, but only when he wants
to, not when others want him to; he should discourage everybody from
giving him advice without being asked; but he should be always asking,
and, moreover, he should listen patiently to the answers, provided they
are truthful. But if he becomes persuaded by someone, for whatever
reason, is not telling him the truth, he should lose his temper. There
are many who think some rulers who have a reputation for being
prudent do not really deserve to be thought so, claiming that the rulers
themselves are not wise, but that they merely receive good advice. But
without doubt they are mistaken. For this is a general rule without
exceptions: A ruler who is not himself wise cannot be given good
advice. Unless, I should say, he hands over all decisions to one other
person and has the good luck to pick someone quite exceptionally
prudent. But such an exceptional arrangement will not last long, for
the man who takes all the decisions will soon take power. But a ruler
who is not wise, if he takes advice from more than one person,
will never get the same advice from everyone, nor will he be able to

105. Also known to Machiavelli.

combine the different proposals into a coherent policy unless he has help. His advisers will each think about his own interests, and he will not be able to recognize their bias or correct it. This is how it has to be, for you will find men are always wicked, unless you give them no alternative but to be good. So we may conclude that good advice, no matter who it comes from, really comes from the ruler's own good judgment, and that the ruler's good judgment never comes from good advice.

Chapter Twenty-Four: Why the rulers of Italy have lost their states.

The policies I have described, if prudently followed, will make a new ruler seem long-established and will rapidly make his power better entrenched than it would be if he had long held office. For the actions of a new ruler are much more closely scrutinized than those of an hereditary ruler; and new rulers, when they are seen to be strong [*virtuose*], attract much more support and make men more indebted to them than do hereditary rulers. For men are much more impressed by what goes on in the present than by what happened in the past; and when they are satisfied with what is happening now, they are delighted and ask for nothing more. So they will spring to a new ruler's defense, provided he plays his part properly. Thus, he will be doubly glorious: He will have begun a new tradition of government, under-pinned and ornamented with good laws, good arms, good allies, and good examples; just as he is doubly shamed who, being born a ruler, has lost power through lack of skill in ruling.

And if you consider those Italian rulers who have lost power in recent years, such as the King of Naples, the Duke of Milan, and others, you will find: First, they all had in common an inadequate military preparation, for the reasons I have discussed above at length; second, you will see that some of them either were at odds with their own populace or, if they had the support of the populace, did not know how to protect themselves from the elite; for without these defects they would not have lost states that were strong enough to put an army in the field. Philip of Macedon (not the father of Alexander, but the Philip who was defeated by Titus Quintius)[106] did not have a large state in comparison with the territory controlled by the Romans and the Greeks who attacked him; nevertheless, because he was a military man and a ruler who knew how to treat his populace and how to protect

106. Philip V, defeated in 197 B.C.

himself from the elite, he was able to sustain a war against superior forces for several years; and if, at the end, he lost control of several cities, he nevertheless retained his kingdom.

So our own rulers, each of whom had been in power for many years and then lost it, should not blame fortune but their own indolence. For when times were quiet they never once considered the possibility that they might change (it is a common human failing not to plan ahead for stormy weather while the sun shines). When difficult times did come, they thought of flight not of self-defense. They hoped the populace, irritated by the insolence of their conquerors, would recall them to power. This plan is a good one if there is no alternative policy available; but it is stupid to adopt it when there are alternatives. No one would be happy to trip and fall merely because he thought someone would help him back to his feet. Either no one comes to your assistance; or if someone does, you are the weaker for it, for your strategy for self-defense has been ignominious, and your fate has not been in your own hands. No method of defense is good, certain, and lasting that does not depend on your own decisions and your own strength [*virtù*].

Chapter Twenty-Five: How much fortune can achieve in human
affairs, and how it is to be resisted.

I am not unaware of the fact that many have held and still hold the view that the affairs of this world are so completely governed by fortune and by God that human prudence is incapable of correcting them, with the consequence that there is no way in which what is wrong can be put right. So one may conclude that there is no point in trying too hard; one should simply let chance have its way. This view has come to be more widely accepted in our own day because of the extraordinary variation in circumstances that has been seen and is still seen every day. Nobody could predict such events. Sometimes, thinking this matter over, I have been inclined to adopt a version of this view myself. Nevertheless, since our free will must not be eliminated, I think it may be true that fortune determines one half of our actions, but that, even so, she leaves us to control the other half, or thereabouts. And I compare her to one of those torrential rivers that, when they get angry, break their banks, knock down trees and buildings, strip the soil from one place and deposit it somewhere else. Everyone flees before them, everyone gives way in face of their onrush, nobody can resist them at any point. But although they are so powerful, this does not mean men, when the waters recede, cannot make repairs and build banks and barriers so that, if the waters rise again, either they will be safely kept within the sluices or at least their onrush will not be so unregulated and destructive. The same thing happens with fortune: She demonstrates her power where precautions have not been taken to resist her [*dove non è ordinata virtù a resisterle*]; she directs her attacks where she knows banks and barriers have not been built to hold her. If you think about Italy, which is the location of all these changes in circumstance, and the origin of the forces making for change, you will realize she is a landscape without banks and without any barriers. If proper precautions had been taken [*s'ella fussi reparata da conveniente virtù*], as they were in Germany, Spain, and France, either the flood would not have had the consequences it had, or the banks would not even have been overwhelmed. And what I have said is enough, I believe, to answer the general question of how far one can resist fortune.

But, turning rather to individuals, note we see rulers who flourish one day and are destroyed the next without our being able to see any respect in which they have changed their nature or their attributes. I think the cause of this is, in the first place, the one we have already discussed at length: A ruler who depends entirely on his good fortune will be destroyed when his luck changes. I also think a ruler will flourish if he adjusts his policies as the character of the times changes; and similarly, a ruler will fail if he follows policies that do not correspond to the needs of the times. For we see men, in those activities that carry them towards the goal they all share, which is the acquisition of glory and riches, proceed differently. One acts with caution, while another is headstrong; one is violent, while another relies on skill; one is patient, while another is the opposite: And any one of them, despite the differences in their methods, may achieve his objective. One also sees that of two cautious men, one will succeed, and the other not; and similarly we see that two men can be equally successful though quite different in their behavior, one of them being cautious and the other headstrong. This happens solely because of the character of the times, which either suits or is at odds with their way of proceeding. This is the cause of what I have described: that two men, behaving differently, achieve the same result, and of two other men, who behave in the same way, one will attain his objective and the other will not. This is also the cause of the fact that the sort of behavior that is successful changes from one time to another. Take someone who acts cautiously and patiently. If the times and circumstances develop in such a way that his behavior is appropriate, he will flourish; but if the times and circumstances change, he will be destroyed for he will continue to behave in the same way. One cannot find a man so prudent he knows how to adapt himself to changing circumstances, for he will either be unable to deviate from that style of behavior to which his character inclines him, or, alternatively, having always been successful by adopting one particular style, he will be unable to persuade himself that it is time to change. And so, the cautious man, when it is time to be headstrong, does not know how to act and is destroyed. But, if one knew how to change one's character as times and circumstances change, one's luck would never change.

Pope Julius II always acted impetuously; the style of action was so appropriate to the times and circumstances in which he found himself that the outcome was always successful. Consider his first attack on Bologna, when Mr. Giovanni Bentivoglio was still alive.[107] The Venetians were not happy about it; nor was the King of Spain; he had discussed such an action with the French, who had reached no decision. Nevertheless, because he was ferocious and impetuous, he placed himself personally at the head of his troops. This gesture made the Spanish and the Venetians hesitate and do nothing: the Venetians out of fear, and the Spanish because they wanted to recover the territories they had lost from the Kingdom of Naples. On the other hand, he dragged the King of France along behind him. For the king saw it was too late to turn back, and he wanted an alliance with him in order to weaken the Venetians, so he concluded he could not deny him the support of French troops without giving him obvious grounds for resentment. So Julius, by acting impetuously, achieved something no other pope, no matter how skillful and prudent, had been able to achieve. For, if he had delayed his departure from Rome until everything had been arranged and the necessary alliances had been cemented, as any other pope would have done, he would never have succeeded. The King of France would have found a thousand excuses, and his other allies would have pointed out a thousand dangers. I want to leave aside his other actions, for they were all similar, and they were all successful. He did not live long enough to experience failure. But, if the times had changed so that it was necessary to proceed with caution, he would have been destroyed. He would never have been able to change the style of behavior to which his character inclined him.

I conclude, then, that since fortune changes, and men stubbornly continue to behave in the same way, men flourish when their behavior suits the times and fail when they are out of step. I do think, however, that it is better to be headstrong than cautious, for fortune is a lady. It is necessary, if you want to master her, to beat and strike her. And

107. In 1506.

one sees she more often submits to those who act boldly than to those who proceed in a calculating fashion. Moreover, since she is a lady, she smiles on the young, for they are less cautious, more ruthless, and overcome her with their boldness.

Chapter Twenty-Six: Exhortation to seize Italy and free her from the barbarians.

Having considered all the matters we have discussed, I ask myself whether, in Italy now, we are living through times suitable for the triumph of a new ruler, and if there is an opportunity for a prudent and bold [*virtuoso*] man to take control of events and win honor for himself while benefiting everyone who lives here. It seems to me so many factors come together at the moment to help out a new ruler that I am not sure if there has ever been a more propitious time for such a man. If, as I said, Moses could only demonstrate his greatness [*virtù*] because the people of Israel were slaves in Egypt; if we would never have known what a great man Cyrus was if the Persians had not been oppressed by the Medes; if the remarkable qualities of Theseus only became apparent because the Athenians were scattered abroad; so now, the opportunity is there for some bold Italian to demonstrate his greatness [*virtù*]. For see the conditions to which Italy has been reduced: She is more enslaved than the Jews, more oppressed than the Persians, more defenseless than the Athenians. She has no leader, no organization. She is beaten, robbed, wounded, put to flight: She has experienced every sort of injury. Although so far there has been the occasional hint of exceptional qualities in someone, so that one might think he had been ordained by God to redeem Italy, yet later events have shown, as his career progressed, that he was rejected by fortune. So Italy has remained at death's door, waiting for someone who could bind her wounds and put an end to the sack of Lombardy, to the extortion of Tuscany and of the Kingdom of Naples, someone who could heal her sores which long ago became infected. One can see how she prays to God that he will send her someone who will redeem her from this ill treatment and from the insults of the barbarians. One can see every Italian is ready, everyone is eager to rally to the colors, if only someone will raise them high.

At the moment, there is nowhere Italy can turn in her search for someone to redeem her with more chance of success than to your own illustrious family, which is fortunate and resourceful [*virtù*], is favored by God and by the church (indeed the church is now at its command). The undertaking is straightforward, if you keep in mind the lives and the deeds of the leaders I have mentioned. Of course those men were exceptional and marvelous; but, nevertheless, they were only men, and none of them had as good an opportunity as you have at the moment. For their undertakings were not more just than this one, or easier, nor was God more their ally than he is yours. This is truly just: "A war is just if there is no alternative, and the resort to arms is legitimate if they represent your only hope."[108] These circumstances are ideal; and when circumstances are ideal there can be no great difficulty in achieving success, provided your family copies the policies of those I have recommended as your models. Beyond that, we have already seen extraordinary and unparalleled events. God has already shown his hand: The sea has been divided; a cloud has escorted you on your journey; water has flowed out of the rock; manna has fallen from on high. Everything has conspired to make you great. The rest you must do for yourselves. God does not want to have to do the whole thing, for he likes to leave us our free will so we can lay claim to part of the glory by earning it.

There is no need to be surprised that none of the Italian rulers I have discussed has been able to accomplish what I believe your family can achieve, or to be disheartened if during all the wars that have been fought, all the political upheavals that have taken place, it has seemed as if the Italians have completely lost their capacity to fight and win [*la virtù militare*]. This is simply because the traditional way of doing things in Italy is mistaken, and no one has appeared who has known how to bring about change. Nothing does more to establish the reputation of someone who comes new to power than do the new laws and the new institutions he establishes. These, when they are well thought out and noble in spirit, make a ruler revered and admired. In Italy we have the raw materials: You can do anything you wish with them. Here we have people capable of anything [*virtù grande*], all they need are leaders who know what to do. When it comes to fighting one-on-one the Italians prove themselves to be stronger, quicker, cleverer. But when it comes to the clash of armies, the Italians are hopeless. The cause lies in the inadequacy of the leaders. Those who know what to do are not obeyed, and everyone thinks he knows what to do. So far there has been no one who has known how to establish an authority, based on fortune and ability [*virtù*], such that the others will obey him. This is the reason why, through the whole of the last twenty years, during all the wars that have taken place in that time, not a single army consisting solely of Italians has done well. Twenty years ago the Italians were defeated

108.   Livy, bk. 9, ch. 1.

at Taro; since then at Alexandria, Capua, Genoa, Vailà, Bologna, Mestre.

So, if your illustrious family wants to follow in the footsteps of those excellent men who liberated the nations to which they belonged, you must, before you do anything else, do the one thing that is the precondition for success in any enterprise: Acquire your own troops. You cannot hope to have more faithful, more reliable, or more skillful soldiers. And if each soldier will be good, the army as a whole will be better still, once they see their ruler place himself at their head and discover he treats them with respect and sympathy. It is necessary, though, to get such an army ready, if we are to be able to defend Italy from the foreigners with Italian strength and skill [*con la virtù italica*].

It is true that the Swiss and Spanish infantries are thought to be intimidating; nevertheless, they both have their defects, so a third force could not only stand up to them, but could be confident of beating them. For the Spanish cannot withstand a cavalry charge; and the Swiss have reason to be afraid of infantry, should they come up against any as determined to win as they are. Thus, we have seen that the Spanish cannot withstand an attack by the French cavalry, and we will see in practice that the Swiss can be destroyed by the Spanish infantry. It is true that we have yet to see the Spanish properly defeat the Swiss, but we have seen an indication of what will happen at the Battle of Ravenna,[109] when the Spanish infantry clashed against the German battalions, for the Germans rely on the same formation as the Swiss. There the Spanish, thanks to their agility and with the help of their bucklers, were able to get underneath the pikes of the Germans and were able to attack them in safety, without the Germans' having any defense. If the cavalry had not driven them off, they would have wiped them out. So, since we know the weakness of each of these infantries, we ought to be able to train a new force that will be able to withstand cavalry and will not be afraid of infantry. To accomplish this we need specially designed weapons and new battle formations. This is the sort of new undertaking that establishes the reputation and importance of a new ruler.

So you should not let this opportunity slip by. Italy, so long enslaved, awaits her redeemer. There are no words to describe with what devotion he would be received in all those regions that have suffered from foreign invasions which have flooded across the land. No words can describe the appetite for revenge, the resolute determination, the spirit of self-sacrifice, the tears of emotion that would greet him. What gates

109. 11 April 1512.

would be closed to him? What community would refuse to obey him?
Who would dare be jealous of his success? What Italian would refuse
to pledge him allegiance? Everyone is sick of being pushed around by
the barbarians. Your family must commit itself to this enterprise. Do
it with the confidence and hope with which people embark on a just
cause so that, marching behind your banner, the whole nation is
ennobled. Under your patronage, may we prove Petrarch right:

> Virtue [*virtù*] will take up arms against savagery,
> And the battle will be short.
> For the courage of old is not yet dead
> In Italian hearts.[110]

---

110.   Petrarch, *Italia mia (Ai Signori d'Italia)*, ll. 93–6.

Selections from the *Discourses*[1]

Niccolò Machiavelli to Zanobi Buondelmonti and Cosimo Rucellai,[2] Greetings

I send you a present which, if it does not measure up to the obligations I have to you, is unquestionably the most valuable thing Niccolò Machiavelli could send you. For in it I have put in words all that I know and all I have learned from an extensive experience of the affairs of the world and endless reading about them. Neither you nor anybody else could ask more of me, so you have no reason to complain if this is all I have given you. Of course you may regret my inadequate intelligence when you find my discussions inadequate, and my poor judgment when, as I often do, I present a mistaken argument. In the circumstances, I am not sure which of us has least reason to be obliged to the other: I to you, who forced me to write a work which I, left to myself, would never have written, or you to me, if, in writing, I have not given you satisfaction. So accept this gift as we accept all gifts from friends, for then we always give more weight to the intention that lies behind the gift than to the quality of the gift itself.

And please believe that my manuscript gives me only one satisfaction, which is when I think that, even if I have been mistaken in many particular matters I discuss, I know that I have not made a mistake in at least one thing: in having chosen you, to whom above all others my *Discourses* are addressed. I feel that in so doing I have expressed some gratitude for the benefits I have received from you. Moreover, I have avoided adopting the normal practice of authors, for they nearly always

1. For an edition of the *Discourses* which provides extensive notes and apparatus see *The Discourses*, ed. and trans. Leslie J. Walker (2 vols., London: Routledge and Kegan Paul, 1950).

2. Buondelmonti and Rucellai were close friends who took part in discussions of politics with Machiavelli in the Oricellari gardens. They were both of distinguished families. Rucellai died in 1519; Buondelmonti in exile in 1527. In the editions of 1531 this letter appears at the end, not the beginning of the *Discourses*. It is possible that Machiavelli intended to substitute it for the preface to book one, or, alternatively, that it survives from an early draft and was intended to be deleted.

dedicate their books to some ruler, and, blinded by ambition and avarice, they praise him as if he had all possible virtuous [*virtuose*] qualities, when they ought to criticize him for having every despicable characteristic. So I, in order to avoid falling into this mistake, have chosen, not princes, but people whose innumerable fine qualities make them worthy to be princes. I have chosen, not rulers who can reward me with titles, honors, and wealth, but private citizens who would reward me if they could. If you want to make sound judgments, you should admire those who are generous in spirit, not those who have the resources to be generous, respect those who know how to rule, not those who have no idea of how to rule, but are in power. Writers praise Hiero of Syracuse more when they describe him while he was still a private citizen than Perseus of Macedon while he was king, for Hiero was fit to be king, even if he had no kingdom, while Perseus had none of the attributes of a true ruler other than a kingdom.[3]

So enjoy this book if you can. You are responsible for what is good in it, and for what is bad. If your judgment is so poor that you continue to enjoy reading me, then I will not fail to complete my commentary on Livy, as I originally promised you I would. Farewell.

Book One

Preface

Men are by nature envious. It has always been as dangerous to propose new ways of thinking and new institutions as it is to seek unknown oceans and undiscovered continents.[4] People are much quicker to criticize than to praise what others have done. Nevertheless, spurred on by an instinctive desire I have always had to do those things that I believe will further the common good and benefit everybody, I have refused to be intimidated. I have resolved to set out on a road no one has travelled before me. My journey may be tiresome and difficult, but I can hope it will prove rewarding, at least if people are willing to judge sympathetically the purpose of my labors. If my limited intelligence, my lack of experience of contemporary politics, and my inadequate knowledge of classical history will make my efforts defective and of very limited use to others, I will at least be pointing out the way to

3. For Hiero, see *The Prince*, chapter six. Perseus, King of Macedon from 179 to 168 B.C., lost his kingdom on the battlefield.

4. Machiavelli presumably had the discoveries of Columbus in mind.

someone with greater ability [*virtù*], more analytical skill, and better judgment, someone who will be capable of achieving what I have aimed at. Perhaps no one will praise my efforts; in any event, I do not deserve to be reproached.

Think of the respect in which we hold antiquity. Often, to take just one example, a single fragment of an antique statue will be purchased at enormous expense by someone who wants to look at it every day. He will give it a place of honor in his house and allow those who aspire to be sculptors to copy it. The sculptors then make every effort to do work comparable to it. Think, on the other hand, of the immensely skillful [*virtuosissime*] deeds the history books record for us, deeds done by ancient kingdoms and classical republics, by kings, generals, citizens, legislators, and others who have worn themselves out for their home-lands. These deeds may be admired, but they are scarcely imitated. Indeed, everybody goes to great lengths to avoid copying them, even if it only concerns an insignificant detail. The result is not a trace of the classical military and political skills [*quella antiqua virtù*] survives. I cannot help but be both astonished and dismayed by this. Especially when I notice that when citizens find themselves caught up in legal disagreements, or when they fall ill, they always appeal to the legal decisions of the ancients, they always follow the medical remedies prescribed by them. For the civil laws are nothing other than decisions handed down by classical jurists, decisions that have been codified, and are now taught to lawyers by our own jurists. Similarly, medicine is simply the experience of classical doctors, on the basis of which contemporary doctors make their decisions. Nevertheless, in organizing republics, in administering states, in ruling kingdoms, in training armies and fighting wars, in passing judgment on subjects, and in planning new conquests, when it comes to all these activities, one does not find a single ruler or republic who tries to learn from the ancients.

I do not believe the cause of this is the feebleness contemporary religion has instilled in the world, nor the evil consequences that a supercilious indolence has had for many Christian countries and cities. The real problem is people do not properly understand the history books. When they read them they do not get out of them the meaning that is in them. They chew on them but do not taste them. The result is countless people read them and enjoy discovering in them the great variety of events they record, but never think of imitating them, presuming it would not be just difficult but would be simply impossible to do as the ancients did. As if the heavens, the sun, the elements, human beings had changed in their movement, organization, and capacities, and were quite different from what they were in days gone by. My intent has been to rescue men from this mistake, so I have decided I must write about all the books of Livy's history that have survived the ravages of time, explaining whatever I think is important if one is to understand them. In doing so, I will draw on my knowledge of ancient and modern affairs. My hope is that those who read my comments will be able without difficulty to draw from them those practical benefits one ought to expect to gain from the study of history. Although my undertaking is a difficult one, nevertheless, helped by those who have encouraged me to embark on this enterprise, I believe I will have so much success that anyone coming after me will only have a little to do before he completes my task.

Chapter One: On the universal origins of any city whatever, and on
              how Rome began.

Those who read how the city of Rome began, who established its laws, and how it was organized will not marvel that so much excellence [*virtù*] was preserved in that city for so many centuries; and that later it gave birth to the vast empire the Roman republic eventually controlled. Since I want to talk first about its birth, I will start by saying all cities are constructed either by men born in the place where the city is built or by foreigners. In the first case, the inhabitants decide to build a city because they have been spread out in many tiny settlements in which they have not felt secure, for each settlement on its own, because of its location and because of the small number of its inhabitants, is incapable of resisting the assaults of an attacker. Nor are they in a position to assemble in joint defense when they see the enemy coming, either because it takes too long, or because, even if they could assemble in time, they would be obliged to abandon many of their settlements and would soon see them plundered by their enemies. So, to avoid these dangers, urged on either by their own individual judgments or by some one member of their group who has greater influence among them, they gather together to live in a single place they have chosen, one that will be more convenient to live in, and that will be easier to defend.

Athens and Venice are among the many cities that originated in this way. Athens, under the leadership of Theseus, was constructed by scattered inhabitants for the sort of reasons I have outlined.[5] Venice was established by numerous little groups who had taken refuge on certain tiny islands at the end of the Adriatic sea.[6] They were trying

5. According to legend, Theseus founded Athens in 1234 B.C.
6. Settlement of Venice is supposed to have begun in 451.

to escape the wars that continually broke out in Italy in the period following the collapse of the Roman empire as a result of the arrival of new groups of barbarians. They organized themselves, without there being any one individual in overall control, to live according to those laws that were, in their view, most conducive to their preservation. Their enterprise was a success because of the lengthy period of peace the site they had chosen ensured for them, for their lagoon was impenetrable, and the tribes who were invading Italy had no ships with which to attack them. So, from the most humble beginnings, they were able to rise to the eminent position they now occupy.

The second case, when foreigners come and build a city, takes two forms, depending on whether the immigrants are free men or men who owe allegiance to others. In the latter case a republic or a ruler may send out colonists in order to reduce the pressure of population in their existing settlements; or because they have recently conquered new territory and want to defend it effectively and inexpensively (the Romans built many such cities throughout their empire); or such a city may be built by a ruler who does not intend to live there, but to immortalize himself through it, as Alexander did by building Alexandria. Because such cities do not start out free, it rarely happens that they make great strides and come to be regarded as the capital cities of their own countries. It is in this category that we should place the construction of Florence, for (no matter whether it was built by Sulla's soldiers or by the inhabitants of the hilltops of Fiesole, who, given confidence by the long peace that the whole world benefited from under Augustus, came down to live in the plain of the Arno) it was built under Roman rule, nor could it, at the beginning, control any territory beyond what was assigned it at the pleasure of the emperor.

Cities are built by free men when a group of people, either under the command of a ruler or acting on their own, are forced to abandon the land of their birth and to seek new territory because of disease, or hunger, or war. They may occupy the cities that already exist in the territory they conquer, as Moses did, or they may build from scratch, as Aeneas did. It is in this latter case that one can fully appreciate the skill [*virtù*] of the architect as it is reflected in the fate of his city, for the history of the city will be more or less marvelous depending on whether its first founder is more or less skillful [*virtuoso*]. The skill [*virtù*] of the founder can be judged by two things: firstly, by his choice of a site for the construction of the new city; secondly, by the laws he draws up for it.

Men act either out of necessity or free choice. Since it seems that men are the most admirable [*maggior virtù*] where they have the least

freedom of choice, one must consider whether it might not be better
to choose an infertile region for the construction of a city so that its
inhabitants will be forced to be industrious and prevented from being
self-indulgent, and so that they will be more united, having less occasion for conflict because of the poverty of their land. We can see this
happened at Ragusa, and in many other cities built in similar locations.
Such a choice of location would be without doubt wiser and would
lead to the best outcome, if men were content to live off their own
possessions and did not want to try to get control of the property of
others. But since men can only secure themselves by building up power, one must avoid building a city in a barren location, but rather settle
the most fertile land, whose fecundity will make possible growth, so
one will be able both to defend oneself against attackers and to defeat
anyone who stands in the way of one's own power. In order to ensure
the location does not lead to self-indulgence, one must design the
laws to force people to do what the location does not force them to do.
Thus, one should imitate those wise men who have lived in countries
that have been delightful and fertile, countries apt to produce lazy men
who are incapable of any manly [*virtuoso*] work. In order to avoid the
disadvantages that would result from the delightfulness of the land if
it caused self-indulgence, they required all those who were liable to
military service to drill, so that by means of such regulations their
inhabitants became better soldiers than those living in territory that is
naturally harsh and infertile. The Kingdom of Egypt is an example of
this: Despite the fact that the country is exceptionally fertile, the artificial necessity imposed by the laws was so effective that Egypt produced
the finest men; and if their names had not been lost in antiquity, we
would be able to see they deserved more praise than Alexander the
Great and many others whose deeds remain fresh in our memory.
And if you had examined the state of the sultan, with its regiments of
Mamelukes and its Turkish militia, before they were abolished by the
Sultan Selim,[7] you would have seen there much drilling of soldiers
and would have learned how much the Turks feared the self-indulgence
the generosity of their country might induce in them, had they not
introduced strict legal penalties to prevent it.

So I conclude it is wiser to choose to settle in a fertile place, provided
the consequences of that fertility are kept within due limits by legislation. Deinocrates the architect came to Alexander the Great when

7. The Mamelukes ruled Egypt from 1252 to 1516, when they were defeated
by the Ottoman Turks.

Alexander wanted to build a city to magnify his own reputation.[8] He showed him how he could build on Mount Athos: The site, apart from being easily defended, could be cut away so the new city would have the shape of a human body, which would be a remarkable and extraordinary thing and worthy of Alexander's greatness. But when Alexander asked him what the inhabitants of the city would live on he replied he had not given the matter any thought. Alexander laughed, and, leaving Mount Athos intact, built Alexandria in a place where people would want to settle because of the fecundity of the countryside and the ease of access to the sea and to the Nile.

Let us now consider the construction of Rome. If you take it that Aeneas was its first founder, you will think of it as one of the cities built by foreigners.[9] If you believe it was founded by Romulus, you will think of it as founded by men born in the vicinity.[10] Either way you will agree it was founded in freedom and was not under any outsider's authority. You will also recognize—we will return to this subject later—the extent to which the laws established by Romulus, Numa, and the other early legislators imposed an artificial necessity upon the inhabitants, so the fertility of the site, the ease of access to the sea, the frequent victories of their armies, and the extensive territory that fell under Roman control could not corrupt them even over the course of many centuries. Their laws ensured they had more admirable qualities [*virtù*] than any other city or republic has ever been able to boast of in its citizens.

The deeds of the Romans that are celebrated in Livy's history occurred either as a result of public or of private decisions and either inside or outside the city. I will begin by discussing those things that happened inside the city and as a result of public decision-making, that I take to be worthy of more detailed discussion, and we will need to explore all the consequences that flowed from them. This first book, or at least this first part, will be taken up with a discussion of these matters.

Chapter Two: On the different types of republic that exist, and on how to categorize the Roman republic.

I want to leave aside any discussion of those cities that were under the authority of outsiders from the beginning, and to discuss only those

8.   Deinocrates designed Alexandria in 322 B.C.

9.   Aeneas's flight from the defeat of Troy to Italy is recounted by Livy.

10.   Livy prefers the story of Romulus and Remus, sons of Mars and wolf-children, but, unlike Machiavelli, he treats it as myth, not history.

that began completely free of external domination and were ruled by their own wills from the beginning, whether as republics or as princedoms. These cities, since they began in a variety of ways, have had a variety of constitutions and legal systems. In some, either at the very beginning or soon after their foundation, a single individual wrote all the laws at once—Lycurgus, for example, gave the Spartans their laws[11]—while others acquired their laws by chance, little by little, according to the circumstances, as happened in Rome. We can call fortunate any republic in which there appears a leader so prudent he is able to give them a code of law they have no need to revise, but under which they can live securely. We know the Spartans obeyed the laws of Lycurgus for eight hundred years without corrupting them and without any serious internal conflict. On the other hand, we can call in some degree unfortunate any city that does not chance upon a prudent lawmaker, and is obliged to revise its laws for itself. And among these cities, moreover, those are most unfortunate that are furthest from having the right laws; and those are furthest astray whose constitution is quite unlike the one that would lead them to their true and ideal goal. For it is almost impossible for a city that finds itself in this situation to have enough good luck to be able to sort itself out. Those others that, if they do not have a perfect constitution, yet have started out in the right direction and are in a position to improve, can, as opportunity presents itself, become perfect. But this is certainly true: One never establishes a constitution without encountering danger. For enough men will never agree to a new law that changes the constitution of the city unless they are persuaded it is essential to pass it, and they will only be persuaded of this if they see themselves to be in danger, so it can easily happen that the republic is destroyed before she arrives at a perfect constitution. The republic of Florence is a good example of this: Defeat in the Battle of Arezzo led to her reorganization;[12] defeat in the Battle of Prato in 1512 led to her dissolution.[13]

I want now to discuss the constitution of Rome and the events that made it possible for her to achieve perfection. Some who have written about constitutions say they are of three types, which they call "monarchy," "aristocracy," and "democracy."[14] They say anyone drawing up

11.   Lycurgus is supposed to have drawn up his laws ca. 884 B.C.

12.   Defeat in 1502, and pressure from Cesare Borgia, led to Piero Soderini being made gonfaloniere for life.

13.   I.e., the restoration of the Medici.

14.   The rest of this chapter is profoundly influenced by Polybius, *Histories*, bk. 6.

the constitution of a city must choose from these the one he thinks most appropriate. Others, who are widely thought to be wiser, say there are six types of constitution, of which three are inherently bad and three are inherently good, although even the good ones are so easily corrupted they, too, can quickly become pernicious. The good ones are the three I have already mentioned; the bad ones are three others that derive from these three, and each of which is so like the good constitution it most resembles that it is easy for one to turn into the other. Thus, monarchies easily become tyrannies, aristocracies become oligarchies, and democracies slide into anarchy. The result is that if a lawmaker establishes a constitution for a city that corresponds to one of the three good forms of government it will not last long, for no precaution is sufficient to ensure it will not slip into its opposite, for the good [*la virtute*] and the bad are, when it comes to constitutions, closely related.

These different types of government developed among men by accident. When the world began, it had few inhabitants, and they lived for a while apart from one another as the animals do. As their numbers multiplied they gathered together, and in order to be better able to defend themselves, they began to defer to one among their number who was stronger and braver than the rest. They made him, as it were, their leader and obeyed him. This was the origin of knowledge of those things that are good and honest as opposed to those that are pernicious and evil. For men saw that, if someone harmed his benefactor, his associates despised him and felt compassion for his victim. They learned to think ill of the ungrateful and to approve of those who were grateful. They came to realize the injuries that were done to someone else could equally be done to themselves. In order to avoid such evils, they gathered together to make laws and to lay down punishments for those who broke them: This was the invention of justice. Thereafter, when they had to choose a ruler, they no longer obeyed the strongest, but he who was most prudent and most just.

Later, however, they began to appoint their ruler by hereditary succession, not by election, with the immediate result that power was inherited by men who were inferior to their ancestors. They no longer acted virtuously [*lasciando l'opere virtuose*], but thought rulers were simply there to outdo other men in extravagance, lasciviousness, and in every other type of vice. The result was that rulers began to be hated, and, because they were hated, to be afraid. Because they were afraid, they went on the attack, and before long kings had become tyrants. These rulers faced the possibility of being destroyed. The conspiracies and plots hatched against them were not begun by those who were fearful or weak, but by those who surpassed their fellows in generosity, spiritedness, wealth, and nobility, for such men could no longer tolerate the dishonorable lives of their rulers. The masses then followed the lead provided by the elite and armed themselves against their ruler, and, when they had got rid of him, obeyed the elite as their liberators. The new rulers hated the idea of one-man rule and, so, established themselves collectively in power.

At first, remembering the evils of tyranny, they governed according to the laws they had established, putting their own interests second and the public good first. They directed and protected both public and private matters with great care. In due course, this government was inherited by their sons, who had never seen power change hands, had never suffered under evil government, and who were unwilling to continue treating their fellow subjects as their equals. They gave themselves over to avarice, to ambition, to chasing other men's wives. So aristocracy degenerated into an oligarchy in which the norms of civilized life were flouted. In a short time, the oligarchs suffered the same fate as the tyrants, for the masses became fed up with their government and gave their support to anyone who was planning any sort of resistance to their rule. Soon someone, with the assistance of the masses, was able to destroy them. Since they could still clearly remember one-man rule, and the harm it had done them, when they destroyed oligarchy they had no desire to restore monarchy, but instead established popular rule. This they organized in such a manner that neither the elite nor a powerful individual could have any influence whatsoever.

In the beginning, all states can command a certain amount of respect, so popular government survived for a while, but not for long, especially once the generation that had established it had passed away. It quickly degenerated into anarchy, in which neither private individuals nor public officials could command any respect. Each person did as he chose, with the result that every day innumerable crimes were committed. So, compelled by necessity, or advised by some good man, or desperate to escape from anarchy, they established once more the rule of one man. And from monarchy, step by step, they degenerated once again into anarchy, repeating the sequence I have already described.

This is the cycle through which all states revolve, and power is still passed, as it always has been, from hand to hand. But it rarely happens that the same people return to power, for scarcely a single state has survived long enough to travel several times through this cycle without being destroyed. Usually, while a state is torn apart by internal dissent, and as a result is weakened and deprived of good leadership, it is

conquered by a neighboring state better organized than it is. But if
this did not happen, then a state could repeat this cycle of constitutions
over and over again.

I conclude all these forms of government are pestilential: The three
good ones do not last long, and the three bad ones are evil. Those
who know how to construct constitutions wisely have identified this
problem and have avoided each one of these types of constitution in
its pure form, constructing a constitution with elements of each. They
have been convinced such a constitution would be more solid and
stable, would be preserved by checks and balances, there being present
in the one city a monarch, an aristocracy, and a democracy.

Lycurgus is the most admirable of those who have established constitutions of this sort. He constructed the constitution of Sparta so that
it gave distinct roles to king, aristocracy, and people, with the result
the state survived for eight hundred years, throughout which time his
name was revered and the city lived in harmony. Matters turned out
differently for Solon, who drew up the constitution of Athens.[15] Because
he constructed a democracy, it survived such a short time that before
Solon died he saw Athens under the tyranny of Pisistratus. Although
forty years later Pisistratus's heirs were driven into exile and freedom
was restored, because the Athenians re-established the democratic
constitution drawn up by Solon, their freedom lasted no more than a
century, despite the fact that in order to preserve it they introduced
numerous reforms Solon had not considered. They did their best to
control the insolence of the powerful and the license of the masses.
Nevertheless, because they did not allow a proper role for one-man
rule and for aristocracy, Athens survived, by comparison with Sparta,
a very short time.

Let us turn to Rome. Even though Rome did not have a Lycurgus
to establish from the beginning a constitution that would enable her
to live free for centuries, nevertheless, she underwent so many political
crises, because of the conflicts between the people and the senate, that
chance eventually brought about something no legislator had been able
to accomplish. For if Rome did not have the first type of good fortune,
she had the second, and although her first constitution was defective,
nevertheless, it did not cause her to turn off the right path that could
lead her to perfection.

Romulus and all the other kings of Rome made many excellent laws,
ones appropriate for a free state. But their goal was the establishment
of a kingdom, not a republic, so when Rome became free she lacked

---

15.   Solon's reforms began in 595 B.C.

many of the laws free government required, for these they had omitted
to decree. And although the kings of Rome lost their power for the
reasons and in the way I have outlined, nevertheless, those who threw
them out quickly established two consuls who played the same role as
the kings, so that they expelled from Rome the name of king but not
the authority of kingship. The new republic was ruled by the consuls
and the senate, so it was a mixture of only two of the three types of
power I have described: of monarchy and aristocracy. It failed to give
any authority to the populace.

When the Roman nobility became overbearing, for reasons I will
explain later, the people rose up against them, with the result that, in
order not to lose all power, the nobles were obliged to concede a share
of power to the people. On the other hand, the consuls and the senate retained enough authority to be able to hold on to a share of power
in the republic. So the tribunes of the people came to be established,
after which the constitution of the republic became more stable, for
now all three types of authority had a fair share in power. And fortune
was so favorable to Rome that, although she passed from monarchy,
to aristocracy, to democracy, going through each of the stages I have
described for the reasons I have outlined, nevertheless, the aristocracy never seized all power from the monarchical element; nor did the
people ever seize all power from the aristocracy; instead, power was
added to power, and the mixture that resulted made for a perfect
republic. Rome achieved this perfection because of the conflict between
senate and people, as I will show at length in the next two chapters.

Chapter Three: On the circumstances under which the tribunes of
the people came to be established in Rome, a
development that made the constitution nearly
perfect.

There is one thing that all those who discuss political life emphasize,
and that is evident from the history of every state: It is essential that
anyone setting up a republic and establishing a constitution for it should
assume that all men are wicked and will always give vent to their evil
impulses whenever they have the chance to do so. Even when some
evil impulse is restrained and concealed for a time, there is always
some hidden reason for this, one we do not recognize because we have
not seen the vicious behavior the evil impulse would normally give rise
to. But time will make clear what it is, for time, as they say, gives birth
to truth.

When the Tarquins were expelled from Rome, there appeared to be a close collaboration between the populace and the senate.[16] The nobles seemed to have given up their pride and to have become democratic in their outlook. One would have thought anyone would have been able to tolerate their rule, even someone from the lowest social class. The hypocrisy of the nobility continued to lie hidden as long as the Tarquins were alive, and during this period the reason for their behavior was invisible. For the nobles were afraid of the Tarquins and afraid, too, that if the populace were badly treated they would form an alliance with them; so they treated the populace well. But as soon as the Tarquins died and the nobles felt they had nothing to fear, they began to treat the populace as outrageously as they had always wanted to, and they now harmed them in every way they could. This confirms what I just said: Men never do anything that is good except when forced to. Where there is a good deal of freedom of choice, and this freedom can be abused, then everything quickly becomes buried in confusion and disorder. Therefore, people say hunger and poverty make men industrious, while laws make them good. Where something works well on its own, without the support of the law, then there is no need for a law. But as soon as good habits break down, then laws at once become necessary. So with the Tarquins gone, fear of whom had kept the nobility in check, it was necessary to think of a new institution that would have the same effect as the Tarquins had had while they were alive. And so, after many conflicts, outcries, and crises had arisen between the populace and the nobility, it was decided to establish the tribunes in order to protect the populace. They were given so much authority and so high a status that thereafter they were always able to act as mediators between the populace and the senate and to control the arrogance of the nobility.

Chapter Four: On the tensions between the populace and the Roman senate, which made that republic free and powerful.

It would be wrong not to discuss those popular disorders that occurred in Rome between the death of the Tarquins and the creation of the tribunes. Afterwards, I will say a few things in reply to the many people who say Rome was a disorderly republic, one full of so much confusion that if good luck and military discipline [*virtù militare*] had not made up for its defects, it would have been inferior to every other republic. I cannot deny good luck and the army were causes of Rome's imperial

16.   The last king was expelled in 510 B.C.

greatness, though it seems to me these people do not realize that where there is a good army there must be a good constitution, and one will nearly always find a good army can make its own good luck.

But let us turn to the other particular characteristics of that city. I maintain those who criticize the clashes between the nobility and the populace attack what was, I would argue, the primary factor making for Rome's continuing freedom. They pay more attention to the shouts and cries that rise from such conflicts than to the good effects that derive from them. They do not take into account the fact that there are two distinct viewpoints in every republic: that of the populace and that of the elite. All the laws made in order to foster liberty result from the tensions between them, as one can easily see was the case in the history of Rome. For from Tarquin to the Gracchi,[17] a period of more than three hundred years, the conflicts that broke out in Rome rarely resulted in men's being sent into exile, and even more rarely led to bloodshed. One cannot judge these conflicts as harmful, or the republic as divided, when over such a long period of time the differences between the parties led to no more than eight or ten citizens' being sent into exile, to a tiny number's being murdered, and indeed to only a few's being fined. Nor can there be any good grounds for calling a republic disorderly when it contains so many examples of individual excellence [*virtù*], for good individuals cannot exist without good education, and good education cannot exist without good laws, and good laws were the result of those very conflicts many people unthinkingly criticize. Anyone who scrutinizes the outcome of these conflicts will find they never led to exiles or murders that were contrary to the public good but always led to laws and institutions that favored public liberty.

And if someone were to argue the methods employed were extralegal and almost bestial—the people in a mob shouting abuse at the senate, the senate replying in kind, mobs running through the streets, shops boarded up, the entire populace of Rome leaving the city—I would reply such things only frighten those who read about them. Every city ought to have practices that enable the populace to give expression to its aspirations, especially those cities that want to be able to rely on the populace at times of crisis. The city of Rome had a number of practices of this kind. For example, when the populace wanted a law passed, either they demonstrated, as I have described, or they refused to enroll for military service, so that in order to pacify them it was necessary to give them at least part of what they wanted. The demands of a free people are rarely harmful to the cause of liberty, for they are

17. From 510 to ca. 121 B.C.

a response either to oppression or to the prospect of oppression. When the populace is mistaken, then there is a remedy to hand in the open-air speech. Some sensible man has to get up and harangue them, showing them how they are wrong. The populace, as Cicero says, although they are ignorant, are capable of recognizing the truth, and it is easy for a man whom they have reason to respect to persuade them to change their mind by telling them the truth.[18]

So people ought to be more sparing in their criticisms of the political system of Rome. If you consider all the good things the Romans achieved, you will have to admit the system that gave rise to such achievements must have been excellent. If popular demonstrations resulted in the creation of the tribunate, they should be praised without reserve, for, beyond giving the populace a role in government, the tribunes were set up to be the guardians of Roman liberty, as the next chapter will show.

Chapter Five: On whether the protection of liberty is best entrusted to the populace or to the elite, and on whether those who want to acquire power or those who want to maintain it are most likely to riot.

Those who have understood how to establish a republic have recognized one of the most urgent tasks is that of identifying a group with an interest in protecting liberty. Depending on whether this task is entrusted to the right group or not, political liberty will be preserved for a longer or a shorter time. Because in every state there is an elite and a populace, the question has been raised as to which group it is best to entrust with the task of protecting liberty. The Spartans and, in modern days, the Venetians have relied on the nobles; but the Romans relied on the populace. So we must ask ourselves which of these republics made the better choice. If we argue from first principles, we will find something to say on either side; but if we look at what happened in practice, we will conclude the nobility are more reliable, for liberty in Sparta and Venice has been longer-lived than in Rome. Let us look at the principles involved and first consider the arguments in favor of Rome's policy.

It would seem one ought to entrust something to people who have no desire to steal it. Now there is no question that if one considers the objectives of the nobles and the non-nobles, one must admit the former are very keen to dominate, and the latter want only not to be dominated. Consequently, the populace have a greater desire to live

18.   Cicero, *De amicitia*, chs. 25–26.

as free men, having less prospect of seizing power for themselves than the elite has. So if you put the populace in charge of protecting liberty, it is reasonable to believe that they will do a better job, and since they cannot hope to monopolize power themselves, they will ensure nobody else does. On the other hand, if you are defending the Spartan and Venetian policy you will say those who entrust the protection of liberty to the powerful accomplish two good things. In the first place, you satisfy some of the nobility's aspirations, and, because they have a greater role in the state as a result of having this power in their hands, they are more likely to be content. In the second, you take away a measure of authority from the populace, who are restless and insatiable. It is the populace who are responsible for innumerable conflicts and clashes in a republic. Their behavior is likely to make the nobility desperate, which in the long run will have evil consequences. You will cite Rome herself as an example. Because the tribunes of the people could claim to be the guardians of liberty, they were not satisfied with ensuring one consul was chosen from among the populace,[19] but insisted both should be. Next they wanted the censor, the praetor, and all the other officials of the city government to be plebeians. Even this was not enough, for, driven on by the same madness, they began in time to worship those men whom they thought were capable of defeating the nobility. The result was the rise of Marius and the ruin of Rome.[20] And indeed, anyone who balanced one set of arguments against the other would have difficulty making up his mind as to which group he should choose as the guardians of liberty, for he would be unable to decide which human aspiration was more dangerous for a republic: defending a status that has already been acquired, or acquiring a status one does not yet have.

In the end, anyone who examines the pros and cons with care will reach the conclusion that you are either thinking in terms of a republic whose goal is to conquer an empire, as Rome's was, or of one that merely wants to defend itself. If the first, then you must do everything as the Romans did; if the second, then you can copy Venice and Sparta, for the reasons I have already given and for others we will come to in the next chapter.

But let us turn to a discussion of which men are more dangerous to a republic, those who want to acquire new power, or those anxious not to lose the power they have. Marcus Menenius was appointed dictator, and Marcus Fulvius general of the horse.[21] Both of them were

---

19. A concession obtained in 367 B.C.

20. Marius was first consul in 107 B.C. and died in 86 B.C.

21. In 314 B.C. See Livy, bk. 9, ch. 26.

plebeians. Their mission was to uncover certain conspiracies against Rome that had been hatched in Capua. The populace also gave them authority to enquire whether there were people in Rome who, out of ambition, were scheming to use extralegal means to be elected to the consulate or to other prestigious offices. The nobility thought the dictator had been given this mandate so he could attack them, and so they spread the word around Rome that it was not the nobles who were driven by ambition to use extralegal means to acquire honors, but the non-nobles. Unable to rely on their own abilities [*virtù*] or their inherited status, it was they who sought to acquire honors by corrupt means. In particular, they attacked Menenius, the dictator. This charge was so damaging that Menenius, having made a speech in which he protested against the calumnies directed at him by the nobles, resigned the dictatorship, and submitted himself to the judgment of the people. When his case had been considered, he was found to be innocent.

In such cases, it is easy to disagree as to who was the more ambitious, those who wanted to hold on to power or those who wanted to acquire it. For either aspiration can easily be the cause of tremendous conflict. Nevertheless, for the most part such conflicts are caused by those who already have power, for the fear of losing it gives them exactly the same ambitions as those who want to acquire power. Men do not feel they are secure in the possession of their property unless they are constantly acquiring more from someone else. Moreover, those who already have power are in a better position to use their influence and their resources to bring about change. In addition, their improper and self-interested behavior excites in the hearts of the powerless the desire to have power, either in order to take their revenge on their enemies by taking what they have from them, or in order to acquire for themselves that wealth and those honors they see their opponents abusing.

Chapter Six: On whether it would have been possible to give Rome a constitution that would have prevented conflict between the populace and the senate.

We have discussed above the effects of the conflicts between the populace and the senate. Since these continued until the time of the Gracchi, when they were the cause of the destruction of political freedom,[22] some may wish that Rome's remarkable accomplishments had been achieved without such internal conflicts. So I thought it

---

22. The Gracchi were followed a generation later by Marius, Marius by Caesar.

would be worth considering whether it would have been possible to give Rome a constitution that would have prevented these conflicts. In order to examine this question we must return to those republics that managed to stay free for a long time without such conflicts and riots, analyze their constitutions, and consider whether key elements from them could have been introduced into Rome.

The crucial example among the ancients is that of Sparta, among the moderns, Venice, as I have already mentioned. Sparta established a king and a small senate to share power. Venice did not divide authority among different institutions, but gave one title, that of gentleman, to all those who had a right to participate in government. This arrangement was the result more of chance than of the forethought of a legislator. A large group of inhabitants having established themselves on the reefs where Venice now stands (for the reasons I described above), they found they had become so numerous that they needed to pass laws if they were to continue to live together, and decided to draw up a form of government. The citizens met regularly in the deliberative councils of the city, and when they felt that there were more than enough of them to sustain a participatory system of politics, they excluded from membership of their assemblies all those who might arrive to live there in future.

As time passed, many of Venice's inhabitants were excluded from power.[23] In order to uphold the status of those who participated in politics, they called them gentlemen, while the others they called commoners. This system of government could come into existence and maintain itself without conflict; for when it was established everyone who at the time lived in Venice had a right to participate in government, so that nobody had reason to complain. Those who came afterwards to live there, finding the constitution well-established and fixed, had no excuse or opportunity to provoke a conflict. They had no excuse, because they had been deprived of nothing; they had no opportunity, because those in power kept them in check and did not employ them in tasks where they could acquire political authority. Moreover, those who came to live in Venice after the constitution was established were not that numerous: Those who governed were not hopelessly outnumbered by those over whom they ruled. In fact, there are as many gentlemen as commoners, if not more. This is the explanation of Venice's ability to establish her constitution and maintain it without internal conflict.

Sparta, as I said, was ruled by a king and a small senate. The

23. As a result of the "closing" of the Great Council in 1297.

constitution survived for such a long time because there were few
inhabitants in Sparta; they had made it impossible for immigrants to
move there; and they had adopted and respected the laws of Lycurgus (for, so long as they obeyed them, they could have no occasion for
conflict). So they were able to live united for centuries. Lycurgus's
laws established more equality of wealth in Sparta than there would
otherwise have been and less equality of status. Everyone was equally
poor, and the populace was less ambitious for power, for only a few
citizens held positions of status, and they lived cut off from the people.
Moreover, the elite did not treat the populace badly, so they never felt
the need to acquire power.

This was a consequence of the particular character of Spartan kingship. The kings were appointed to office and surrounded by the nobility;
so they had no better means of preserving their authority than protecting
the people from any injury. The result was that the people did not
fear their rulers and did not want to rule. Because they had no power
and did not fear those who did, they did not feel in competition with
the nobility, so there was no occasion for conflict. They were able to
live together harmoniously for centuries. There were two principal
causes of this harmony: The fact that Sparta had few inhabitants meant
that power could be concentrated in the hands of a few; and the fact
that there was a ban on immigration meant that the subjects had little
opportunity to become corrupt, or to become so numerous that they
could not be managed by the elite who governed them.

So, having considered these matters, we can see that the legislators
who drew up the constitution of Rome would have had to do one of
two things if they wanted to ensure that Rome was as harmonious as
the two republics we have been discussing. Either they would have
had to exclude the populace from the army, as the Venetians did, or
to prevent immigration, as the Spartans did. They did neither, which
meant that the populace were strong and grew in numbers, and so had
innumerable opportunities to riot. But if the Roman political system
had been more orderly, it would have had the unfortunate consequence
that Rome would have been weaker and she would no longer have
been able to achieve that greatness she did in fact achieve. If Rome
had avoided those tensions that led to conflict, she would also have
prevented herself from acquiring new territory.

In all human affairs we see, if we analyze things carefully, that you
cannot get rid of one cause of trouble without introducing another.
Thus, if you want to make a populace numerous and well-armed, so
that they can conquer a vast empire, then you must accept that you
will not be able to get them to do everything you want. If you keep

the population small or unarmed so that you can get them to do what you want, then if you do conquer territory you will not be able to hold on to it, and your subjects will become so feeble that you will be defenseless when anyone chooses to attack you. So in all discussions about policy, we should decide which course of action has the fewest disadvantages and we should regard that policy as the best, for you will never find a policy that gives you no grounds for anxiety, that involves no costs. Rome could, like Sparta, have appointed a ruler for life, and made its senate small; but if it wanted to have an empire, it could not, like Sparta, prevent the number of its citizens from growing. Unless it had done this, however, a king for life and a small senate would have been of little use in ensuring harmony.

So if someone wanted to organize a republic from scratch, he would have to ask himself if he wanted it to grow in power and territory as Rome did or to remain limited in both. If he chose the first, then he would have to organize it along the same lines as Rome and take into account as best he could the inevitability of riots and large-scale conflicts. Unless he was prepared to have many inhabitants and to arm them well he could not hope to have a republic that would grow, or, if it grew, would be able to defend itself. If he chose the second, then he could organize it like Sparta and Venice; but because territorial expansion is fatal to such republics, he would be obliged, in every way that he could, to prevent his republic from acquiring new territory. For such acquisitions, if undertaken by a weak state, are bound to bring about its destruction, which is what happened to both Sparta and Venice. In the case of Sparta, which had conquered almost the whole of Greece, a little local difficulty exposed the weakness of its power base. After the successful rebellion of Thebes under the leadership of Pelopidas, the other cities all rebelled, too, destroying the whole Spartan empire.[24] Similarly, Venice occupied a large proportion of Italy, acquiring most of it not on the battlefield but through cunning and bribery, and when she finally had to prove her strength, she lost everything in a single battle.[25]

I certainly think that if one wanted to establish a republic that would last for centuries one ought to imitate the constitution of either Sparta or Venice, and one ought to situate one's city somewhere where it would be easy to defend, giving it sufficient military might to ensure that no one would think they could conquer it in a hurry, while on the other hand

24. In 379 B.C.
25. The Battle of Agnadello or Vailà, 1509.

not giving it so much that its neighbors would feel threatened by it. Such a state could flourish for centuries. For there are two reasons why one attacks another state: in order to rule over it, or out of fear that it will invade you. A state organized as I have described would provide scarcely any motivation for someone to attack it for either reason. For granted my presupposition that it has well-prepared defenses, it will be difficult to seize, and so it will be rare indeed for anyone to think he can devise a way of conquering it. If it stays within its own boundaries, and people see from experience that it is not interested in making conquests, then no one will ever go to war against it out of fear of being attacked by it. This will be all the more true if the constitution or laws of this republic prohibit the acquisition of new territory. I have no doubt that if you could establish a balance between weakness and strength in this way, then you would have a city that was genuinely harmonious and within which you could lead an ideal civic life.

But in life nothing stands still. Since things cannot stay in the same place, they must be either rising or falling. There are many things that you would not choose to do, but that you are obliged to do. So if you set up a republic that was well-equipped to defend itself without expanding its territory, and then circumstances forced expansion upon it, you would see the foundations of its strength undermined, and it would quickly be destroyed. On the other hand, if heaven so smiled upon it that it was under no necessity to go to war, then idleness would lead either to internal divisions or to effeminacy; either of these, or both of them together, would bring about its collapse. So in my view it is impossible to find a balance between weakness and strength; impossible to find a middle way successfully. In drawing up the constitution of a republic one should, therefore, aim high and construct it in such a fashion that if circumstances force it to expand it will be able to hold on to what it has acquired.

To return to the original question, I think one is obliged to copy the Roman model, and that it would be wrong to imitate any other republic; nor do I think there is a compromise to be found between the two types of republic. Those conflicts that may break out between the populace and the senate have to be tolerated and accepted as a price that must be paid if one wants to attain the grandeur of Rome. For, besides the reasons I have already given for thinking that the authority of the tribunes was a necessary bastion of liberty, one can easily recognize the benefits the republic derived from the right of public accusation, which was one of the rights held by the tribunes, a right I will discuss in the next chapter.

Chapter Seven: On how essential it is that there should be a right
                             of public accusation in a republic if it is to retain
                             its freedom.

There is no authority more useful and necessary for those who are
entrusted by a city with the task of guarding its liberty than the right
of publicly accusing, before the people or before some magistrate or
council, citizens who do anything that is a threat to public liberty. This
right has two extremely useful consequences for any state. The first
is that citizens, for fear of being accused, dare not attempt to do
anything that might harm the state, and if they do try to do anything
they are immediately and impartially crushed. The other is that one
gives an outlet to those resentments that build up in a city, for whatever
reason, against individual citizens; otherwise, when these resentments
have no institutionalized outlet, they cause people to act outside the
law, which leads to the collapse of the whole political system. There
is nothing that makes a republic more stable and more solid than that
its laws should provide for the expression of those resentments that
have built up within the community. There are lots of examples that
illustrate this. The best is Livy's account of Coriolanus.[26] There he
says that the Roman nobility had lost patience with the populace because
it seemed to them that the populace had acquired too much authority
as a result of the establishment of the tribunate, which was biased
in their favor. Rome, as occasionally happened, was acutely short of
foodstuffs, and the senate had sent to Sicily for grain. Coriolanus, who
was hostile to the popular faction, argued that the time had come when
the people could be punished and when the authority they had acquired
to the detriment of the nobility could be reclaimed from them. They
should be allowed to starve, and supplies of grain should be withheld
from them. When the populace heard what Coriolanus had said, they
were so indignant that a mob of them would have killed him as he was
coming out of the senate, had the tribunes not cited him to appear
before them and answer charges. This incident confirms what I said
above: It is useful and necessary that republics should have laws that
enable the mass of the population to give vent to the hostility it feels
towards a particular citizen, for when there are no institutionalized
mechanisms to allow this, extralegal methods will be employed, and
without doubt these have much worse consequences than legal ones.

If the law makes it possible for an individual citizen to be executed
when he does not deserve to be, this does little or nothing to undermine

26.   Livy, bk. 2, chs. 33–35.

the political stability of the republic. The law is enforced without private violence or foreign troops being involved, and it is these that destroy political freedom. It is the ordinary power of the state that is employed. This power is confined within established limits; it does not breach them and place the political system in danger. There are examples that can be cited to support this view. As far as ancient history is concerned, the case of Coriolanus is sufficient: Everyone should consider the evil consequences for the Roman republic if he had been killed in a riot, for this would have been an attack by private individuals on a private individual. Numerous people would have been frightened as a result; because they were frightened, they would have prepared to defend themselves; in order to defend themselves, they would have sought out allies. Consequently, they would have banded together into factions within the city, and such factional strife can destroy a city. But because the appropriate authorities took charge of the matter, all those evil consequences that could have resulted from unauthorized violence were avoided.

In our own day, we have seen upheavals within the Florentine political system because the masses could not give vent to their hostility towards a particular citizen through institutionalized means, for example at the time when Francesco Valori was more or less ruler of the city.[27] Valori was thought by many to be ambitious, and believed to be someone whose audacity and boldness would lead him to destroy political freedom. There was no legal mechanism that could be employed against him; the only thing to do was to build up a faction in opposition to his own. The result was that he, having nothing to fear except an illegal attack, began to surround himself with supporters prepared to defend him; on the other hand, his opponents had no legal recourse against him, but had to consider extralegal action; in the end the two sides came to blows. If it had been possible to appeal to the courts against Valori, his power could have been destroyed and he alone would have had to pay the price; because extralegal means had to be employed, he was not the only one who suffered, but many other members of the elite suffered with him.

In addition, in support of my argument, I could cite the incident that happened in Florence with regard to Piero Soderini. This only occurred because Florence has no mechanism for bringing charges against powerful citizens suspected of seeking to undermine the consti-

27. From 1494 to 1498. Valori was a supporter of Savonarola and was murdered in the early stages of the coup d'état that led to Savonarola's execution. Shortly after this, Machiavelli entered government service.

tution. It is not sufficient for a republic to have a panel of eight judges before whom a powerful man can be accused; you need to have a large number of judges, for an elite will always share the viewpoint of other members of the elite. If there had been an adequate mechanism for bringing Soderini to justice, either the citizens would have charged him, if he deserved it, and in this way, without calling in the Spanish army, they would have been able to vent their anger; or, if he did not deserve it, they would not have dared move against him, for fear they themselves might be charged. One way or another, the hostility towards him would have been appeased, and a crisis would have been avoided.[28]

So we can reach the following conclusion: Whenever we see foreign troops being called in by one faction living within a city, we can conclude that there is something faulty in the constitution, for otherwise there would be internal mechanisms that, without recourse to extralegal means, would enable men to give vent to their bitter feelings. All one needs is to allow charges to be brought before a large enough number of judges and to give these judges adequate authority. In Rome, such excellent provision was made for this that, despite all the conflicts that there were between the populace and the senate, neither the senate, nor the populace, nor any individual citizen ever thought of turning to outside forces. For they had a remedy to hand, so they did not have to look abroad for one.

Although the examples I have already given are quite enough to make my point; nevertheless, I will add one more, which appears in Livy's history.[29] He reports that in the city of Clusium, at that time one of the wealthiest in Tuscany, one of the sisters of a man called Aruns was raped by a Tuscan noble.[30] Aruns could not obtain redress because the assailant was too well connected, so he went to the French tribes that at that time controlled the territory now called Lombardy. He urged them to bring their troops to Clusium, explaining to them how they would benefit while helping him obtain redress for the injury done his family. If Aruns had believed that he could obtain redress by appealing to the city's laws, he would not have involved himself with barbarian forces. But just as it is important that a republic should have mechanisms to enable people to bring charges against the powerful,

28. The crisis is that of 1512, when Florence was defeated at Prato, Soderini forced into exile, the Medici restored, and Machiavelli lost his job.

29. Livy, bk. 5, ch. 33. The date is 391 B.C.

30. Machiavelli uses the technical term for an Etruscan noble, *lucumone*. Here and elsewhere I have used Tuscan where we would now say Etruscan because, as in the case of Gauls and Frenchmen, Machiavelli sees no distinction.

so it is dangerous and harmful if irresponsible individuals can slander
other citizens, as I will explain in the next chapter.

Chapter Eight: On how slander is just as damaging to a republic as
public accusations are beneficial.

Despite the fact that the excellent qualities of Furius Camillus, after
he liberated Rome from the oppression of the French tribes, were so
generally recognized that all the citizens of Rome deferred to him
without feeling that in doing so they were diminishing their own reputation or status, Manlius Capitolinus could not tolerate the fact that his
rival was given so much respect and so much glory.[31] It seemed to him
that, as far as the safety of Rome was concerned, his own achievement
in saving the Capitol was as admirable as anything Camillus had done,
and that he deserved just as much praise as Camillus did if the other
aspects of their military careers were compared. So he was eaten up
with jealousy and could not rest content while Furius Camillus was
admired. Seeing that he had no hope of spreading hostility to him
among the senators, he turned to the populace and spread among them
various rumors that placed Camillus in a bad light. One of the things
he said was that the treasure that had been collected to give to the
French, but that in the end had not been given to them, had been
embezzled by private citizens, and that if it was restored it could be
put to public use, reducing the burden of taxes on the populace, or
paying off their private debts. The populace was very taken with this
claim: They began to gather in crowds and, as often as they felt like
it, they rioted in the city. The senate was not pleased, and, believing
the situation to be urgent and dangerous, established a dictator to
sort the matter out and put a halt to Manlius's attacks. The dictator at
once summoned Manlius. They went to meet each other in public, the
dictator surrounded by the nobility, Manlius by the populace. Manlius
was asked what he had to say on the question of who had the treasure
he had been talking about, because the senate was as eager as the
populace to hear him on the subject. Manlius did not reply directly
to the question, but avoided it by saying that there was no need to tell
them what they already knew. So the dictator had him locked up.

This example serves to show how detestable slanders are, both in
free cities and in other types of political system. In order to suppress

---

31. Manlius Capitolinus had saved the Capitol in 390 B.C., but Camillus
was acknowledged Rome's second founder for defeating the Gauls. Relations
between the two reached a crisis in 386 B.C.

them, one should not omit any legislation that may be of use. Nor can there be any more effective way of suppressing them than by providing numerous channels through which charges can be laid, for slanders are as bad for republics as public accusations are good. Between the two there is this difference: Slanders do not need a witness to be believed, nor do they have to pass any test before they are regarded as proven, so that anyone can be slandered by anyone. But it is not the case that anyone can bring charges against anyone else, for in order to bring a charge you have to produce evidence and give grounds for thinking that the charge is well founded. Men bring charges against each other in front of the magistrates, the councils, the public assembly; they slander each other on street corners and in places of business. Slander is more common where public accusations are less common and where the legal system is ill-adapted to the bringing of charges. So someone drawing up a constitution for a republic ought to ensure that one can bring charges in it against any citizen, without intimidation and without favoritism. If this principle is properly recognized in practice, he should then punish harshly those who spread slanders. They will have no grounds to complain when they are punished, for there were courts to hear their accusations, so there was no excuse for spreading them around the streets. And where proper provision is not made in this matter there will always be serious disorders, for slanders upset people without punishing them; and those who have been upset think of getting their revenge, for the things that are said against them do not so much frighten them as anger them.

In this matter, as I have said, the Romans did things in the right way, while in our city of Florence they have always been handled badly. Just as in Rome their arrangements had excellent consequences, so in Florence our failure to make arrangements has had evil consequences. If you read the histories of this city, you will see how many slanders have been, in every period, directed at those citizens who have played an important role in the city's affairs. One was accused of stealing the city's money; another was said to have lost a battle because he had taken a bribe; a third to have done things that were bad for the city because he stood to gain increased power by it. The result was that hatred was whipped up on all sides; hatred led to division; division led to factions; factions led to ruin. If there had been provision in Florence for individuals to bring charges against citizens and for slanderers to be punished, then innumerable political crises that have occurred would have been avoided. For individual citizens, whether they were condemned or cleared of the charges, would have been unable to do harm to the city and would have been brought to trial less often than they were attacked by rumor, for, as I have said, you have to have some grounds to justify bringing charges, while you can slander anyone you choose.

And among the other means citizens have used to accumulate power has been that of spreading slanders. They have used them to considerable effect against powerful citizens who opposed their wishes, for they have claimed to be taking the side of the people, and, by confirming them in the bad opinion they had of the city's political leaders, won their allegiance. One could point to quite a few examples, but I will restrict myself to one only. The Florentine army laying siege to Lucca was commanded by Mr. Giovanni Guicciardini who held the post of commissioner.[32] Either his bad planning or his bad luck was responsible for the fact that the city did not fall. Whatever the real cause, it was Mr. Giovanni who took the blame, for people said that he had been bribed by the city of Lucca. This slander, which was spread about by his enemies, made Mr. Giovanni so depressed he was close to suicide. Although in order to clear his name he gave himself up to the chief of police, nevertheless, he could never establish his innocence, for the republic of Florence provided no procedure through which he could defend himself. This state of affairs was the cause of a good deal of tension between the allies of Mr. Giovanni, who included most of the political elite, on the one hand, and those who favored political innovation on the other. This tension, for this and other similar reasons, grew so acute that it brought about the ruin of the republic.[33]

So Manlius Capitolinus was a slanderer, not someone prepared to bring charges; and the Romans showed by the way they treated him exactly how slanderers ought to be punished. For one should require them to bring charges, and, if their charges are upheld, either reward them or at least not punish them; but if they are not upheld, one should punish them, as Manlius was punished.

Chapter Nine: On how it is necessary to act alone if you want to draw up the constitution for a new republic from scratch, or reform an old one by completely changing its established laws.

Perhaps some people will think that I have jumped too far ahead in the history of ancient Rome, for I have not yet said anything about the men who drew up the Roman constitution, nor have I discussed those laws that dealt with religion or with military service. Since I do not

32. In 1430 to 1433.
33. With the restoration of the Medici in 1432.

want to keep those who want to read something about these matters waiting any longer, let me say that many will probably think the founding of Rome presents a bad example, for Romulus, in order to establish constitutional government, first killed his brother and then agreed to the killing of Titus Tatius, the Sabine, who had been elected to share office with him. You might think that the citizens of a state founded in this manner could claim that they were only following the example of their ruler if they attacked those who opposed their wishes while they sought to acquire power and authority. You would be right to think this, so long as you did not stop to consider the reasons that had led him to commit murder.

One ought to recognize this as a general principle: It rarely (if ever) happens that a republic or a kingdom has good institutions from the beginning, or is completely reformed along lines quite different from those on which it was previously organized, unless one person has sole responsibility. So one person alone must decide on the strategy, and he must make all the key decisions. A wise legislator when establishing a republic, if he wants to serve not his own interests but the public good, not to benefit his own heirs but the nation as a whole, should make every effort to ensure that all power lies in his own hands. A wise man will never criticize someone for an extralegal action undertaken to organize a kingdom or establish a republic. He will agree that if his deed accuses him, its consequences excuse him. When the consequences are good, as were the consequences of Romulus's act, then he will always be excused, for it is those who are violent in order to destroy who should be found guilty, not those who are violent in order to build anew.

A legislator should, however, use care and skill [*virtuoso*] to ensure that the power he has seized is not inherited by a successor; for, since men are more inclined to do evil than good, his successor is likely to use for selfish purposes the power he has been using for the public good. Moreover, one person alone may be best at drawing up plans, but the institutions he has designed will not survive long if they continue to depend on the decisions of one man. They will do better if many share the responsibilities, and if many are concerned to preserve them. For just as it is a bad idea to have many people plan something, for they will not agree about what is best, since there will be many differing opinions among them, so, too, when once they know what is right, they will not be able to agree to act contrary to it. Romulus deserved to be pardoned for the death of his brother and his colleague, for his actions were aimed at the public good and not at self-advancement. This is evident from the fact that he quickly established a senate to whose views he listened and whose advice he took. If you analyze the powers Romulus kept in his own hands, you will find that the only powers he kept were those of commanding the armies once war had been declared and of summoning the senate. This became apparent when Rome acquired freedom by driving out the Tarquins, for the Romans did not alter their established constitution at all, beyond replacing an hereditary monarch with two consuls elected annually. This shows that the original institutions of Rome were better adapted for a constitutional and participatory political system than for an absolute and tyrannical one.

There are an infinite number of examples that could be produced in support of what I have said in this chapter, such as Moses, Lycurgus, Solon, and other founders of monarchies and republics who could, because they had laid claim to a certain personal authority, establish laws aimed at the common good. But I want to leave these aside, as the point is obvious. Let me give only one additional example, not such a well-known one, but worth considering if one wants to establish a good constitution. Agis, King of Sparta,[34] wanted to confine the Spartans within the limits that had been established for them by the laws of Lycurgus. He felt that his city, because it had in some measure deviated from its original constitution, had lost a good deal of its traditional excellence [*antica virtù*] and, with it, much of its strength and power. He had no sooner begun his reforms than he was assassinated by the Spartan ephors[35] on the grounds that he was trying to establish a tyranny. But Cleomenes was appointed king to succeed him,[36] and he developed the same aspirations, for he came across some memoranda and memoirs written by Agis. From them he learned the true opinions and intentions of his predecessor. He recognized that he could not do his country the service he intended if he did not concentrate all power in his own hands, for he thought that human beings were so self-interested that one could not do good to the majority if faced with the opposition of a powerful minority. So he seized on a suitable opportunity and had all the ephors and anyone else in a position to oppose him killed. Then he completely overhauled the laws of Lycurgus. This would probably have given Sparta a new lease on life and established for Cleomenes a reputation as great as that of Lycurgus, if the Macedonians had not been establishing their predominance, and if the other Greek cities had not been incapable of resisting them. For after Cleomenes' reforms, the Spartans were attacked by the Macedonians

34. King from 244 to 240 B.C.
35. The ephors, like the Roman tribunes, were elected by the people.
36. He ruled from 237 to 221 B.C.

and discovered that, on their own, they were not strong enough to resist them. Their forces had nowhere to retreat and were defeated.[37] So Cleomenes' plans, although wise and admirable, never came to fruition.

Having considered all these matters, I conclude that in order to establish the constitution of a republic one needs to have sole power; and that Romulus should be forgiven, not blamed, for the deaths of Remus and of Titus Tatius.

Chapter Ten: On how, just as the founders of a republic or a kingdom deserve praise, so the founders of a tyranny should be held in contempt.

Of all the types of men who are praised, it is the heads and founders of religions who are the most highly praised. After them come those who founded either republics or kingdoms. After them, the most famous are those who have commanded armies and have expanded either their own territory or that of their nation. To these we may add authors. These are of different types, and each is celebrated according to its ranking. All other men who are praiseworthy—and there are an infinite number of them—acquire a measure of reputation through their skill or craft. On the other hand, those who destroy religions, undermine kingdoms and republics, are hostile to excellence, to literature, and to all the arts and crafts that are useful or honorable to mankind, these men are infamous and detestable. These are the impious, the violent, the ignorant, the good-for-nothings, the lazy, the base. There never will be anybody so crazy or so wise, so devilish or so saintly, that, offered a choice between the two types of man, will not praise those who deserve to be praised and criticize those who deserve to be criticized. Nevertheless, almost all men, misled by a false idea of what is good and a false notion of what is praiseworthy, slip, either willfully or foolishly, into the ranks of those who deserve more blame than praise. Put in a position where they can win eternal praise by founding either a republic or a kingdom, they become tyrants and do not even realize how much reputation, glory, honor, security, peace of mind, and satisfaction of spirit they are giving up, and how much infamy, vituperation, criticism, danger, and unease they are going to incur.

It is impossible for a private citizen living in a republic, if he reads his history books and makes good use of the records of past events,

37. In 222 B.C.

not to want to live in his homeland as a Scipio[38] rather than a Caesar.
If by chance or skill [*virtù*] he becomes a ruler, he is bound to prefer
being an Agesilaus,[39] a Timoleon, a Dion,[40] to being a Nabis,[41] a
Phalaris,[42] or a Dionysius. For everyone can see that the latter are held
in complete contempt, while the former are immoderately praised.
They also see that Timoleon and the others had no less authority in
their countries than Dionysius and Phalaris had in theirs, but they had
a great deal more security.

There is nobody who is taken in by the glory of Caesar, even when
they see him praised in the highest terms by those who write about
him; for those who praise him have been corrupted by his success and
frightened by the long endurance of the Roman empire. Since the
rulers of that empire continued to call themselves Caesars, writers
could not discuss Caesar freely. But if you want to know what writers
would say about him if they were free to speak their minds, look at
what they say about Catiline.[43] Caesar is more to be censured than
Catiline; just as he who does evil is more blameworthy than he who
merely tries to do it. Look, too, at the praise with which authors refer
to Brutus. Afraid to criticize Caesar because of his power, they acclaim
his enemy.

If you become an absolute ruler in a republic you should also consider
how much more praise, once Rome was ruled by emperors, was
awarded to those emperors who abided by the laws and were benevolent
than to those who were the opposite.[44] Note that Titus, Nerva, Trajan,
Hadrian, Antoninus, and Marcus had no need of praetorian guards or
of multitudes of legions to defend themselves, because their own way

38. Scipio (234–183 B.C) defeated the Carthaginians.

39. King of Sparta from 398–360 B.C. and praised by Plutarch.

40. First Dion (d. 354 B.C.) and then Timoleon (d. 337 B.C.) led successful
revolts against the tyranny of Dionysius II of Syracuse, who ruled from 367
to 343 B.C. Again, the source is Plutarch.

41. Tyrant of Sparta from 207 to 192 B.C. The source is Polybius, bk. 13.
chs. 6–8.

42. Tyrant of Agrigentum from 570 to 554 B.C., referred to by Aristotle in the
Politics and the *Rhetoric.*

43. Catiline conspired to overthrow the government from 66 to 63 B.C., when
he was killed at the head of an uprising. Cicero's attacks on him were well-known
rhetorical models.

44. In this paragraph, Machiavelli discusses the emperors up to and including
Marcus Aurelius (d. 180). Their successors are discussed in *The Prince*, ch.
nineteen.

of life, the good will of the populace, and the love of the senate served to defend them. On the other hand, the entire armies of the eastern and western empires were not large enough to protect Caligula, Nero, Vitellius, and many other wicked rulers against the enemies they had acquired by their foul practices and evil lives. Any ruler who gives due consideration to the history of these emperors will be taught clearly enough which is the way to acquire glory, and which the way to deserve censure; what to do in order to be safe, and what to do to live a life of fear.

Of the first twenty-six emperors, from Caesar to Maximinus,[45] sixteen were assassinated, and ten died of natural causes. It is true that among those who were killed the odd good ruler is to be found, Galba for example, or Pertinax, but their deaths were the result of the corruption among the soldiers they had inherited from their predecessors. Among those who died of natural causes the occasional wicked ruler is to be found—Severus, for example—but these were men of extraordinary good fortune and skill [*virtù*]: Few men can count on both of these. He will also learn by reading the history of Rome how one should organize a good kingdom, for all the emperors who inherited power, with the exception of Titus, were wicked; those who were appointed to succeed without being blood relatives were all good, for example the five emperors from Nerva to Marcus.[46] When power fell once more into the hands of hereditary rulers, the empire declined once again.

Let our ruler consider the period of time that runs from Nerva to Marcus and compare those rulers with those who went before and those who came after; then let us ask him when he would rather have been born, and over which type of state he would rather rule. When the empire was governed by good men, he will find rulers lived in security, surrounded by their citizens who had nothing to fear, and he will find that the world was peaceable and that justice prevailed. He will see that the senate had its due authority, the magistrates their honors, that the rich citizens were able to enjoy their wealth, and that nobility and virtue [*virtù*] were admired. Everything was peaceable, and all was right with the world. Rancor, license, corruption, and ambition, for their part, were nowhere to be found. These were golden times, when everyone could hold and defend whatever view he wished. In short, everybody benefited: The prince was treated with reverence

45.   Caesar died in 44 B.C. (though he was never officially emperor); Maximinus in 238.

46.   That is, from 96 to 180.

and esteem, the people were loving and secure. If he then looks carefully at the periods before and after this one, he will find them horrifying because of the frequent wars, unstable because of the frequent seditions, and full of cruelty during both peace and war. Everywhere he looks he will see rulers murdered, civil wars, international conflicts. He will see Italy afflicted and full of unprecedented misfortunes, her cities ruined and sacked. He will see Rome burned, the Capitol destroyed by her own citizens, the ancient temples desolate, religious ceremonies corrupted, the cities full of adultery. On the seas, ships carry men into exile; the rocks on the shores are stained with blood. In Rome itself innumerable atrocities occur; breeding, wealth, previous honors, and above all virtue [*virtù*] are thought to be capital offenses. Slanderers are rewarded, slaves are bribed to turn against their masters, servants against their employers. Those who are not overwhelmed by their enemies find their own friends will do them down. Then he will really know just how much Rome, Italy, and the whole world owe to Caesar.

Doubtless, if he has blood in his veins, he will be appalled at the thought of imitating the evil times and will burn with an immense desire to copy the good. Truly, if a ruler wants to acquire worldly glory, he ought to want to rule over a corrupt city, not in order to destroy it completely, as Caesar destroyed Rome, but to re-establish it, as Romulus did. In truth, the heavens cannot offer a man a greater opportunity to win glory, nor can men desire any reputation more than this one. If, in order to establish a good constitution for a city, there were no alternative to giving up power, then there would be some excuse for anyone who, in order to hold on to power, failed to introduce a good constitution. But since one can introduce a good constitution and still retain power, there is no excuse for such people at all. So those to whom heaven gives such an opportunity should recognize that they stand at a crossroads: One path leads to security in this life and to glory after death; the other leads to continuous anxiety in this life and to perpetual infamy after death.

Chapter Eleven: On the religion of the Romans.

Rome's first founder was Romulus, and she owed her birth and education to him, as a child is indebted to its father. Nevertheless, fate took the view that the institutions established by Romulus were not adequate for the vast empire that Rome was to have; so it inspired the Roman senate to appoint Numa Pompilius as Romulus's successor, so that those things Romulus had omitted to take care of could be dealt

with by Numa. The Romans of his day were completely wild, not
domesticated; he wanted to train them to live a sociable life and to
practice the arts of peace. So he turned to religion because it is essential
for the maintenance of a civilized way of life, and he founded a religion
such that for many centuries there was more fear of God in Rome
than there has ever been anywhere else. Such piety was of considerable
assistance whenever the senate or one of Rome's great leaders undertook any enterprise. If you look over the whole record of Roman history,
taking into consideration both the Romans as a community and the
behavior of individual citizens, you will find that the citizens of Rome
were a good deal more afraid of the consequences of breaking their
oaths than of breaking the laws, for they were more afraid of God's
power than man's.

This is evident from the cases of Scipio and Manlius Torquatus.
After Hannibal had routed the Romans at Cannae[47] many of the citizens
gathered together and, despairing of their homeland, resolved to abandon Italy and retreat to Sicily. When Scipio heard this he went to meet
them and, with a naked sword in his hand, forced them to swear never
to abandon the land of their birth. Lucius Manlius, father of Titus
Manlius, who was later called Torquatus, had been accused by Marcus
Pomponius, tribune of the people. Before the day of judgment came,
Titus went to find Marcus and threatened to kill him if he did not
promise to lift the charges against his father.[48] He forced him to swear
that he would do so, and Marcus, having sworn out of fear, kept his
word. Thus, those citizens who could not be kept in Italy by love of
country or fear of the laws were held there by an oath they had been
forced to take against their wills; and that tribune set aside the hatred
he had for the father, ignored the injury the son had done him, and
sacrificed his honor, in order to keep an oath he had been forced to
take. The sole cause of this behavior was the religion Numa had
established in the city.

Anyone who reads the history of Rome with care will recognize how
useful religion was when it came to commanding armies, to inspiring
the populace, to keeping men on the straight and narrow, to making
criminals ashamed of themselves. So that if one had to debate to which
ruler Rome owed more, to Romulus or to Numa, I rather think that
Numa would come in first. For where religion is well-established it is

47. In 216 B.C.
48. In 362 B.C. Among the charges was that he had been cruel to his own
son.

easy to introduce military prowess; but where there is military prowess
without religion it is hard to introduce piety. One can see that there
was no need for Romulus, who was trying to establish the senate and
construct other civil and military institutions, to claim that his actions
were authorized by God; but this was a claim Numa was obliged to
make. He pretended to be on friendly terms with a nymph who advised
him on everything before he made recommendations to the people.
This came about because he wanted to establish new and unaccus-
tomed institutions in Rome, and he feared his own authority might be
insufficient.

Indeed, there has not been a single founder of an exceptional constitution for a nation who has not had recourse to divine authority, for
otherwise it would have been impossible for him to win acceptance for
his proposals. For there are many fine principles that a wise man will
acknowledge but that are not sufficiently self-evident to be accepted
by ordinary people. So intelligent men who want to overcome this
problem turn to God. This is what Lycurgus did, and Solon, and many
others whose objectives were the same as theirs. The Roman populace,
astonished at Numa's goodness and wisdom, fell in with every proposal
he made. It is certainly true that in those days people were very religious,
and that the people with whom Numa had to deal were unsophisticated. This made it much easier for him to accomplish what he set out to
do, for he could easily manipulate them in any way he chose. Doubtless
anyone who in our own day set out to construct a republic would find
it easier to do it among the inhabitants of the mountains, who are
completely uncivilized, than he would among those who are accustomed
to living in the cities, who are civilized but corrupt. A sculptor finds
it easier to make a fine sculpture out of a rough block of marble than
out of one that has been poorly worked on by somebody else.

Taking everything into account, I conclude that the religion introduced by Numa was one of the primary reasons for the success of
Rome, for a good religion leads to good institutions, good institutions
lead to good fortune, and good fortune ensures the success of everything
one undertakes. And, just as religious worship is the foundation of the
greatness of a republic, so the neglect of it will bring about its ruin.
For where the fear of God is missing, either the state will collapse, or
if it is held together it will only be by fear of a ruler who is able to
make up for an inadequate religion. And since rulers do not live long,
such a state is bound to fail soon, once the force [*virtù*] holding it
together is gone. So those states that depend entirely on the strength
[*virtù*] of a single individual do not last long, for his strength cannot

outlive him. It is rare for his successor to be able to take over where he leaves off, as Dante has the good sense to note:

> It is rare for human integrity to be inherited.
> God wants it this way, so that people will turn to him for it.[49]

The best thing for a republic or a monarchy is not to have someone in charge who governs well for as long as he lives; it is better to have someone who organizes the state so that when he dies it will continue without him.

Although it is easier to persuade unrefined men to adopt a new institution or a new belief, this does not mean it is impossible to persuade people who are sophisticated and who pride themselves on being refined to do so. The people of Florence do not think of themselves as either ignorant or unsophisticated; nevertheless, Friar Girolamo Savonarola persuaded them that he talked with God. I do not want to say if I think this was true or not; for one should talk with reverence of such a great man. But I certainly will say that innumerable people believed him, although they had not seen anything extraordinary that might lead them to think it true. His way of life, his doctrine, and his message were enough to make them believe him. No one should despair of being able to achieve things that others have achieved before them, for men, as I said in my preface, are born, live, and die in the same way as they always have done.

Chapter Twelve: On how important it is to give due weight to
religion, and on how Italy, having been deprived of
faith by the Church of Rome, has been ruined
as a consequence.

Those rulers and those republics who want to keep their political systems free of corruption must above all else prevent the ceremonies of their religion from being corrupted and must keep them always in due veneration. For one can have no better indication of the prospective ruin of a society than to see that divine worship is held in contempt. It is easy to see why this is so, since we saw above that religions are established wherever men are born. Every religion grounds its spiritual life in one particular doctrine or practice. The religious life of the pagans was based on the replies given them by their oracles and on the cult of divination and augury. All their other ceremonies, sacrifices,

---

49. Dante, *Il Purgatorio,* Canto 4,11. 121–3.

and rites depended on these, for it was easy for them to believe that a god who could foretell the good or evil that was going to happen to you could also determine your fate. It was this belief that gave rise to temples, to sacrifices, to prayers, and to all the other ceremonies with which the gods were venerated. They were authorized by the oracle of Delos, the temple of Jupiter Ammon, and by other celebrated oracles who were universally admired and worshipped. These oracles in time came to speak as they were instructed to by the powerful, and the deception involved was recognized by the populace. Thus, men came to be sceptics and became inclined to overthrow every good institution.

So the rulers of a republic or of a kingdom should uphold the basic principles of the religion to which they are committed. If they do this it will be easy for them to keep their state religious and, as a consequence, law-abiding and united. Everything that happens that fosters religious faith, even if they privately judge it to be false, they should support and encourage; the more prudent they are, the more scientific their outlook, the more they should do this. It is because sensible men have adopted this policy that belief in miracles has taken hold, even in religions that we know to be false. For wise men supported them without worrying about the truth of their claims, and their authority served to encourage belief in society as a whole.

There were many such miracles reported in Rome: for example, when the Roman soldiers were sacking the city of Veii[50] some of them entered the temple of Juno. They went up to her statue and said, "Do you want to come to Rome?" Some thought she nodded in response; others heard her say yes. Since these men had a genuine religious faith (Livy's account makes this plain, for he reports that they entered the temple without being raucous, but acting devoutly and full of reverence)[51] they thought they had heard the reply to their question that they had, perhaps, expected. This simple-minded belief was unhesitatingly encouraged and favored by Camillus and by the other rulers of the city.

If, when Christianity first became a state religion, such piety had been encouraged (as the founder of the religion instructed it should be), the Christian states and republics would now be more united and a good deal happier than they are. Nor is there any clearer indication of the decline of Christianity than the fact that those peoples who live closest to Rome, whose Church is the head of our religion, have the least faith. If you look back to the founding principles of Christianity,

50. Veii fell after a ten-year siege in 395 B.C.
51. Livy, bk. 5, ch. 22.

and contrast them with present practices, you will be bound to conclude that our religion will soon be destroyed or scourged.

Since many are of the view that the welfare of the cities of Italy depends on the Roman church, I want to argue the contrary case, employing those reasons that occur to me. I will appeal to two powerful arguments that, I believe, are compatible with each other. The first is that the wicked examples presented by the papal court have caused the whole of Italy to lose all piety and all religious devotion. This has innumerable unfortunate consequences and is the cause of numerous disorders. For just as respect for religion has a whole range of beneficial consequences, so contempt for religion has a whole range of evil consequences. Thus, we Italians owe this much to our Church and to our clergy: They have made us irreligious and wicked.

But this is not the half of what we owe them, for there is another reason why the Church is the cause of our ruin: the Church has been and still is responsible for keeping Italy divided. In truth, no geographical region has ever been unified or happy if it has not been brought under the political control of a single republic or ruler, as has happened in France and Spain. And the only reason why Italy has not been unified as they have been, the only reason why she does not have a republic or a prince who has been able to acquire control of the whole territory, is the existence of the church. The pope lives in Italy and has a temporal authority there, but he has not been powerful or skillful [*virtù*] enough to acquire absolute power throughout Italy and make himself her ruler; but on the other hand he has never been so weak that, faced with the prospect of losing his temporal possessions, he has been unable to call on some other state to defend him against whatever power has been on the rise in Italy. There is plenty of evidence for this in the past, for example when the papacy employed Charlemagne to kick out the Lombards, who had become rulers of almost the whole of Italy.[52] In our own day the papacy destroyed the power of the Venetians by obtaining the support of the French;[53] and then got rid of the French with the help of the Swiss.[54] So the church has not been powerful enough to conquer Italy, but has prevented anyone else from conquering her. This is the reason why Italy has never been united under one ruler, but has been divided among numerous princes and rulers, which has resulted in so much division and weakness that she has been reduced to being the victim, not only of powerful foreign

52. In 774.
53. Battle of Agnadello, 1509.
54. Campaign of 1512.

states, but of anyone who cares to attack her. We Italians owe all this to our Italian church and to no one else.

If you wanted to have an incontrovertible test of the truth of my argument, you would need to be powerful enough to transport the court of Rome, with its temporal authority, from Italy to Switzerland. For the Swiss are the only people who still live as the ancients did, being uncorrupted in both their religion and their military service. You would see that in a short time the evil habits of the court of Rome would introduce more disorder into the territory of the Swiss than anything else that could ever happen there.

Chapter Thirteen: On how the Romans used religion to reorganize their city, to carry out their enterprises, and to put a stop to internal dissensions.

I think it might be helpful if I gave a few examples of occasions when the Romans used religion to reorganize their city and to carry out their enterprises. Although there are lots of examples to be found in Livy, nevertheless, I intend to confine myself to the few that follow. In the year after the Roman populace established tribunes with consular authority, all of whom, with one exception, were plebeians, there was plague and famine, and a number of prodigious events occurred.[55] The nobles took advantage of this when it came to the election of new tribunes. They said the gods were angry because Rome had ill-treated its constituted authorities, and that there was no way of placating the gods except to elect the proper people as tribunes. The result was that the populace, unable to argue against these pious sentiments, elected tribunes who were all nobles.

Again, one can see how, when the city of Veii was under siege, the military commanders made use of religion to keep the soldiers ready for an attack. That same year[56] the Alban lake had expanded remarkably. The Roman soldiers were weary with the lengthy siege and wanted to return home. Their commanders discovered that Apollo and some other oracles had declared that the year that Veii would be taken would be the year that the Alban lake overflowed its banks. This made the soldiers willing to put up with the frustrations of the siege, for they were seized with the hope that they would be able to take the town. They were willing to go on with the task, with the result that Camillus, once he was made dictator, took that city after it had been under siege

55. In 399–398 B.C.
56. I.e., 398 B.C.

for ten years. So religion, skillfully employed, helped the Romans seize Veii and helped, too, to restore the tribunate to the nobility. Without its help it would have been difficult to accomplish either objective.

I would not want to omit another example relevant to this subject. Terentillus, when he was tribune, provoked numerous conflicts in Rome.[57] He wanted to propose some legislation for reasons I will outline below in the appropriate place. One of the first means employed by the nobility to resist him was religion, which they put to work in two different ways. In the first place, they had the Sibylline books consulted; they were interpreted as saying that the city was in danger of losing its liberty that year as a result of civil conflict. Although the tribunes exposed this as a stratagem, nevertheless, the prophecy so frightened the populace that they cooled in their support for Terentillus. The second was a response to the fact that a certain Appius Herdonius, with a throng of exiles and slaves, four thousand men in all, had occupied the Capitol by night, giving grounds to fear that if the Aequi and the Volsci, who were longstanding enemies of the Romans, took the opportunity to attack, they would be able to seize the city. Despite this, the tribunes did not let up in the determined insistence with which they advocated the adoption of Terentillus's law, dismissing Herdonius's attack as a fake. So a certain Publius Ruberius, a citizen whose manner was solemn and authoritative, came out of the senate and addressed the populace. Using words that were partly affectionate and partly threatening, he pointed out to them the danger in which the city stood and the untimely nature of their demands. He succeeded in compelling the populace to swear an oath that it would not go against the wishes of the consul. Restored to obedience, the populace retook the Capitol by force. But Publius Valerius, one of the consuls, died during the attack, and Titus Quintius was hurriedly appointed to replace him. He, in order to prevent the populace from catching its breath, and in order to ensure they did not have time to turn their thoughts to Terentillus's law, ordered them to march out of Rome against the Volsci, saying that the oath they had taken to stand by the consul obliged them to follow him. The tribunes argued against him, saying that the oath had been taken to the dead consul and not to him. Nevertheless, Livy describes how the populace, for fear of religion, preferred to obey the consul rather than believe the tribunes. He says this in praise of the old religion: "That negligence towards the gods that characterizes our own age had not yet developed. People did not yet feel free to reinterpret oaths and laws to suit

---

57.   In 462 B.C.

themselves."[58] Because of this, the tribunes were afraid that they would lose all their authority if they held out. They agreed with the consul that they would remain obedient to him, and that for one year there would be no more talk of the law of Terentillus, while the consuls agreed that for one year they would not lead the populace out to war. And so religion made it possible for the senate to overcome problems that, without its assistance, they would never have been able to overcome.

Chapter Sixteen: On how a people who have been accustomed to being ruled by one man, if by some chance they become free, have difficulty in holding on to their liberty.

There are numerous examples to be found in ancient history that show how difficult it is for a people who are accustomed to being ruled by one man to preserve their liberty if by some chance they acquire it, as Rome acquired its liberty when it threw out the Tarquins. This is as you would expect, for such a people are no different from a wild beast which, although by nature savage and untamed, has been raised from birth in a prison and in slavery. If it is then allowed to wander freely in the countryside, because it has no experience of hunting for its food and no knowledge of where to take refuge, it will be recaptured by the first person who sets out to hunt it down.

The same thing happens with a people. Being used to living at the command of others, having no experience of debating questions of strategy, whether of defense or offense, having no knowledge of the neighboring rulers, and being unknown to them, they quickly succumb once again to a ruler's yoke and usually end up under a harsher tyranny than the one from which they have just escaped. They encounter these problems even if their character is not corrupted. For a people who have been entirely corrupted cannot live free for even a short period of time, not even for a moment, as I will explain later. So here I want to discuss those peoples who are not extensively corrupted and who have more that is good in them than is rotten.

In addition, there is another problem, which is that a state that becomes free acquires bitter enemies, but not loyal allies. All those who benefited under the previous tyranny, who fed off the wealth of the ruler, become bitter enemies. They have lost the opportunity to become rich, and so cannot live content. Each one of them is forced to try to reconstruct the old tyranny in order to recover his old influ-

58. Livy, bk. 3, ch. 20.

ence. On the other hand, the new state does not acquire, as I said, loyal allies, because political freedom distributes honors and rewards for honest and impartial reasons, and no one gets honored or rewarded who does not meet the criteria. When someone has the honors and benefits he thinks he deserves, he does not feel indebted to those who gave them to him. Moreover, no one feels grateful to anyone for those benefits of freedom that all share in common, at least so long as they enjoy them. They are able to enjoy their own property without fear of losing it; they do not have to fear that their women will be seduced or their sons corrupted, or be anxious for their own safety. But no one ever feels obliged to anyone else merely because they have left them in peace.

So, as I have already said, a state that has recently acquired freedom acquires bitter enemies without acquiring loyal allies. If you want to find a remedy for these problems and for the conflicts that the above-mentioned difficulties bring with them, there is no more effective solution, none that is more justifiable, reliable, and necessary, than to kill the sons of Brutus.[59] They, as history records, were provoked to conspire with other young Romans against their fatherland by the simple fact that they could not monopolize influence under the consuls as they had been able to under the kings. The freedom of the nation seemed to be the cause of their own enslavement. If you set out to rule over a multitude, whether you do so within a system of political freedom or as sole ruler, and you fail to neutralize those who are hostile to the new constitution, then you are building a state that will be short-lived. It is true that, in my view, those who rule alone and who, in order to consolidate their system of government, have to employ extra-legal means, are unfortunate, for they will find themselves opposed by the populace as a whole. If you are opposed by a minority, it is easy to neutralize them, and your actions need not cause much resentment; but if you are opposed by the vast majority, then you are never going to be safe, and the more blood you shed, the weaker your hold on power becomes. So the best policy you can pursue is to try to win the allegiance of the populace.

What I have just said is something of a digression, for I have been discussing the problems of sole rulers, where I set out to talk about republics. Nevertheless, because I do not want to have to come back to this subject again, let me briefly finish what I have to say about it. If a ruler wants to win over a populace that is hostile to him—I am

59. Killed by their father shortly after the expulsion of the last king in 510 B.C.

speaking about a ruler who has become a tyrant in his own homeland—
I would say he should first ask himself what the populace wants. He
will always find that there are two things it wants: In the first place, it
wants to revenge itself on those who brought about its enslavement;
and in the second, it wants to be free again. As far as their first wish
is concerned, their ruler can satisfy it completely; the second he can
only partially satisfy. There is a good example of a prince letting his
subjects have their revenge. Clearchus had been tyrant of Heraclea
but had been driven into exile.[60] The populace and the elite within
the city fell out among themselves. The elite, finding themselves on
the losing side, began to support Clearchus and conspired with him
to restore him to power in the face of popular opposition. So they took
the people's liberty away from them. Clearchus found himself caught
between the insatiable demands of the elite, whom he could find no
way of either satisfying or reforming, and the hatred of the people,
who were furious at having lost their liberty. He decided to free himself
of the elite, who had become a nuisance, and win over the people. So
he seized an appropriate opportunity and hacked all the members of
the elite into pieces, much to the delight of the populace. By this means
he satisfied one of the two desires that such populaces have, the desire
to revenge themselves.

But as far as the populace's other desire, the desire to regain its
liberty, is concerned, a sole ruler cannot satisfy it, so he should ask
himself why it wants to be free. He will find that a very small number of the people want to be free in order to exercise authority; but all
the rest, who are the vast majority, want liberty in order to live in security.
For in all republics, no matter what particular type of constitution they
have, at the most forty or fifty citizens get to occupy positions of
authority. Because this is such a small number, it is easy to neutralize
this group of people, either by killing them or by offering them positions so attractive (when compared to what they might expect in a free
political system) that most of them decide they are better off accepting the status quo. As for the rest, who merely want to live in security, it
is easy to satisfy them by constructing institutions and passing laws
such that your own power is reconciled with the security of the public.
If a ruler does this, and the populace sees that he is careful not to
break any of these laws no matter what happens, they will quickly come
to feel secure and to be content. An example of this is provided by
the Kingdom of France, where people only feel secure because the
kings of France have obliged themselves to respect innumerable laws,

60. His rule began in 365 B.C. and is described in Justin, *Histories*, bk. 16.

laws that provide for the security of all their subjects. The constitution of that kingdom allows the king to do as he pleases in matters of war and taxes; but in all other affairs his actions are constrained by the laws.

So a ruler, whether prince or republic, who does not have secure control of the state at the beginning, must, as the Romans did, take the first opportunity to secure his position. If you let that moment slip by, you will later regret not having done what you ought to have done. Because the people of Rome were not yet corrupt when they recovered their freedom, and because they killed the sons of Brutus and eliminated the Tarquins, they were able to hold on to what they had won and to make good use of all those institutions and practices that I have already described. But if the people are corrupt, then they will be unable to discover (no matter who they are, Romans or non-Romans) policies that are effective in preserving freedom: This is the subject of the next chapter.

Chapter Seventeen: On how a corrupt people who come to be free can only hold on to their freedom with the greatest of difficulty.

In my view, if the kings of Rome had not been abolished, Rome would in a very short time have become weak and worthless. For if you consider the extent of the corruption that had set in among the kings, you will recognize that if there had been two or three generations of such rulers, then the corruption of the rulers would have infected the body of the nation. Once the society as a whole was corrupt, it would never again have been possible to reform it. But because the head was struck off before the body was infected, it was easy for them to accustom themselves to a free and well-organized political system. One should recognize as an indubitable truth that if a corrupt city, accustomed to one-man rule, acquires freedom and sees its ruler and all his relatives killed, it will never know what to do with its newfound liberty. It would be better for it to have a new ruler step into the shoes of the old. Without a new ruler it will never settle down, unless some individual who combines exceptional goodness with exceptional skill [*virtù*] keeps freedom alive in its midst; but this freedom will only survive as long as he does.

This is what happened at Syracuse with Dion and Timoleon. They both had the skill [*virtù*], under differing circumstances, to keep freedom alive in their city while they lived; but as soon as they died the old tyranny was restored. But the best example is that of Rome. When the Tarquins were thrown out the Romans were able to seize and maintain their freedom; but when Caesar was killed, when Gaius

Caligula was killed, when Nero was killed, when the whole house of Caesar had been eliminated, at no point were they able so much as to lay claim to freedom, let alone maintain it. Events took a very different course, although all this happened in the same city, simply because, in the days of the Tarquins, the Roman people were not yet corrupt, while in later centuries they were rotten to the core. In the early days, in order to keep themselves firm of purpose and determined to prevent the restoration of the monarchy, all that was necessary was that they should swear that they would never agree to there being a king in Rome; in later centuries the authority and severity of Brutus,[61] backed up by all the legions of the eastern empire, were insufficient to keep them committed to preserving the liberty that he, like the first Brutus, had restored to them. This was the result of the corruption that the faction of Marius had introduced into the populace; Caesar, having put himself at the head of this party, had been able to blind the populace to the fact that they were being enslaved, even as he himself placed the yoke upon their necks.

Although this example from the history of Rome is more important than any other, nevertheless, I would like to introduce some further examples of popular corruption drawn from contemporary history. I would say that nothing that could happen, no matter how destructive and violent, could accustom the peoples of Milan and of Naples to freedom, for those societies are completely corrupt. This was apparent after the death of Filippo Visconti,[62] for although the Milanese sought to re-establish liberty, they could not do so, and had not the least idea of how to maintain it. Rome was therefore extremely lucky that her kings became corrupt quickly, so that they were soon kicked out, before their corruption had spread to the guts of the city. It is because the populace of Rome was not corrupt that the innumerable conflicts that broke out in Rome did not harm but actually helped the republic, for her citizens at least had the right objectives.

So we can draw this conclusion: Where the individuals are not corrupt, conflicts and other crises do no harm; where they are corrupt, the best-planned laws are useless, unless the laws are imposed by someone who uses ruthless methods to make people obey him, until the individuals themselves become good. I do not know if this has ever happened, or if it could ever happen. In practice one finds, as I said just before, that where a city has gone into decline because the individuals who make it up are corrupt, if it ever happens that it acquires freedom,

---

61. This is the Brutus who killed Caesar in 44 B.C.
62. In 1447.

it happens because of the skill [*virtù*] of one individual who is present by chance, not because of the strength [*virtù*] of the population as a whole, which is what is needed to maintain good institutions. As soon as the one leader dies, the city returns to its old habits. This is what happened in Thebes which, because of the skill [*virtù*] of Epaminondas, was able, so long as he was alive, to maintain a republican structure and to hold down an empire; but, as soon as he died,[63] Thebes returned to its old internal conflicts. The problem is that an individual cannot live long enough to have time to discipline properly a city that has long been spoiled. One leader of exceptional longevity or two skilled [*virtuose*] leaders succeeding each other are not enough to establish order; but without one or the other, as I have said, there is no hope. By the time you discover this, however, you have undergone many dangers, and much blood has been spilled, and still liberty is not reborn. For this sort of corruption, this sort of incapacity for political freedom, is the result of the social inequality that has developed within the city. In order to restore equality, one would have to use quite exceptional measures. Few know how to use them, or, if they do know, are prepared to face what is involved, as I will explain in greater detail elsewhere.

Chapter Eighteen: On the way to preserve political freedom in a corrupt but free city; or to establish it in a corrupt and unfree city.

I think it is relevant to what we have been discussing, and it would not be out of place, to consider whether one can preserve political freedom in a corrupt but free city, or whether one can establish it in a corrupt and unfree city. On this subject, I say that it is very difficult to do either one or the other; and although it is almost impossible to formulate general rules, for one would have to adjust one's policies in the light of the extent of the corruption, nevertheless, since it is good to think through every problem, I do not want to omit a discussion of this one. Let us assume we are dealing with an extremely corrupt city, so that we can consider the most difficult case. Indeed, the case would seem hopeless, for there are neither laws nor institutions that will serve to restrain a universal corruption. For just as good habits need good laws if they are to survive, so good laws will only be obeyed if the subjects have good habits.

Moreover, the institutions and laws that have been established in a republic at the time of its foundation, when the individuals who made

63. In 362 B.C.

it up were good, are no longer appropriate when they become bad. If the laws of a city are relatively easily changed to take account of changing circumstances, the institutions, on the other hand, never change, or do so only at long intervals. The result is that the new laws are insufficient, because the institutions that remain unchanged distort their impact. In order to make clearer what I mean, let me explain what the institutions of the government, or rather of the state, were in Rome, and then I will outline the laws with which the magistrates held the citizens in check. The fundamental institutions of the state were embodied in the respective powers of the people, the senate, the tribunes, and the consuls; in the ways in which magistrates were chosen and appointed; and in the ways in which legislation was passed. This fundamental constitution changed little or not at all as circumstances changed. What did change were the laws that restricted the actions of citizens, such as the laws on adultery, the laws controlling extravagance, those on political corruption, and many others, which were altered as the citizens became progressively more corrupt. But since the institutions of the state remained unchanged, although they were no longer appropriate once the citizens had become corrupt, the revision of particular laws was insufficient to prevent the progress of corruption; the outcome would have been different if not only the laws had been changed, but the constitution as well.

That I am justified in claiming that such institutions were not the right ones for a corrupt city is particularly apparent if we look at two topics: the election of magistrates and the passage of legislation. The people of Rome did not give the consulate and the rest of the highest offices in the city except to those who sought them. This system was good at first, for only those citizens who thought themselves worthy of high office stood for election. Since defeat was shameful, each candidate behaved well in the hope of being judged worthy of election. However, this system was disastrous when the city had become corrupt. For then it was not the most virtuous [*virtù*] but the most powerful who stood for election, and the weak, even if virtuous [*virtuosi*], were too frightened to run for office. Things degenerated to this point not all at once but bit by bit, as happens with all cases of degeneration. Once the Romans had subdued Africa and Asia, and had compelled almost the whole of Greece to acknowledge their authority, they became confident that no one would conquer them, and they no longer thought they had any enemies of whom they ought to be afraid.[64] This sense of security, this absence of enemies who inspired respect, meant that

---

64. Roughly, after 146 B.C., when Carthage fell.

the people of Rome, in electing consuls, no longer paid attention to competence [*virtù*], but judged only on the basis of charm. They elected those who were best at flattering Rome's citizens, not those who were best at defeating Rome's enemies. Later, even charm was not enough, and the people sank to the point that they voted for those who had the most patronage to distribute; so that good men, because the system was faulty, never stood a chance.

Similarly, a tribune, or indeed any other citizen, could propose a law to the people. Every citizen then had the right to speak for or against the proposal before a vote was taken. This was a good system, so long as the citizens were good, for it is always a good principle that anyone should be free to put forward a proposal of benefit to the public; it is also a good principle that everyone should be able to express his opinion on the subject, so that the people, when they have heard everyone's opinion, can then make the right decision. But once the citizens became corrupt this system became disastrous, for only the powerful proposed laws, and they did so not in order to further the liberty of all, but only in order to build up their own power. Everyone was too frightened to speak against their proposals, so that the people were either taken in, or else compelled to choose policies that would lead to their own destruction.

If one had wanted to preserve liberty in Rome despite the progress of corruption, it would have been necessary to go beyond passing new laws from time to time and to construct new political institutions. For the institutions and ways of life one needs to establish if men are corrupt are different from those that are appropriate if they are good; if one has different materials with which to work, one must build a quite different structure. But these institutions would either have had to be reformed all at once, as soon as it was realized that as a whole they were no longer appropriate, or else they would have had to be revised little by little, as each particular institution was seen to be in need of reform. Both of these procedures are, in my view, almost impossible to carry out. For if you want to revise institutions little by little and one by one, you need to have some wise man proposing change, someone who sees problems almost before they have developed and catches them at the moment of their birth. In the whole history of a city there might easily prove to be not a single person as wise as this. And even if there were such a person, he would never be able to persuade others to recognize the truth of his arguments, for men who have been used to living in a particular way have no desire to change it, especially when they do not find themselves standing toe-to-toe with a problem, but rather are asked to accept its existence on the basis of someone else's conjectures and hypotheses. On the other hand, if one hopes to change the institutions at a stroke, when everyone has come to recognize that they are defective, then I maintain defects that are easy to recognize are hard to correct. For such reforms, ordinary measures are insufficient, for we are dealing with a situation where the ordinary measures have proved defective. So one has to adopt extraordinary measures, such as resorting to violence and civil war. One's primary goal must be to become sole ruler of the city, so that one can do with it as one pleases. In order to reconstruct the constitution of a city so that it fosters political liberty, one needs to be a man with good intentions; but people who resort to arms in order to seize power in a republic are people whose methods are bad. So you can see that there will hardly ever be an occasion when a good man, using wicked means, but using them in the service of good ends, will want to become sole ruler; or when a wicked man, having become sole ruler, wants to do good. It will not occur to him to use for good the power he has acquired by wicked means.

So I have now explained the difficulties that would have to be overcome if one were to try to preserve liberty in a corrupt city or to attempt to establish it from scratch. These difficulties are, in effect, insuperable. Even if one had the opportunity to carry out reform or revolution, one would have to introduce a constitution that was more monarchical than democratic. For men who were so ill-behaved that they could not be kept in order by the laws would need to be kept in check by a more or less arbitrary authority. If one sought to find some other way of making them good, one would either fail completely, or have to resort to extreme cruelty, as I explained above when discussing Cleomenes. He, in order to be sole ruler, had to kill the ephors, just as Romulus, for the same reason, had to kill both his brother and Titus Tatius the Sabine. They went on to use their power well. But you have to take into account the fact that neither of them was dealing with subjects who were as eaten away with corruption as those we have been discussing in this chapter. So it was not unreasonable for them to hope to build a free state; and they were able to turn their aspirations into reality.

Chapter Twenty-One: On how much those rulers and republics
                             that do not have their own armies deserve
                             to be criticized.

Those contemporary rulers and modern republics that do not have their own soldiers for defense and for offense ought to be ashamed of themselves. They should think of Tullus, and they will see that this

shortcoming is not caused by a shortage of men fit for military duty,
but by their own failure, for they should have known how to turn their
subjects into soldiers. For Tullus became King of Rome when the city
had been at peace for forty years.[65] He could not find a single man
who had ever been in battle. Nevertheless, when he decided he wanted
to go to war, he did not think of hiring the Samnites, or the Tuscans,
or of turning to others who were accustomed to military service. Instead,
being a man of great wisdom, he decided to use his own troops. He
was so skilled in his leadership [*fu tanta la sua virtù*] that it was possible
for him to train the most excellent soldiers from scratch. This is truer
than anything else: If a state has men but no soldiers, then the fault
is the ruler's. There is no point in blaming the nature of the territory
or the character of the inhabitants.

Here is a very recent example that confirms my claim. Everyone
knows that only very recently the King of England attacked the King
of France, and did so relying entirely on his own native troops.[66] Now
the English had been more than thirty years without fighting a war, so
that their king could not recruit either soldiers or officers with experience of warfare; nevertheless, he did not hesitate to rely on untried
troops to attack a kingdom full of experienced officers and disciplined
soldiers, for the French army had for years past been continuously at
war in Italy. The explanation for this is simply that the King of England
was a prudent man, and his country was well administered, for during
the years of peace they had continued to prepare for war.

Pelopidas and Epaminondas, the Thebans, when they had liberated Thebes and freed it from domination within the Spartan empire,[67]
found themselves ruling a city used to obeying, surrounded by a people who had become effeminate. But they did not hesitate, so well did
they understand their business [*tanta era la virtù loro*], to call them to
the colors and to march out with them against the Spartan armies
whom they defeated. The historian of these events[68] comments that
these two very quickly showed not that men born in Lacedaemonia
had the makings of good soldiers, but rather that wherever men are
born, good soldiers are to be found, provided you can find someone
who knows how to train them for military service, as we have seen
Tullus knew how to train the Romans. Virgil makes the point better

65. In 672 B.C.
66. In 1513.
67. In 379 B.C.
68. Plutarch.

than anyone else could, and in doing so shows that he agrees with it, when he says:

Tullus will herd the lazy men into the army.[69]

Chapter Twenty-Six: On how a new ruler, in a city or territory
over which he has gained control, should
make everything new.

Anyone who becomes the ruler of a city or of a territorial state—especially if the foundations of his power are weak, and he is not concerned to establish constitutional rule, whether of a monarchical or republican type—the best policy he can follow if he wants to hold on to power is, since he is a new ruler, to remake everything else in the state from scratch. In cities he should establish new governments and put in charge new men with new titles and new powers. He should make the rich poor and the poor rich, as David did when he became king, "who filled the hungry with good things, and the rich he sent empty away."[70] Moreover, he should build new cities and destroy those that already exist. He should move populations from one place to another. In short, he should leave nothing as it was in the whole territory. There should be no office, no rank, no authority, no wealth which is not acknowledged by its possessor as being his gift. He should take as his model Philip of Macedon, the father of Alexander, who transformed himself from a princeling into the ruler of all Greece by using such policies. Those who write about him say that he removed whole populations from one province to another, as herdsmen drive their herds.[71]

Such methods are horrific and destructive not merely of a Christian way of life but of a merely human existence. Nobody ought to willingly adopt them. Anyone should prefer to remain a private citizen rather than become a king through the destruction of so many people's lives. Nevertheless, anyone who does not want to choose the option of doing good, if he wants to stay in power, will find himself well-advised to adopt these evil methods. But instead, men pursue policies that are neither good nor bad, and these are extremely dangerous. They do

69.   Virgil, *Aeneid*, bk. 6, ll. 813–4.
70.   Machiavelli is, in fact, quoting the Magnificat (1 Luke 53), which echoes David's Psalm 33.11.
71.   Philip II ruled from 360 to 336 B.C. Machiavelli's source is Justin, bk. 8.

not understand how to be either entirely wicked or completely good, as I will explain in the next chapter.

Chapter Twenty-Seven: On how it is only on very rare occasions
that men know how to be either
completely bad or completely good.

Pope Julius II went to Bologna in 1505 to overthrow the Bentivogli, who had been rulers of the city for a hundred years. He also wanted to get rid of Giovampagolo Baglioni, who was tyrant of Perugia, because he had plotted against all the tyrants who controlled cities within the papal states. When he reached Perugia, realizing that everyone knew what his intention was, he had no expectation of being allowed to enter the city accompanied by his army, but he did get permission to enter without any troops, despite the fact that Giovampagolo was in the city with plenty of troops whom he had collected together to defend himself. So, swept along by the frenzy with which he undertook everything he did, Julius put himself into the hands of his enemy with only his personal guard to protect him.

Shortly afterwards, he left the city taking Giovampagolo with him, leaving a governor behind who would rule Perugia on behalf of the church. Astute men who were with the pope remarked on his rash boldness and on the cowardice of Giovampagolo.[72] They could not understand how it came about that Giovampagolo had not made himself famous for evermore by getting rid of his enemy with a single blow. He would have been able to make himself wealthy from the plunder, for all the cardinals were travelling with the pope, and they had all their luxuries with them. They could not believe that he had held back out of goodness, nor that his conscience had restrained him. He was a violent man, who kept his sister as his mistress, and had killed cousins and nephews to take power. Compassion could not have made such a man hesitate. So they concluded the explanation was that men do not know how to be either admirably wicked or completely good. A truly wicked deed has its own grandeur or involves a certain nobility of conception: Most men are consequently not up to it.

So Giovampagolo, who thought nothing of committing incest and murdering his relatives in public, did not know how to carry out an enterprise that would have caused everyone to admire his spirit. He had a legitimate opportunity, but to tell the truth he did not dare, though he would have won eternal fame for being the first person to

72. Machiavelli himself was there.

show the clergy just how little one should respect people who live and govern as they do. He could have done something whose grandeur would have more than compensated for any disgrace or any danger that might have resulted from it.

Chapter Twenty-Nine: On whether ingratitude is more characteristic of a people or a ruler.

It seems to me relevant to the subject we have been discussing to ask whether it is peoples or rulers who commit acts of the most striking ingratitude. In order to discuss this question better, I will begin by remarking that this vice of ingratitude is the result either of stinginess or of suspicion. For when either a people or a ruler has sent a general out on an important expedition, and the general has been victorious and acquired a good deal of glory, then that ruler (or that people) is obliged to reward him when he returns. And if, instead of rewarding him, he dishonors him or attacks him, and does so because he is stingy and does not want to give him what he deserves because he is too miserly, then he makes a mistake that cannot be excused. Such a mistake brings with it eternal infamy. Nevertheless, there are many rulers who commit this crime. Cornelius Tacitus explains why in the following sentence: "It is easier to respond to an injury than to a good deed, for gratitude is thought of as an obligation, revenge as pure profit."[73]

When, on the other hand, a ruler (or a people) does not reward him or, to put it better, attacks him, not because he is stingy, but because he is suspicious, then there is some excuse for his behavior. Of this sort of ingratitude, motivated by suspicion, one reads often enough; for a general who has brilliantly [*virtuosamente*] conquered an empire for his employer, overcoming his enemies, covering himself with glory, and loading his soldiers down with riches, inevitably acquires such a reputation—with his soldiers, with his enemies, and with his ruler's own subjects—that his victory cannot taste good to the ruler who sent him out. Because it is in human nature to be ambitious and suspicious, and not to know how to place either good fortune or bad in perspective, it is inevitable that this suspicion, which begins to stir in a ruler as soon as a general has won a victory, appears to be justified by something that the general himself does or says that seems disrespectful. So the ruler can think of nothing but of how to protect himself against him. In order to do this, he considers either killing him or blackening his

73. Tacitus, *Histories*, bk. 4, ch. 3.

reputation with his army and with his fellow subjects. He must use every effort to show that this victory is the result, not of his general's skill [*virtù*] but of good luck, or the cowardice of the enemy, or the wisdom of the other officers that participated in the campaign.

Vespasian, while in Judea, was declared emperor by his army.[74] So Antonius Primus, who was in command of another army in Illyria, declared his support for him and marched into Italy against Vitellius, who controlled Rome. He brilliantly [*virtuosissimamente*] destroyed two of Vitellius's armies and occupied Rome. Mucianus, sent there by Vespasian, found that through Antonius's skill [*virtù*] everything had been taken care of, and every difficulty overcome. Antonius's reward was to see Mucianus quickly deprive him of authority over his army, and he found that little by little he was being confined to Rome and deprived of all power. So Antonius set out to meet Vespasian, who was still in Asia. Vespasian gave him such a welcome that within a short time, deprived of all rank, he died, perhaps of despair. History is full of cases like this. In our own day, everyone still remembers with what effort and skill [*virtù*] Gonsalvo Ferrante, campaigning in the Kingdom of Naples against the French on behalf of Ferdinand, King of Aragon, conquered and defeated that kingdom,[75] and knows his reward for victory was that Ferdinand left Aragon and, having arrived in Naples, began by taking away his authority over his troops,[76] then deprived him of his fortresses, and soon took him back with him to Spain, where he quickly died, unhonored.[77]

This suspicion on the part of rulers is so natural that they cannot help but give in to it. It is impossible for them to express gratitude to someone whose victories, while he is in command of their armies, have brought extensive new territories under their control. If a ruler cannot help but give in, it is scarcely remarkable if a popular government cannot either, and one should lay no more stress on its failings than on a prince's. For a city that rules itself has two objectives: One is to acquire new territory, the other to defend its freedom. It is to be expected that it will make mistakes because of its excessive preoccupation with these objectives. As for mistakes made in acquiring territory, I will discuss them in their proper place. These are some of the mistakes made in defending liberty: to attack those citizens whom one ought to reward, and to be suspicious of those in whom one ought to have

74. In 69. The source is Tacitus, bk. 3.
75. In 1495–6.
76. In 1507.
77. In 1515.

confidence. Although these types of behavior, in a republic that has become corrupt, result in great evils, and although often a general seizes by force the rewards that ingratitude has denied him, with the result that the republic ends up under the rule of a tyrant, as Rome ended up under the rule of Caesar, nevertheless, in a republic that has not been corrupted they result in great benefits and ensure that freedom is preserved. For a little longer the citizens continue to be good and free of ambition, if only out of fear of punishment.

It is true that, among all the peoples who have ever controlled an empire, Rome was, for the reasons I have explained above, the least ungrateful, for one may claim that there is only one example of Roman ingratitude, that of Scipio.[78] For Coriolanus and Camillus were driven into exile, not out of ingratitude, but for offenses that both had committed against the populace.[79] Coriolanus was not pardoned because he had always had a hostile attitude towards the populace; but Camillus was not only recalled, but throughout the remainder of his life he was honored as if he were sole ruler. But the ingratitude shown towards Scipio was the result of a suspicion the citizens began to have about him, one they had not had about the others. This was because Scipio had defeated such a mighty enemy, and victory in so long and dangerous a war had given him such a remarkable reputation, which was enhanced by the speed of his success and by the esteem that his youth, his prudence, and his other remarkable virtues [*virtudi*] had acquired for him. These factors were so important that the constituted authorities in Rome, not to mention anyone else, were frightened of his personal authority. This state of affairs displeased all wise men, as something completely unheard of in Rome. His position seemed so exceptional that Cato the Elder, who was regarded as a saint, was the first to attack him, the first to say that a city could not call itself free if one of its citizens could intimidate the authorities.[80] If the people of Rome followed Cato's advice in this matter, then they should not be blamed for it, since, as I said above, peoples and rulers who are ungrateful because they are suspicious have no choice. Let me conclude this chapter by repeating that this vice of ingratitude is derived either from stinginess or from suspicion; but one can see that popular governments will never be guilty of it from stinginess, and they will be less often guilty of it because they are suspicious than rulers will be, for they have less reason to be suspicious, as I will explain below.

78. See Livy, bk. 38, chs. 50–60.
79. Coriolanus in 491 B.C., Camillus in 391 B.C.
80. In 189 B.C.

Chapter Thirty-Two: On how a republic or a ruler should not
postpone treating its subjects well until the
government's time of need.

A policy of being generous to the populace in times of danger worked
out well for the Romans. When Porsenna came to attack Rome in
order to restore the Tarquins, the senate was concerned the populace
might prefer to have monarchy restored rather than bear the burden
of the war. In order to ensure its support, they removed the tax on
salt and other duties, saying that the poor did enough to benefit the
public if they fed their own children.[81] In gratitude for this assistance,
the populace proved ready to bear siege, hunger, and war.

But it would be wrong for anyone, relying on this precedent, to
postpone until danger is at hand the measures necessary to win the
support of the populace, for he will never succeed with this policy,
even though it worked for the Romans. For each person will conclude
that he does not have you to thank for the good you do him, but your
enemies. They will all be afraid that, when the crisis has passed, you
will take back whatever you have been forced to give them. They will
feel no obligation to you at all. The reason why this policy worked out
well for the Romans was that their government was new and not yet
well established. The populace had seen that other laws to benefit
them had already been passed, such as the law giving a right of appeal
to the people. So they could persuade themselves that the good that
had been done them was not so much caused by the arrival of the
enemy as by the senate's desire to treat them well. Moreover, people
had a fresh memory of what it was like to be ruled by kings. They
remembered having been scorned and ill-treated in numerous ways.
Because similar circumstances rarely obtain, it will not often be the
case that similar policies will be successful.

So anyone who holds power, whether in a republic or as a ruler,
ought to ask himself ahead of time what hostile circumstances he may
find himself in and what sorts of men he may have to turn to for
support in tough times, and then treat these people in the fashion in
which he judges he will be obliged to treat them then, when facing
unfavorable conditions. Anyone who acts differently, whether ruler or
republic, but especially a ruler, and then believes, on the strength of
this example, that when danger comes he will be able to win back
support by treating people well, is making a mistake, for not only will
he not be able to win over support, but his attempts to do so will
accelerate his own destruction.

81. In 508 B.C.

Chapter Thirty-Four: On how dictatorships were beneficial, not harmful, for the Roman republic; and on how powers that are seized from the hands of the citizens against their will are destructive of political freedom, but those they freely vote to give up are not.

Those Romans who found a way to introduce the institution of the dictator to their city have been criticized by some writers, for it has been held responsible for the eventual development of tyranny in Rome. They point out that the first tyrant to establish himself there ruled under the cover of this office of dictator, and they say that without this pretext Caesar would never have been able to find any public appointment that would have provided legitimacy for his tyranny. But those who hold this view have not examined the question carefully, and those who believe them have been misled. For it was neither the name nor the office of dictator that enslaved Rome, but the right that dictators claimed, without authorization from the citizens, to stay in office for a lengthy period. If there had been no title of dictator in Rome, Rome's overmighty citizens would have made up an alternative one, for power easily acquires a title, while titles do not convey power. If you look you will see that the dictators, as long as they were appointed according to the constitutional procedures, and did not appoint themselves, were always good for the city. Those appointments made and those powers claimed by non-constitutional means harm republics; but those that are constitutional do no harm. So in Rome centuries passed without a single dictator doing anything but good to the republic.

The reasons for this are obvious. First, for a citizen to want to break the law and claim for himself extralegal authority, he must have many qualities he simply never would have in a republic that was not corrupt. For to form this intention he must needs be extraordinarily rich, and he must have the support of numerous supporters and adherents, which he could not have if the laws were obeyed. Even if he could have, men of this sort are so intimidating that in a free election men will not willingly vote for them. Moreover, the dictator was appointed for a fixed period and not for life, and he was appointed to deal solely with the particular problem that had made necessary his appointment. He was given authority to take decisions on his own in order to deal with an urgent crisis, to act as he saw fit without consulting others, and if he decided to punish you, you had no right of appeal. But he could not do anything that would undermine the state, such as reduce the powers of the senate or the populace, or abolish the ancient institutions of the city and make new ones. So, taking together the short time of his dictatorship, his limited powers, and the fact that the people of Rome were not corrupt, it was impossible for him to exceed his powers and do harm to the city, and the record shows that he always left things better than he found them.

The truth is that this is one of the institutions that deserves to be added to the list of factors that helped cause the greatness of the Roman state, for without such an institution it is difficult for cities to cope with exceptional events. The established institutions in republics move slowly, for no single committee or official can on its own take charge of everything. Most of the time they have to cooperate to get things done, and time slips by while they try to agree on what to do. The result is that it is terribly dangerous to leave matters in their hands when there is a crisis to be dealt with that leaves no time for delay. So all republics should establish a similar institution. The Venetian republic, which is the best of the modern ones, has ensured that in times of emergency a small group of citizens can take the necessary decisions, provided they are unanimous, without further consultation.[82] If a republic does not have some provision of this sort one is faced with a choice between being destroyed while obeying the constitution or avoiding destruction by violating the constitution. No republican should ever reconcile himself to the notion that it might be necessary to govern by extralegal means. Even if acting outside the constitution may have good consequences in the short term, in the long run it represents a dangerous precedent. People begin to make a habit of ignoring the constitution when it gets in the way of doing good; later they use this to legitimate ignoring the constitution when it gets in the way of their doing harm. No republic can claim to be perfect if its laws do not make provision for any possible eventuality, if they do not lay down correct procedures for dealing with unforeseen events.

So I conclude by saying those republics that do not allow for the establishment of a dictatorship or some other form of emergency rule in time of danger will always go under when the crisis comes. It is worth noting the procedures the Romans established for electing a dictator when they invented this new office,[83] for they dealt with the matter wisely. The problem was that the creation of a dictatorship was a blow to the status of the consuls in office at the time, for they were downgraded from being the supreme magistrates to having to take orders like everyone else. Because there was concern that this would

82. The Council of Ten, created in 1310.
83. Livy thinks in 501 B.C.

be a cause of hostility between citizens, it was decided that the consuls should be the ones with the authority to elect a dictator, for it was felt that in a crisis where Rome had need of an absolute ruler the consuls would be eager to appoint one, and that, if it were they who had taken the decision, then they would have less reason to resent it. For those wounds you inflict on yourself by choice and of your own free will cause a great deal less pain than those others inflict on you, and the same goes for every other setback. However, in the last years of the republic, the Romans, instead of appointing a dictator, used to give arbitrary authority to one of the consuls by passing the motion: "Let the consul ensure that the republic comes to no harm."[84] To return to my subject, I conclude that Rome's neighbors, in trying to defeat her, pushed her into changing her constitution with the result that she was not only better able to defend herself but was able to attack them with more strength, better judgment, and greater unity.

Chapter Forty-Two: On how easy it is for men to be corrupted.

One should also note, while we are discussing the Decemviri, how easy it is for men to be corrupted.[85] Their characters are quickly transformed, no matter how good and well-trained they were. Think of how the young men that Appius had gathered around him began to be well-disposed towards tyranny because they stood to gain some small benefit by it, and of how Quintus Fabius, one of the second group of Decemviri, who was one of the best of men, was blinded by a little bit of ambition, and was persuaded by Appius's malice to change his good habits into evil ones, and become like his new mentor. If they consider such matters carefully, those who pass laws for republics or for kingdoms will be all the more eager to put a brake on human appetites, and deprive men of any hope that they can go wrong without being punished.

Chapter Forty-Three: On how those who fight for their own glory
make good and faithful soldiers.

One should also consider, while thinking over what I have said above, what a fundamental difference there is between an army that is content and fights for its own glory and one that is ill-disposed and fights to

---

84. The first occasion appears to be in 121 B.C.
85. The Ten were first elected to reform the laws in 452 B.C.; when a commission was again elected in 451 they proceeded to establish a virtual dictatorship.

satisfy someone else's ambition. For while the Roman armies were in the habit of always winning so long as Rome was ruled by the consuls, under the Decemviri they always lost. From this example one can get some indication of why mercenary soldiers are useless, for they have no reason to stand firm apart from the little bit of pay that you give them. This is not and cannot be a strong enough motive to make them faithful, and it cannot make them so devoted to you that they are prepared to die for you. In an army where the soldiers do not feel enough affection for the ruler for whom they fight to become his eager supporters, you will never find sufficient firmness of purpose [*virtù*] for them to withstand an enemy who is at all determined [*virtuoso*]. And because this love and this eagerness can only develop among your own subjects it is essential, if you want to hold on to power—the argument applies equally to republics and to kingdoms—to enlist your own subjects. It is a simple fact that all those who have made major gains with their armies have done this. The Roman armies when the Decemviri were in charge were no less skillful [*virtù*] than before; but they no longer had the same attitude, and so they did not achieve what they were accustomed to achieving. But as soon as the rule of the Decemviri came to an end, and they began to fight again as free men, they recovered their old spirit, and, as a result, their undertakings once more had happy outcomes, as they always had done in the past.

Chapter Forty-Six: On how men advance from one aspiration to an-
                    other. At first they want only to defend
                    themselves; later, they want to attack others.

When the Roman people had recovered their liberty, and returned to their original condition, except improved in so far as they had made many new laws that reinforced the authority of the populace, it seemed reasonable that Roman politics would quiet down for a while. In practice, however, the opposite proved to be the case, for every day new conflicts and discords broke out. Because Titus Livy very sensibly explains why this happened, it seems to me relevant at this point to report to you his precise words.[86] He says that it was always the case that if the populace were humiliated, the nobles grew haughty, and vice versa. Because the populace remained peaceably within their assigned limits, the young nobles began to insult them, and the tribunes were able to do little to defend them, for they, too, were under attack. The nobility, for its part, even though it thought that its younger members

86.   Livy, bk. 3, ch. 65.

were overdoing it a bit, nevertheless was not distressed at the idea that if one group was going to make gains at the expense of the other, then it was they who stood to make gains at the expense of the populace. So the desire to defend their rights meant that each group advanced to the point where it oppressed the other.

The way these things work is this: When men are simply trying to avoid having reason to fear their opponents, they begin to give their opponents grounds to fear them. In defending themselves against attack, they attack others and put them on the defensive, as if there were no choice but to be either the attacker or the victim. So you can see one way in which republics fall apart; and also how men advance from one aspiration to another. There is nothing truer than the opinion Sallust attributes to Caesar: "All bad outcomes derive from good beginnings."[87] As I have said, those citizens who live in a republic and are ambitious for themselves start out by trying to ensure that they cannot be attacked. They want not only to be safe from other private citizens, but even to be immune from prosecution. In order to accomplish this, they seek allies. These they acquire in ways that seem outwardly honest, either by lending private citizens money or by defending them against the powerful. Because this seems like a good way to behave [*pare virtuoso*], everyone is easily taken in by it, and so nothing is done to put a stop to it. So, an individual who carries on in this fashion, without being stopped, soon accumulates so much influence that other private citizens are afraid of him, and even government officials have to give him special treatment. Once he has got into this position, without anyone having taken the measures needed to put a stop to his accumulation of influence, it becomes very dangerous to do anything about it, for the reasons I explained above. It is dangerous to try to tackle a problem in a political system once it has become well-established.

In the end, it becomes straightforward: You must either eliminate him and run the risk of destroying yourself before you know it, or allow him to continue to accumulate power, in which case it will become obvious that he has mastered you, unless his death or some other lucky accident comes to your rescue. For once you have reached this point where both citizens and government officials are frightened of going against his wishes or even those of his allies, then it is relatively straightforward for him to ensure that everyone makes the decisions he wants made, and everyone turns against those he wants attacked. So a republic ought to have among its institutions one whose task it is to ensure citizens cannot do harm under the pretence of doing good, and that

87. Sallust, *Bellum Catalinarium*, ch. 51.

they can only establish reputations that help support, not undermine, political freedom. I will discuss how to accomplish this in another chapter.

Chapter Forty-Nine: On how those cities that are free at the time
of their foundation, as Rome was, have
difficulty in determining which laws will
make it possible for them to preserve their freedom; consequently, it is almost
impossible for those cities that are under
someone else's authority at the very
beginning to establish the right laws.[88]

Just how difficult it is when one is drawing up the constitution of a republic to put in place all those laws needed to preserve its freedom is well illustrated by the development of the constitution of Rome. For, although first Romulus, then Numa, next Tullus Hostilius and Servius, and finally the commission of ten citizens appointed for that purpose all drew up numerous laws, new problems were constantly becoming apparent to the rulers of the city, and new constitutional legislation was constantly having to be introduced. So, for example, the office of censor had to be introduced;[89] the censors were one of the innovations that helped keep Rome free, for a while at least. The censors had authority over the manners and morals of the Romans, and this was an important factor slowing down the progress of their corruption.

It is true they made a mistake when they appointed the first censors, for they were given a five-year term of office; but it was not long before this mistake was put right thanks to the wisdom of the dictator Mamercus who introduced a new law to restrict their term of office to eighteen months.[90] The censors who were in office at the time were so angry at this that they expelled Mamercus from the senate: an action that was sharply criticized, both by the populace and the senators. The historical record does not indicate that Mamercus had any recourse, so either our historian has slipped up, or there was something wrong with the constitutional provisions of Rome in this area. For a republic ought not to have a constitution under which a citizen who introduces a new law that fosters political liberty can find himself as a consequence facing enemies against whom he has no defense.

88.   I.e., even when they become free.
89.   In 443 B.C.
90.   In 433 B.C.

But to get back to our subject, my point is that the creation of this new office of censor should serve to bring home to us that if cities like Rome that were free when they were founded, and have governed themselves from the beginning, find it very difficult to establish the right laws to protect their freedom, it is not surprising those cities that have been from the beginning under the authority of an outsider, face, not just difficulties, but virtual impossibilities whenever they attempt to establish a constitution that will make it possible for them to live a peaceful and civilized life.

The history of Florence is a good example of this. Because she began life under the authority of Rome, and because she had always lived subordinated to an outsider, for a long time she had no self-respect and gave no thought to her own welfare. Then, when her chance came to do as she pleased, she began to construct her own institutions. But her new institutions were mixed up with old ones, and as these were bad, the new ones could do no good. So Florence has ruled herself for at least the two hundred years for which we have reliable records without having once had a constitution that properly entitled her to be called a republic. And the difficulties that she has had are merely representative of those faced by all cities that have begun in circumstances similar to hers. And although on many occasions there have been public and free elections to appoint a small group of citizens with ample authority to reform the constitution, nevertheless, they have never introduced reforms that served the general interest but always ones that served the interests of their faction. The result has been not a new order but a new disorder in the affairs of the city.

Let us take a particular instance. I maintain that among the matters someone establishing a constitution for a republic ought to consider is that of deciding who is to have the right to pass sentence of death on his fellow citizens. The Romans handled this well, for normally a convicted citizen could appeal to the populace; and if because of some exceptional event it was dangerous to defer the execution to allow time for an appeal, then they had the option of appointing a dictator who could carry out immediate executions. And they never had recourse to this option unless it was absolutely necessary.

But in Florence and the other cities born in servitude, it was an outsider who had the right to pass sentence of death; someone who had been sent by their ruler to exercise judicial authority. When they later acquired their freedom, they retained this practice of giving judicial authority to an outsider, who was given the title of *Capitano*. This was a very bad arrangement, for the *Capitano* could easily be corrupted by powerful citizens. But this institution was altered as political revolutions occurred. They created a commission of eight citizens who carried out the functions previously performed by the *Capitano*.[91] In doing so, they went from bad to worse, for the reasons I have given above: Elites always look after the interests of elites, and concentration of power always serves the interests of the powerful.

Venice avoided this mistake. She has a commission of ten citizens who can pass sentence on any citizen, and against whose judgment there is no appeal. But in case they proved incapable of taking action against the powerful, even though they had the authority to do so, they established the commission known as the Forty;[92] and moreover they provided the senate, the most powerful commission, with authority to punish them. The result is that as long as there is someone willing to bring charges, there is a court capable of keeping the members of the elite in check.

Thus, we should not be surprised to see that in Rome, which drew up its own constitution, and which had so many wise men among its political leaders, new problems arose almost every day that necessitated the establishment of new institutions to foster political freedom; or to see that in other cities, which started out with less satisfactory institutions, so many problems arise that they never get a chance to establish a functional constitution.

Chapter Fifty: On how a single committee or official ought not to be able to bring the government of the city to a halt.

Titus Quintius Cincinnatus and Gaius Julius Mento were the consuls in Rome.[93] Because they disagreed with each other they had brought all the business of the republic to a halt. Seeing this, the senate urged them to appoint a dictator, so that he could carry out the business that their disagreements prevented them from handling. But the consuls, who disagreed about everything else, were agreed only on this: Neither wanted to appoint a dictator. So the senate, having no other options, was obliged to turn to the tribunes for help. They, supported by the authority of the senate, forced the consuls to obey. The first thing to note here is the usefulness of the office of tribune; it was useful not only to place a brake upon the aspirations of the powerful in their dealings with the populace, but also in their dealings with each other.

91.   In 1477.
92.   Established in 1179.
93.   The year is 431 B.C.

Second, we see that one should never organize a city so that a few individuals can hold up any of those decisions that are, in the normal course of events, necessary for the preservation of the republic. For example, if you give a committee authority to make a distribution of honors and employments, or you appoint a magistrate to administer some activity, then you should either make it obligatory for them to fulfill their function no matter what, or provide that if they are not willing to do it, then someone else can and must substitute for them. Otherwise, your constitution will be defective and will endanger the city, as we have seen the Roman constitution would have been if it had not been possible to overcome the obstinacy of the consuls by appealing to the authority of the tribunes.

In the Venetian republic, the Grand Council[94] distributes honors and employments. On occasion this assembly, out of frustration or because of some misunderstanding, has failed to appoint successors to the officials who govern the city and to those who are sent out to administer Venice's empire. This was a serious breakdown in government, for all of a sudden both the subject territories and the capital city were without duly-appointed authorities, and absolutely nothing could be done if the general assembly of the Council was not either appeased or persuaded of the seriousness of the situation. This constitutional defect would have had serious consequences for the city if some of the wiser citizens had not taken appropriate measures. They found an opportune moment to introduce a law stating that no official, present or future, either within the city or without, should lose his authority until appointments had been made and his successor was ready to take office. In this way the Grand Council lost its ability to endanger the republic by bringing the conduct of public business to a halt.

Chapter Fifty-Three: On how the populace often seeks its own ruin, taken in by some plan with a misleading appearance of being in its interests; and on how great hopes and cheerful promises easily influence it.

When the city of Veii had been conquered, the populace of Rome persuaded itself that the city of Rome would benefit if half the Romans went to live in Veii.[95] It argued that since that city was in a fertile

94. An assembly of all the nobles.
95. 395 B.C.

region, had fine buildings, and was close to Rome, half the citizens of
Rome could be made better off, while, since they would still be nearby,
they could continue to play their part in Roman politics. The senate
and the more sensible citizens thought that this plan was pointless and
potentially damaging. They openly said that they would rather be put
to death than agree to such a proposal. The result was that, as the
debate on the question became heated, the populace became so furious
with the senate it was on the point of resorting to arms, which would
have led to bloodshed. But the senate took refuge behind a number
of old and revered citizens; respect for them made the populace pause,
and it went no further in their disobedience towards the authorities.

Here there are two things we need to note. The first is that the
populace is often taken in by some plan with a misleading appearance
of being in its interests, and seeks its own ruin. Unless someone who
has its confidence makes it understand why the plan is a bad one and
what policy ought to be followed instead, the republic will run into an
infinity of dangers and suffer innumerable losses. Of course, there are
times when nobody has the confidence of the populace, for it may have
already been disillusioned either by events or by its leaders. Then you
are unlucky; your city is bound to be destroyed. Dante remarks on this
subject, in his discourse *On Monarchy*, that the populace often cries
out: "Kill us quick! Off with our heads!"[96] This popular scepticism
with regard to good advice means that republics often fail to reach
sound decisions. I have already discussed the case of the Venetians
who, when under attack by so many enemies, could not agree to save
something before all was lost by returning the territory they had taken
from their neighbors (which was the reason why they were under attack,
and the cause of the alliance of powers against them).[97]

However, if you ask yourself what decisions it is easy to persuade a
populace to take, and what decisions it is difficult, these categories are
helpful: Either the policy you propose appears at first sight to involve
gains or losses; alternatively, it either appears brave or cowardly. When
you propose something to the populace that appears to involve gain,
even if hidden behind the appearance of gain there is a real loss, and
when you propose something that seems courageous, even if the real
consequence is likely to be the destruction of the republic, then it is
easy to persuade the masses to agree with you. On the other hand, it
is always difficult to persuade them to adopt policies that seem to

96.   In fact, Dante, *Convivio*, I.11, 1. 54.
97.   The War of the League of Cambrai, 1505–09.

involve cowardice or loss, even if they are likely to lead, in fact, to security and to gain.

Innumerable examples could be cited to confirm this, both Roman and non-Roman, both ancient and modern. Thus, this is the explanation of the hostility with which Fabius Maximus came to be regarded in Rome. He could not persuade the Roman populace that the republic would benefit by drawing the war out and by allowing Hannibal to advance without meeting him in battle. The populace thought this policy was cowardly, and did not understand the real benefits that would come from it. Fabius could not find arguments strong enough to convince it. The populace is often blinded by its sense of honor. Thus, the people of Rome not only made the mistake of giving Fabius's commander of the cavalry permission to engage the enemy, even though Fabius disapproved, and even though there was a danger that the resulting conflict of authority would tear the Roman army apart unless Fabius was astute enough to find a way of resolving the problem; they did not learn their lesson, but went on to make Varro consul, not because of any good qualities he had, but simply because he had gone around Rome telling everyone he met in the streets and squares that he would defeat Hannibal as soon as he was given permission to engage him in battle. This led straight to the Battle of Cannae[98] and the rout of the Roman army, and it very nearly caused the defeat of Rome.

On this subject I want to introduce one more example from Roman history. Hannibal had been in Italy for eight or ten years. He had slaughtered Romans from one end of the peninsula to the other. Then Marcus Centenius Penula, a man of contemptible family background (although he had risen to a senior rank in the army), stood up in the senate and said that if they gave him permission to form an army of volunteers wherever he wanted in Italy he would either capture or kill Hannibal in no time at all. The senate thought that his proposal was reckless; but they also feared that if they turned it down, and the populace later got to hear of Penula's offer, then there might be a riot, for the populace would be provoked to hatred and ill-will towards the senatorial class. So they accepted his proposal, preferring to endanger the lives of all those who enrolled under Penula than to risk provoking new hostility towards themselves within the populace. For they understood how easy it would be to persuade the populace to approve of a proposal of this sort, and how difficult it would be to persuade it to reject it. So Penula set out with a disorderly and undisciplined mob

98. In 216 B.C.

to confront Hannibal. The battle was no sooner begun than it was over, and he and all his followers were defeated and killed.

Let us turn to Greece, and in particular to Athens. There Nicias, a man of remarkable wisdom and good sense, could never persuade the populace that it was a bad idea to set out to attack Sicily. They voted for it, despite the opposition of those who were sensible, and the result was the complete defeat of Athens. Again, Scipio, when he became consul, wanted to have command in Africa, claiming he would be able to destroy the Carthaginians.[99] Fabius Maximus persuaded the senate that this was a bad idea; but Scipio threatened to propose it to the populace, knowing perfectly well that proposals of this sort appeal to the common sort.

There are relevant examples to be found in the history of our own city. For instance, there was the occasion when Mr. Ercole Bentivoglio, commander, along with Antonio Giacomini, of the Florentine armies, defeated Bartolommeo d'Alviano at San Vincenti, and so went on to attack Pisa.[100] The populace voted in favor of this campaign on the basis of the optimistic promises made by Mr. Ercole, although many wise citizens criticized it. Nevertheless, there was nothing they could do to stop it, for the vast majority were all in favor of it, having taken at face value the optimistic promises of the commander. I conclude that there is no easier way to destroy a republic where the populace holds power than to encourage it to engage in bold enterprises. For where the populace have any influence, such proposals will always be adopted; and those who are opposed to it will find themselves marginalized. But if the outcome is often the destruction of the city, it is even more often the ruin of the individual citizens who put forward such enterprises. For the populace is led to expect victory; when it faces defeat it does not blame fortune, nor does it excuse its military commander on the grounds that he had insufficient resources at his disposal. It concludes he was stupid or malicious. Usually, he is either assassinated, or imprisoned, or put under house arrest; this was the fate of innumerable Carthaginian commanders and of many Athenian ones. Any victories they had in the past are discounted; today's defeat cancels them out. This is what happened to our Antonio Giacomini who, having failed to take Pisa as the populace expected and as he had promised, became the object of such contempt among the people that, despite the fact that he had done innumerable good deeds in the past, he was allowed to live only because the political authorities took pity

99.   205 B.C.
100.   In 1505.

on him, and not because the populace could see any reason why he should be pardoned.

Chapter Fifty-Four: On the ability of a senior statesman to restrain an agitated mob.

The second thing worth remarking about the text cited in the last chapter is that there is nothing more likely to restrain an agitated mob than the respect it has for some senior and experienced statesman who is prepared to meet it face-to-face. Virgil is right to say:

> But if by chance they find themselves in front of a man who has
> a reputation for piety and trustworthiness,
> They fall silent and listen attentively.[101]

Consequently, if you are in command of an army about to mutiny or in charge of a city on the verge of a riot, then you should face the mob, making yourself seem both as friendly and as authoritative as possible. In order to inspire respect, you should surround yourself with all the trappings of the office you hold. A few years ago Florence was divided into two factions, the *frateschi*[102] and the *arrabiati*,[103] as they were called. They came to blows and the *frateschi* were defeated. Pagolantonio Soderini was on the losing side; at the time he was thought of as one of the leading citizens. During the rioting, the mob, weapons in hand, went to his house to loot it. Mr. Francesco, his brother, who was then Bishop of Volterra and is now a cardinal, happened to be in the house. As soon as he heard the shouts and saw the crowds approaching, he put on his most distinguished robes, put on his bishop's rochet over them, and went out unarmed to meet the mob. His demeanor and his words stopped them in their tracks. For many days afterwards his achievement was talked about and admired throughout the city.

The conclusion I draw from this is that there is no more reliable or more essential technique for controlling an agitated mob than to put in front of it someone whose appearance suggests he is entitled to respect and who does in fact inspire it. To go back to the original text, note how determined the Roman populace were to adopt the proposal to move to Veii, since they thought they would benefit from it, and

101. Virgil, *Aeneid*, bk. 1, ll. 151–2.
102. The followers of the friar, Savonarola.
103. The crazies, i.e., the aristocratic faction.

were unable to recognize the evil consequences that would result from it. Demonstrations would surely have turned into riots if the senate had not brought their fury under control by employing senior statesmen who were widely respected.

Chapter Fifty-Five: On how easy it is to reach decisions in cities where the multitude is not corrupt; and on how it is impossible to establish one-man rule where there is social equality; and on how it is impossible to establish a republic where there is inequality.

Although we have already discussed at some length what one should expect, be it good or bad, in corrupt cities, nevertheless, I do not think it would be a digression if we considered a debate that took place in the senate over a motion introduced by Camillus. He proposed giving one-tenth of the plunder seized in Veii to the temple of Apollo.[104] Since this plunder had fallen into the hands of the Roman populace, and since there was no other way of knowing what it was worth, the senate passed a decree that everyone should hand over to the treasury one-tenth of the loot that he had seized. This decree was never enforced, for the senate later adopted another proposal, and found a different way of compensating Apollo on behalf of the Roman people. Nevertheless, the very fact that it was passed is an indication of the extent to which the senate had confidence in the trustworthiness of the populace. In their opinion, everyone could be relied on to give an accurate account of all that he owed under the terms of the decree. As for the populace, they did not think for a moment of evading the decree by simply handing over less than they owed; they sought to have it repealed by openly protesting against it.

This example, along with many others that we have already discussed, shows the extent to which the Roman populace had a sense of public duty and of religious obligation, and how justified were those who had confidence in them. It is a simple fact that where such a sense of public duty is not to be found, one is entitled to be pessimistic. There is no point in being optimistic if you live in one of those regions that, in our own day, have become corrupt. Italy is the most far gone of them all; even France and Spain have been infected. If we do not see quite so many disorders in those countries as break out in Italy every day, the reason is not so much that the populace has a sense of public duty,

104.   The chief deity of Veii. The year is 395 B.C.

for the truth is that their peoples are for the most part corrupted; rather it is because each has a king who keeps it united, not only because he is a strong leader [*non solamente per la virtù sua*], but because the institutions of those kingdoms are still intact. In the territory of Germany, it is evident that a sense of public duty and of religious obligation is still widespread among the populace; the result is that many self-governing republics survive there. They observe their own laws so well that nobody dares try to invade them from without or to subvert them from within.

In order to show that I am right to claim that the sense of public duty we associate with the ancients still predominates in them, I want to give one example comparable to the one I gave earlier concerning the senate and the Roman populace. In the German republics, it is customary, when they find they need to spend a considerable amount of money on public business, for the appropriate magistrates or councils to impose a tax on the inhabitants of the city of one or two percent of each person's assets. Once a decree has been passed according to whatever procedures are required by the local constitution, each person makes an appearance before the officials assigned to collect the tax, and, having taken an oath to pay what he owes, places in an official chest the sum of money that he, having consulted his conscience, thinks he ought to pay. He himself is the only witness to how much he pays. From this you can get some idea of how far a sense of public duty and of religious obligation is still to be found among these men. One is bound to think that each person pays what he really owes; for if he did not, the tax would not yield as much as they expected, judging by its yield on previous occasions over a long period of time; if it did not yield as much, the public would know they had been defrauded; and if they knew they were being defrauded they would change their method of collecting taxes. Such public spiritedness is all the more to be admired in our day and age because it is so rare.

Indeed, it survives only in Germany, and there are two reasons for this. The first is that the Germans do not have numerous contacts with their neighbors, for their neighbors rarely visit them, and they rarely visit their neighbors. They have been content with the products of the local economy, eating food grown and raised nearby, and dressing in wool from their own sheep. This removes the primary reason for contact with foreigners, and with it, the primary source of all corruption. They have avoided being infected with the customs of the French, the Spanish, or the Italians; and these three nations between them are the source of corruption throughout the world. The second reason is that those republics that have preserved popular sovereignty and resisted corruption do not tolerate any of their citizens to style himself a gentleman, or to live like one. So they maintain among themselves a genuine equality, and they are bitterly hostile to those lords and gentlemen who do exist in their region. If by chance some of them fall into their hands, they regard them as the germs of corruption and the causes of every possible immorality, and kill them.

In order to clarify the meaning of this term "gentleman," let me say that men are called "gentlemen" if they live in luxury without working. Their income arises from their estates, but they do not have to worry about cultivating them or going to any other trouble to make ends meet. Such people are pernicious influences in any republic and, indeed, in any part of the world. But even worse are those who, in addition to being wealthy, have a castle at their disposal and have subjects who obey them. Gentlemen of both types are to be found throughout the kingdom of Naples, in the papal states, in the Romagna, and in Lombardy. This is the reason why no republic has ever been established in those regions, nor any other form of popular sovereignty. For such types of men are totally hostile to a civilized way of life. To want to set up a republic in regions with this sort of social structure is to want the impossible; if one wanted to introduce a new political system in such regions, supposing one had gained control of them, there would be no choice but to establish a monarchy. The reason is as follows: Where the individuals are so corrupt that the laws alone will not restrain them, then you need to establish alongside the laws a force greater than theirs, that is to say, the heavy hand of a king, who can use an absolute and unlimited power to put a halt to the unlimited ambition and corruption of the elite.

This argument is confirmed by the example of Tuscany. There you find that for a long time there have been three republics—Florence, Siena, and Lucca—crammed into a small geographical space. And the other cities of the region are either accustomed to subordination, as is apparent both from the character of their citizens and from their constitutions, or else defend, or at least would like to defend, their liberty. The reason is simple: In that region there are no lords of castles to be found and no (or at any rate very few) gentlemen. There is so much social equality that it would be easy for a wise man with some knowledge of ancient civilizations to establish some form of popular sovereignty. But it has been their great misfortune that, right down to the present, they have not chanced upon a leader who has been able to do it or has understood how to do it.

From this discussion I draw the following conclusion: Anyone who wants to set up a republic in a place where there is a fair number of gentlemen can only do it if he begins by killing them all. On the other hand, anyone who wants to set up a monarchy or a system of one-man rule in a place where there is a fair amount of social equality will never manage to do it unless he lifts out of that equality many individuals who are ambitious and restless, and makes them into gentlemen in fact if not in name, giving them castles and estates, and giving them control of men and property. Then he will be surrounded by an elite whom he can rely on to uphold his power, while they can rely on him to further their aspirations. As for the rest of the population, they will be obliged to submit to a yoke nothing but force could persuade them to tolerate. This way, those doing the forcing will be more than a match for those being forced, and so people will stay obediently in the ranks assigned to them. The task of making a region suited to monarchy into a republic, or one suited to republican government into a monarchy, is one for somebody of quite exceptional intelligence and force of personality. There have been many who have tried to do it, but very few have known how to carry it out in practice. For the scale of the enterprise is daunting in itself, and it means that often people fail when they have scarcely begun.

I believe that this opinion of mine—that where there are gentlemen one cannot establish a republic—may appear to be contradicted by the history of the Venetian republic, for there only those who are gentlemen are allowed to be elected to office. But my reply is that this example does not tell against me, for the gentlemen of Venice are rather gentlemen in name than in fact. For they do not have large incomes from country estates since their great wealth is founded on commerce and trade. Moreover, none of them has a castle or has any private jurisdiction over other men. In their case the name "gentleman" is a purely honorific title, one that has nothing to do with the factors that determine whether or not you are called a gentleman in any other city. Just as all republics have social distinctions that they refer to by one name or another, so Venice is divided into the gentlemen on the one hand and the populace on the other. They insist that the gentlemen have a monopoly, both in practice and in theory, of all the offices, while the rest are completely excluded from them. This does not lead to conflict in that territory, for the reasons I have explained. So we see that a republic can only be established where there is considerable social equality or where men are made to be equal; by contrast, the rule of one man requires considerable social inequality. If you ignore this principle you get a lopsided construction, and one that will not stand for long.

Chapter Fifty-Eight: On how the masses are wiser and more loyal than any monarch.

There is nothing more worthless and more unreliable than the masses. So says our Titus Livy, and all the other historians agree with him. For it often happens that, as one follows a political narrative, one sees the masses condemn someone to death, and then next moment lament his death, and long for his return. This is how the Roman populace behaved towards Manlius Capitolinus whom they first condemned to death and then longed for him to be alive.[105] This is what Livy says: "As soon as he was no longer a danger, the populace wanted him back."[106] And elsewhere, when he describes the events that took place in Syracuse after the death of Hieronymus, nephew of Hiero, he says: "This is the nature of the masses: Either they obey humbly, or they domineer arrogantly."[107]

I am not sure if I want to embark on an undertaking that is so hard and full of so many difficulties that I will either have to give up in disgrace or, if I carry on, be made to pay dearly for my persistence. I am not sure if I want to defend a view that, as I have said, is rejected by all the authorities. Nevertheless, I do not think, and never will think, that one should be blamed for putting forward an argument, so long as one relies on reason and has no intention of resorting to citing authorities or to force. In my view, then, the defect for which authors criticize the masses is a defect to be found in all men, considered as individuals, and, above all, in rulers. For anyone who is not constrained by the laws will make exactly the same errors as will the unbridled masses. One can easily recognize the truth of this, for there are and have been plenty of rulers but there are few who have been good and wise. I am speaking of rulers who have been able to break the bounds that ought to restrain them. I do not mean to include those kings who were to be found in Egypt when, at the beginning of recorded history, that territory was governed according to laws; or those who were to be found in Sparta; or those who in our own day have ruled in France. For government in France is more moderated by legal constraints than in any other presently-existing kingdom about which we are well-informed. The rulers who hold power under such constitutions are not to be included in the category I am discussing, for we want to

---

105. Manlius had saved the Capitol from the Gauls in 390 B.C., but was condemned to death in 384.

106. Livy, bk. 6, ch. 20.

107. Livy, bk. 24, ch. 25.

consider the nature of individual men taken on their own and see if it is similar to that of the masses. Otherwise, we would have to consider the masses when they are similarly constrained by the laws so that we could compare them with constitutional monarchs. In such cases you would find the masses just as well-behaved as the monarchs, and you would find that they neither arrogantly domineer nor humbly obey.

Take for example the Roman populace who, for as long as the republic survived uncorrupted, never humbly obeyed and never arrogantly domineered; instead, they maintained their proper status honorably, respecting their institutions and obeying their governors. When it was necessary for them to join forces against an internal enemy, they did so, as they did against Manlius Capitolinus, against the Decemviri, and against others who tried to oppress them. But when it was necessary to obey dictators and consuls in order to preserve the republic, they did so. And if the Roman populace wished Manlius Capitolinus were alive once he was dead, it is not surprising; what it missed were his virtues [*virtù*], which were so great that remembering them made everyone regret his death. The same memories would have had the same consequences in a monarch, for all authors agree that virtue [*virtù*] is praised and admired even in one's enemies. If Manlius had been brought back to life while the populace mourned his death, it would have passed the same sentence on him as it did when it let him out of prison and shortly afterwards condemned him to death. So, too, we find examples of monarchs who are thought of as wise but have had someone put to death, and then bitterly regretted it. Alexander killed Cleitus[108] and other friends of his; Herod killed Mariamne.[109] But what our historian says about the nature of the masses is not intended to refer to those masses who are constrained by the laws, as the Roman populace was, but to those who are unbridled, as the populace of Syracuse was; they made the same errors as individuals who are enraged and unconstrained, the same errors as Alexander the Great and Herod made in the instances I have mentioned. Consequently, one should no more blame the masses in general than one does rulers in general, for both groups and individuals make mistakes when they have opportunities to go wrong and nothing prevents them. There are plenty of other examples of this beyond the ones I have mentioned, both among the Roman emperors and among other tyrants and monarchs. One finds far more examples of unreliable behavior and of shifts of policy and attitude among them than among any populace.

---

108. In 328 B.C.
109. In 29 B.C. The source is probably Josephus.

I conclude, therefore, that the common opinion, which holds that the populace, when they are in power, are unreliable, changeable, and disloyal is wrong. I maintain that they are no more guilty of these vices than are individual rulers. If someone were to criticize both multitudes and individuals who hold power, he might be right; but if he makes an exception of the individuals, then he makes a mistake. For a populace in power, if it is well ordered, will be as reliable, prudent, and loyal as an individual, or rather it will be even better than an individual, even one who is thought wise. On the other hand, an individual who is not restrained by the laws will be even more disloyal, unreliable, and imprudent than a populace. The difference in their behavior would be a consequence, not of a difference in their natures, for all men are alike, and if any type of person is better than the rest, it is the common man who is; but would reflect whether they had more or less respect for the laws under which both prince and populace are supposed to live.

If you consider the Roman populace, you will see that for four hundred years they were hostile to the idea of monarchy, and were in love with the glory and the common good of their homeland; there are innumerable instances of their behavior that testify to both commitments. And if anyone cites against me the ingratitude that they showed towards Scipio, I would reply with what I said at length on this question above, when I showed that the populace was less ungrateful than an individual ruler.

But as far as prudence and predictability are concerned, I say that the populace is generally more prudent, more predictable, and has better judgment than a monarch. It is with good reason that people compare the voice of the populace to the voice of God, for one can see that there is a widespread belief that the predictions of a populace are uncannily accurate; indeed, it seems as if it has an inexplicable capacity [*occulta virtù*] to foresee what will bring it good fortune and what bad. As far as exercising their judgment is concerned, one sees that it is rare indeed that the people hear two speeches upholding different policies, and do not, if the speeches are equally effective [*virtù*], choose the better policy. They are almost always able to understand those truths that are explained to them. I have already admitted they sometimes make mistakes in matters involving their pride or what they take to be their interests. But monarchs often make mistakes when their passions are aroused, which happens much more often with a single ruler than it does with the populace. One also sees that, when it comes to making appointments to government offices, the populace makes much better choices than rulers do. You will never persuade the populace that it is a good idea to promote to an office a man who has a bad reputation and lives a decadent life. But rulers are easily persuaded to do this for all sorts of reasons. One sees a populace begin to be committed to opposing something, and then not change its mind for several centuries; the same cannot be said for rulers. For both the good judgment of the populace and its enduring commitments, I will rely simply on the example of the Roman people who, over a period of hundreds of years, during which they elected vast numbers of consuls and tribunes, did not make more than two or three appointments they afterwards had cause to regret. And they were, as I have said, so hostile to the idea of monarchy that no matter how much they were indebted to one of their citizens, if he aspired to be crowned king, then he could not hope to escape the lawful penalties.

One may also note, in addition, that cities where the populace is in power are capable of making immense territorial gains in very short periods of time, much greater than any that have been made by an individual ruler. This is what Rome did after it had expelled its kings, and Athens after it freed itself from Pisistratus. The only possible reason for this is that the populace is better at ruling than individuals are. Neither can I allow you to argue against my view by appealing to the things our historian says in the text I began by quoting and in other similar places. For if you go over all the cases of bad government by the populace, and all those by monarchs, all the achievements of the populace, and all those of monarchs, you will find the populace to be much superior in both goodness and glory. If individuals are superior to the populace in drawing up laws, establishing civic forms of life, creating constitutions and institutions, then the populace is equally superior to an individual when it comes to maintaining the institutions once they have been established. No doubt its achievements in this respect get credited to the original legislators.

So finally, to conclude my discussion, I say that just as some states based on one-man rule have endured over time, so have some republics. Both monarchies and republics need to be regulated by laws, for a king who can do whatever he wants is a madman on the loose, and a populace that can do what it wants is never wise. However, if we were to discuss the relative merits of a monarch who is obliged to obey the law and a populace restrained by legislation, you would find that the populace made a better ruler [*si vedra più virtù nel popolo*] than the monarch. If we were to discuss both types of government unconstrained by the law, you would find that the populace makes fewer mistakes than a monarch, and the ones it makes are less significant and easier to put right. For a populace that is licentious and disorderly needs

only to be talked to by someone who is good, and he will find it easy
to set it on the right path. A bad monarch will not listen to anyone,
and the only way to correct him is to kill him. This enables one to judge
the relative importance of the faults of the two types of government.
To cure the faults of the people, you need only words; to cure those of
a monarch, you need cold steel. Now it is obvious that a disease that is
hard to cure is worse than one that is easy.

When a populace breaks free from restraint, there is no need to fear
the foolish things it may do. It is not the present evil one has to worry
about but the evil that may develop out of popular government, for a
tyrant may seize power in the midst of the confusion. But the opposite
is the case with bad monarchs. With them, one fears the present evil
and hopes for some future improvement, for men persuade themselves
that the evil deeds of their ruler may provoke people to lay claim to
their freedom. So you can see that the difference between them is that
under one type of government you fear what exists, under the other
what might come to pass.

The cruel deeds of the multitude are directed at those whom it fears
will endanger the common good; those of a monarch are directed at
those whom he fears will endanger his own interests. Why then do
people think ill of the populace? Because everyone freely speaks ill of
them; they can do so without fear even when they are in power. But
about monarchs one always speaks with great caution, and one is always
fearful of the consequences. It does not seem to me irrelevant, since
my present subject has led me towards it, to discuss in the next chapter
which alliances one can most safely put one's trust in, those made with
republics, or those made with monarchs.

Book Two

Preface

Men always praise the olden days and criticize the present, but they
do not always have good reason for doing so. They are so biased in
favor of the past that they do not celebrate only those periods they
know about because of the surviving descriptions of them written by
men alive at the time; they also, once they have become old, praise
the way they remember things having been in their youth. When their
praise of the past is mistaken, as it usually is, there are, I think, several
reasons why history plays tricks on them.

I believe the first is that we are not told the whole truth about the past. For the most part, people keep quiet about those events it would be shameful to record, while those deeds that will make them seem glorious in the eyes of posterity they portray in the most favorable light possible. Most writers place themselves in the service of victory. In order to make fortune's victories glorious they not only exaggerate the skillful [*virtuosamente*] things the victors did, they even improve on the actions of their enemies, with the result anyone who is born in future ages in either of the territories, either that of the victors or that of the vanquished, has good reason to be amazed at the actions of those men and the character of those times, and has no choice but to praise them to the skies and to love them.

Secondly, men hate things either out of fear or jealousy. But these two powerful motives for hatred cease to apply as time passes, for what is past can no longer hurt you, and you no longer have reason to be jealous of it. The opposite is true of those things you can still touch and see for yourself. Because you know them through and through, and nothing is hidden from you, you recognize their good features, but at the same time there are many aspects of them that displease you. So you conclude things were much better in the past, even when in reality actions in the present are much more deserving of fame and of glory. I am not talking about scientific and artistic activities, for their qualities are so transparent there is little time can do to take away or add to the reputation that they properly deserve. I am talking, rather, about the manners and morals of men, reports of which are much harder to assess.

I ought to admit that although the habit of praising the past and condemning the present is as widespread as I have said, nevertheless, people are not always mistaken when they think the past superior to the present. Sometimes their judgment is bound to be justified. Human affairs are always changing, and when they change it must be either for better or worse. One sees a city or a territory organized for a constitutional government by some one excellent individual; for a while, thanks to the skill [*virtù*] of this founder, the political system will get steadily better and better. Someone who is born in such a state, if he praises the olden times more than his own day, makes a mistake; and he makes this mistake for the reasons I have explained above. But later generations in this same city or territory, born when things have gone into decline, are not mistaken. Thinking about how these things work, I reached the conclusion that the world is always in the same overall condition. There has always been in it as much good as bad, but both the good and the bad are redistributed from territory to territory.

One can see this from what we know about the ancient monarchies.

Good and bad were redistributed among them as manners and morals changed, but the overall condition of the world remained the same. There was only this one difference: Where virtue [*virtù*] had at first been resident in Assyria, it later moved to the Kingdom of the Medes, and then to Persia, until eventually it came to Italy, and to Rome. Since the Roman empire, it is true, there has been no lasting empire, and virtue [*virtù*] has not remained concentrated in one place; nevertheless, you can see it was scattered among many nations, each of whom came to live virtuously [*virtuosamente*]: the Kingdoms of France and Turkey; the Sultanate of Egypt; and now the peoples of Germany. Above all, virtue was to be found among the sect of the Saracens, who accomplished so much, occupied so much territory, and were indeed responsible for the destruction of the Roman empire in the east.

In all these territories, then, and in all such sects, virtue [*virtù*] was to be found after the Romans had gone into decline, and still is to be found in some parts of them that still aspire to greatness; there she is deservedly praised. If you are born in one of these virtuous places and praise the olden days more than the present, you may be making a mistake. But if you are born in Italy or in Greece, and if you have not become (if you are Italian) an admirer of the northerners, or (if you are Greek) a supporter of the Turks, then you are right to criticize your own times and praise the past. For in the past, there were plenty of things that deserved admiration; in the present, there is nothing at all to mitigate unalloyed misery, disgrace, and contempt. Now there is no respect for religion, for the law, or for military service; everything is splattered with filth. These vices are all the more detestable because they are most prevalent among those who hold government office, who order everyone else around, and want to be treated like gods.

But let us get back to our subject. I meant to point out that if men's judgment is unreliable when it comes to judging the relative merits of the present and the distant past in matters where one cannot have such detailed knowledge of the past as one can of the present, this does not explain why old men are poor judges of the relative merits of the times of their youth and their old age, for they have had an equal knowledge and experience of the one and the other. Or at least they would have if men throughout their lives had the same capacity to make judgments and were governed by the same appetites. But men change as they grow older, even if their circumstances do not; so things look different to them, even if they have in fact stayed the same, for men have different appetites, different pleasures, different preoccupations in old age from the ones they had when young. For men, as they grow older, become weaker, but at the same time more prudent and astute in their judgment.

So those things that seemed to them tolerable, even excellent, when they were young, as they grow old seem to them intolerable and wretched. Where they ought to blame their own changing judgment, they blame the changing times.

Moreover, there is another reason: Human appetites are insatiable. It is in man's nature to be able to and to want to desire all things; it is in the nature of circumstances that he can only realize a few of his desires. The result is that men are always finding themselves discontented and discovering themselves to be dissatisfied with what they possess. This makes them have a low opinion of the present, praise the past, and put their hope in the future, even though they have no good reason for thinking things were better or will improve.

I do not know, however, if I deserve to be included among those whose judgment is flawed, though I might be thought to praise the ancient Romans too much and criticize our own times too severely in these discourses. Indeed, if the excellence [*virtù*] that was the norm then, and the inadequacy that is to be found everywhere today, were not as plain as day, then I would express myself more cautiously, for fear I might slip into this error for which I criticize others. But the matter is so obvious anyone can recognize the truth, so that I am entitled to speak frankly and express myself bluntly on the differences between our own times and those of the ancient Romans, in the hope any young men who read what I write will be encouraged to reject the world they live in and will want to try to imitate the ancients, should fortune ever give them the opportunity to do so. For it is a worthy undertaking to teach others how to do those admirable things that you, because of corrupt circumstances and hostile fortune, have been unable to perform. If many acquire the ability to do what is needed, then one, if fortune smiles upon him, may be successful.

Having, in the previous book, talked about the decisions the Romans took in matters relating to the internal affairs of the city, in this book we will discuss those things the Roman populace did in order to expand the territory under their control.

Chapter One: On whether skill [*virtù*] or good fortune was a more significant factor in the Romans' acquisition of an empire.

Many have been of the opinion—among them Plutarch who is an author whose judgment is always to be respected[1]—that the Roman

1. Plutarch, *Opera moralia*, 44: *De fortuna Romanorum*.

162

people, in acquiring an empire, benefited more from good fortune than from skill [*virtù*]. One of the various reasons they put forward to support this view is that it is evident, they say, from the actions of the Romans themselves that they attributed all their victories to good luck, for they erected more temples to the goddess Fortune than to any other god. It would seem Livy was more or less of this opinion, for it is rare for him, whenever he has a Roman speak about skill [*virtù*], not to couple skill with luck.

But I do not want to admit the truth of this opinion under any circumstances, and I do not believe there are good arguments to support it. For if there has never been a republic that has made as extensive gains as Rome did, it is also evident there has never been a republic better organized to make gains than Rome was. It was the skill [*virtù*] of their armies that enabled them to conquer an empire, and it was their way of going about things, which dates back to their first legislator, that enabled them to hold on to what they had conquered, as I will explain at length below, over the course of a number of chapters. Some people say it was good fortune and not skill [*virtù*] that ensured the Roman people never had to face war against two powerful enemies at the same time. Thus, they only found themselves at war with the Latins, when, if they had not really defeated the Samnites, they were at least able to call on their support, for in fighting the Latins they were helping the Samnites. They did not campaign against the Tuscans until they had first conquered the Latins and had almost completely crippled the Samnites by defeating them again and again. If two of these powers had allied when they were fresh and undefeated, then without doubt one could reasonably have predicted they would destroy the Roman republic.

But, however it came about, it is true they never had to fight two extremely powerful enemies at one time. It seems the rise of one always caused the decline of another, or the decline of one made possible the rise of another. This is apparent from the chronology of the wars they fought, for, leaving aside those that took place before Rome was seized by the French, one can see that while they were at war with the Aequi and the Volsci,[2] and so long as those tribes remained powerful, nobody else attacked them. Only after they had been subdued did the war with the Samnites begin,[3] and although the Latin tribes rebelled against the Romans before that war was over,[4] nevertheless, when that rebellion took place the Samnites entered into a league with the Romans and

2. 493–380 B.C.
3. 343 B.C.
4. 340–338 B.C.

sent their troops to help the Romans punish the Latins for their insolence. Once they were subdued, the war against the Samnites began
again.[5] When the Samnites had been beaten in battle after battle, the
war with the Tuscans began;[6] and when that had been settled, the
Samnites rebelled again as a result of the invasion of Italy by Pyrrhus.[7]
When he had been forced to retreat into Greece, they began the first
war with the Carthaginians;[8] no sooner was this war over, but all the
French, on both sides of the Alps, allied against the Romans, until
they were defeated and butchered in large numbers between Popolonia
and Pisa, where now stands the tower of St. Vincent.[9]

After this war, there was a period of about twenty years when they
were not involved in any major conflicts, for they only fought against
the Ligurians[10] and against those remnants of the French who held
out in Lombardy. This relative peace lasted until the beginning of the
Second Carthaginian War in which Italy was embroiled for sixteen
years.[11] Having brought this to a glorious conclusion, they found themselves at war with Macedon,[12] and, after that was over, with Antiochus
and with Asia.[13] And after they had been victorious in that war there
was not a ruler or a republic in the whole world who, either alone or
in alliance with others, could hope to defy the Roman armies.

But anyone who considers the chronology of the wars before this
final victory and who studies the policies of the Romans will realize they
did not simply rely on fortune. They also employed a quite remarkable
prudence and skill [*virtù*]. For if you ask yourself why they were so
fortunate the answer will be obvious. It is evident that when a ruler
or a people acquire a reputation such that every neighboring prince
and people is spontaneously afraid of attacking them and fearful of
being attacked by them, then it will always be the case that no state
will ever attack them unless it has no alternative.

The result is that the dominant state will have almost a free choice
when it comes to deciding with which of its neighbors it wants to fight

5.   327–314 B.C.
6.   310–300 B.C.
7.   281–275 B.C.
8.   264–241 B.C.
9.   In 225 B.C.
10.   223–222 B.C.
11.   218–201 B.C.
12.   200–196 B.C.
13.   193–188 B.C.

a war, and will be able, with a little effort, to pacify the others. They, partly out of fear of the dominant power and partly taken in by the techniques it will employ to give them a false sense of security, will be easy to pacify. The other powers who are not immediate neighbors and who do not have dealings with the victim, will regard the whole business as taking place a long way away and think it no concern of theirs. They will keep making this mistake until they are next in line. By which time they have no defense available except to rely on their own troops. But by then their own troops will be inadequate, for the dominant power will have become overwhelmingly strong.

I will not delay to discuss how the Samnites stood by and watched while the Romans defeated the Volsci and the Aequi, and, in order to be brief, I will confine myself to the case of the Carthaginians. They were very powerful and widely respected at the time the Romans were fighting against the Samnites and the Tuscans, for they already controlled the whole of Africa along with Sardinia, and Sicily, and part of Spain. Because they were so powerful, and because their territory was some distance from that of the Romans, it never occurred to them to attack them, or to come to the assistance of the Samnites and the Tuscans. Thus, they behaved as one does if one thinks time is on one's side, allying with the Romans, and trying to win their good will. They did not recognize their mistake until the Romans had conquered all the peoples between themselves and the Carthaginians, and had begun to challenge them for control of Sicily and Spain.

The same thing happened to the French as to the Carthaginians, and the same thing again to Philip, King of Macedon, and to Antiochus. Each one of them believed, while the people of Rome were occupied with one of the others, that Rome's enemies would win, and that there was plenty of time to defend themselves, either through diplomacy or war, against Rome's advancing power. So I am of the view that the good fortune the Romans had in never having to fight against two enemies at the same time is available to any ruler who acts as the Romans did and is as skillful [*virtù*] as they were.

It would be relevant here for us to explain the policies pursued by the Roman people when occupying newly acquired territory if we had not discussed this question at length in our treatise on Princedoms. You will find an extensive discussion of this question there. I will only say this much in passing: The Romans always tried hard when they were acquiring new territory to have the support of an ally who could serve as a ladder over the defenses, or as a gate through the walls, or as an assistant in retaining control once it was acquired. So they used the Capuans to get entry to Samnium,[14] the Camertini to get into Tuscany;[15] the Mamertini helped them in Sicily,[16] the Saguntines in Spain,[17] the Masinissa in Africa,[18] the Aetolians in Greece,[19] the Eumenes and other rulers in Asia,[20] the Massilians and the Aedui in France.[21] They were never short of such allies to assist them in their undertakings and to help them acquire and hold new territories. Governments that systematically follow this policy will find they have less need of good fortune than those who do not.

So that everyone can clearly recognize how much more important skill [*virtù*] was than good fortune in the acquisition of the Roman empire we will discuss in the next chapter the character of the peoples they had to fight against, and will see just how determined they were to defend their liberty.

Chapter Two: On the peoples the Romans had to fight against, and on their determination in defending their liberty.

Nothing made it harder for the Romans to overcome the peoples immediately around them and, indeed, some in more distant territories, than the love many societies in those times had for liberty. They defended their liberty so stubbornly that they could never have been conquered except by a people of quite exceptional strength [*virtù*]. For there are many examples that show the dangers these societies were willing to endure in order to defend or recover their liberty; and show, too, the revenge they sought to exact on those who had taken their freedom from them.

One learns, too, from the study of history the losses both peoples and cities suffered as a result of their enslavement. While at the present time there is only one geographical region where one can say there

14.   340 B.C.
15.   310 B.C.
16.   264 B.C.
17.   218 B.C.
18.   205 B.C.
19.   211 B.C.
20.   193 B.C.
21.   154 and 122 B.C.

are free cities to be found,[22] in classical times there were numerous peoples in every region who lived in complete liberty. One sees how, in the times we are discussing at the moment in Italy there were nothing but free peoples from the Appennines, which now mark the boundary between Tuscany and Lombardy, right down to the southern tip: the Tuscans, the Romans, the Samnites, and many other societies which lived in that section of the peninsula. Nor is there any report of there being any kings other than those who ruled in Rome, plus Porsenna, King of Tuscany—history does not record how many successors he had. But it is evident that when the Romans went to war with Veii, Tuscany was free. Indeed, the Tuscans were so enamored of liberty and so hated the title of king, that, when the inhabitants of Veii, who had appointed a king to take charge of their defense, asked them for help in resisting the Romans, they decided, after much debate, not to come to their assistance. They argued that, so long as they obeyed a king, there was no point in defending the freedom of people who had already given their freedom away.

It is easy to understand how a people acquires such a love of political freedom, for we see by experience that city-states have never been successful, either in expanding their territory or in accumulating wealth, except when they have been free. And really one is bound to be astonished if one considers the extraordinary accumulation of power and wealth in the hands of Athens in the hundred years that followed her freeing herself from the tyranny of Pisistratus.[23] But it is even more breathtaking to consider the astonishing success of Rome once she had freed herself from her kings. It is easy to work out why, for cities become great by pursuing, not the interests of private individuals, but the interests of the community as a whole. And there is no doubt the public interest is never a guiding principle except in republics. There, everything that furthers the common good is carried out, even if one or two private individuals suffer by it. The vast majority have interests that coincide with the public interest, and so they are able to pursue it, even in face of the resistance of the small minority who suffer by it. But the opposite occurs when a city is under the rule of one man, for usually what serves his interests hurts the city, and what would benefit the city is contrary to his interests.

The result is that as soon as a tyranny is established in a city where once there has been political freedom, the least bad outcome for the inhabitants is that their city ceases to make progress and stops

22. Germany.
23. 510 B.C.

accumulating either power or wealth; but usually, indeed nearly always, they begin to lose what they have won. If by chance it were a competent [*virtuoso*] tyrant who took power, who had the courage and military strength [*virtù*] to extend the territory under his control, still his society would not benefit at all from his achievements. He would be the only beneficiary. For he would not be able to reward any of his citizens who are strong and good. He must keep such men in servitude for fear they might be a threat to him. Nor can he make the cities he conquers subordinate to his home city or have them pay tribute to it, for if he makes his own city strong he endangers himself. It is in his interest to keep his state divided into distinct territories and to ensure each city and each province answers to him directly. So, naturally, he is the only one who benefits from his conquests, while his homeland is no better off. If you want to see my opinion confirmed and to read numerous arguments in support of it, read the treatise Xenophon wrote *On Tyranny.*

Thus, it is not at all surprising that in classical times peoples hunted down tyrants with such bitterness and were so enamored of political freedom, and that the very idea of liberty was held in such respect among them. See, for example, what happened when Hieronymus, the nephew of Hiero of Syracuse, was killed in the city of Syracuse.[24] News of his death reached his army, which was not far away. At first they began to form a mob, seizing weapons to go to kill his murderers; but, when they heard that in Syracuse people were crying out "Liberty!," the word itself was enough to mesmerize them, and at once they quieted down, put aside their anger against the tyrannicides, and began to ask themselves how one could institutionalize political freedom in their city.

Again, it is not at all surprising that peoples pursued extraordinary vendettas against individuals who had taken their liberty from them. There are plenty of examples of this. I intend to refer only to one case that happened in Corcyra, a Greek city, at the time of the Peloponnesian War.[25] Greece was divided between two alliances, one of which was led by the Athenians, the other by the Spartans. The result was that in many cities where there were already internal divisions one faction allied itself with the Spartans, the other with the Athenians. In Corcyra the nobles got the upper hand and deprived the populace of their liberty. The popular party, thanks to Athenian assistance, took back control and seized all the nobles, locking them up in a prison big

24. Hieronymus was murdered in 215 B.C. after being in power for a year.
25. In 427 B.C. Machiavelli's source is Thucydides, bk. 4, chs. 46–48.

enough to hold them all. From there they took them out in groups of eight or ten at a time, pretending they had been sentenced to exile in different places, and tortured them to death in the public view. When those who were still alive realized what was happening, they decided to do their best to escape such an ignominious death. Arming themselves with whatever they could find, they fought with those who wanted to enter the prison, defending the gateway against them. The populace, hearing the noise of the struggle, came running; they wrecked the upper floors of the building and buried their captives under the rubble. Many other similar events, both horrible and remarkable, took place in Greece. They show people go to greater lengths to take revenge on those who have taken their liberty from them than on those who have merely tried to do so.

You may wonder why, in those classical times, peoples were more in love with liberty than they are now. I think the reason is the same as why men in our day are less strong. In my view, both result from the difference between our upbringing and that of classical times, which is rooted in the difference between our religion and theirs. Because our religion has taught us the truth and the right way to salvation, it makes us less concerned with our reputation in this world. The pagans, on the other hand, were much more concerned with reputation and regarded it as the highest good, with the result their deeds were more savage. There are lots of their institutions that could serve as indications of this—one might begin with a comparison between the magnificence of their religious ceremonies and the simplicity of ours. Ours make a show of refinement rather than magnificence and include no actions that require savagery or courage. Their rituals were full of pomp and ceremony, but in addition they sacrificed numerous animals in ceremonies full of blood and savagery. These were cruel rites, and from them the worshipers learned to be cruel men.

Moreover, classical religion only deified men who had already been heaped with worldly glories, men such as generals of armies and rulers of states. Our religion, by contrast, glorifies men who are humble and contemplative, rather than those who do great deeds. In fact, it regards humility, self-abasement, and contempt for worldly goods as the supreme virtues, while classical religion valorized boldness of spirit, strength of body, and all the other qualities that make men redoubtable. It is true our religion requires that you be strong, but it wants you to demonstrate your strength by undergoing suffering without complaint, rather than by overcoming resistance. This set of values, it would seem, has turned the men of our own day into weaklings and left them unable to defend themselves against the ravages of the wicked. The wicked have no difficulty in handling their fellow men, for they know the average individual wants rather to endure their blows than to strike back, for he hopes to go to heaven.

Although it seems we have all been made effeminate, and God himself allows injustice to flourish, it is of course the fault of the sinful nature of mankind, which has caused them to interpret the teachings of our religion as suits their lazy temperament and not as brave men would have done [*non secondo la virtù*]. For if they had taken into account the fact that our religion allows us to praise and defend our homeland, they would have realized that if we are religious we ought to love and honor our country and to prepare ourselves to be the sort of people who will be capable of defending it. The upbringing we get, and these false interpretations of our religion, have the consequence that there are not so many republics to be found in the world as there were in classical times; nor, it follows, does one find in the peoples of our day as much love of liberty as there was then.

Another, and perhaps better, explanation is that the strength and military might of the Roman empire destroyed all the republics and all the free cities. And although that empire later collapsed, the cities within it were not able to reconstruct political freedom or rebuild institutions that would foster liberty, except in a very few places. Whatever the real cause, the Romans, no matter where they went, found republics allied together, armed to the teeth, and determined to defend their freedom to the end. Which shows that the Roman people, had they not been of exceptional and extreme strength [*virtù*], would never have been able to defeat them.

I want to give one example among them all and will confine myself to the case of the Samnites. It seems astonishing, but they were so powerful and so effective on the battlefield, that they could, as Livy admits, resist the Romans right down to the time of the consul Papirius Cursor,[26] son of the first Papirius, that is, for a period of forty-six years, despite having been defeated on the battlefield again and again, having had their crops destroyed repeatedly, and having their people massacred in their homes. Especially when one sees that their territory, where there were once so many cities and such a dense population, is now almost uninhabited, while in those days the people were so strong and so well organized it would have been impossible to overcome them, had they not been attacked by troops with the strength [*virtù*] of the Romans.

It is easy to establish where the organization they had then came from, and why we are now disorganized. For it is all the result of the

26. 298 B.C.

fact that in those days they lived as free men, while now we live as slaves. For all the lands and territories, wherever they may be, that live in freedom experience, as I have already said, immense benefits. There you see denser populations, for men are freer to enter into marriage and keener to do so. People are happy to engender children if they think they will be able to feed them and do not fear their family wealth will be confiscated from them. They are happier if they know they will not only be born free, not slaves, but, if they have the right qualities [*virtù*], they will be able to grow up to share in government. There, people see wealth steadily accumulate, both wealth from agriculture and wealth from industry and commerce. For each person tries hard to build up savings and pile up goods if he believes he will have a chance to enjoy what he has acquired. As a result, men are eager to pursue both private and public benefits, and both types of interest are advanced extraordinarily quickly.

The opposite of all this happens in those countries where the people are enslaved. Then their traditional standard of living diminishes in proportion to the severity of their enslavement. Of all harsh enslavements, the harshest is to be enslaved to a republic: in the first place, because republics are more durable, and you have less hope of escaping from their control; in the second, because the objective of a republic is to weaken and consume all other communities in order to strengthen its own. This is not the objective of an individual ruler who forces you to submit to him, unless he is a barbarian, someone who lays waste the countryside and destroys civilized urban life. Oriental rulers act like this. But if he has normal human sentiments, then in most cases he loves all the cities subjected to him equally and leaves them with their commerce intact and with by far the greater part of their ancient institutions, so that if they cannot advance as they could while they were free, they are not ruined because they are enslaved. Here I am talking about the enslavement cities enter into when they are subjected to a foreign ruler, for I have already discussed above the case of cities subjected to one of their own citizens.

If you think about everything I have said, you will not be astonished at the power the Samnites had when they were free, or at the feeble state they were reduced to when they were enslaved. Livy testifies to this at several points, and particularly in his account of the invasion of Hannibal, where he reports the Samnites were being oppressed by a Roman legion based in Nola. They sent ambassadors to Hannibal to ask him to come to their assistance.[27] During their speech they said

27.   215 B.C. Livy, bk. 23, ch. 42.

they had fought against the Romans for a hundred years, relying on their own soldiers and their own commanders. Many times they had stood firm against two consular armies commanded by both consuls; but now they were reduced to such a low condition they could scarcely defend themselves, even against the insignificant Roman legion that was in Nola.

Chapter Three: On how Rome became a great city by ruining the cities round about and by allowing foreigners easy access to her privileges.

"Meanwhile Rome grew on the ruins of Alba."[28] Those whose aim is that a city should acquire a large empire should make every effort to ensure it is full of inhabitants; for without this abundance of manpower you will never succeed in making a city great. There are two ways of doing this: by attraction and by compulsion. By attraction, you keep the routes open and safe for foreigners who wish to come and live in your city, so that everyone is keen to live there. By compulsion, you destroy the neighboring cities and compel their inhabitants to move to your city. These policies were so effectively pursued by the Romans that when the sixth king was on the throne[29] there were eighty thousand men living in Rome who were able to bear arms. For the Romans modelled their behavior on that of a good farmer. So that a fruit tree will grow, will produce a good crop of fruit and carry it until it is ripe, he cuts off the first branches that appear. Its strength [*virtù*] remains in the trunk, so that later it will have more numerous branches and bear more fruit.

This policy for enlarging a city and building an empire is demonstrated to be necessary and effective by the examples of Sparta and Athens. These two republics were heavily armed and administered under excellent laws; nevertheless, they never acquired an empire as large as that of Rome, despite the fact that Rome seemed to suffer more internal conflicts and to be less well administered than they were. For this there is no explanation other than the one I have just given. Rome, because it had grown bulky by pursuing these two policies, could at one point put in arms two hundred and eighty thousand men, while Sparta and Athens were never able to arm more than twenty thousand each. This was not because Rome's location was more favorable than theirs, but simply because Rome pursued different policies.

28. Livy, bk. 1, ch. 30.
29. Servius Tullius ruled from 578 to 535 B.C.

For Lycurgus, the founder of the Spartan republic, believing nothing could more easily lead to the decay of his constitution than immigration, did everything he could to prevent foreigners from having dealings with Spartans, and, apart from preventing intermarriage and refusing to allow them to take out citizenship, apart from obstructing the development of those links that cause men to meet together, he decreed that in his republic the money be made of leather, thus ensuring no one would want to come there to sell goods or to establish any industry. As a result the city of Sparta could never increase its population.

Everything we do has to imitate natural processes. Just as it is neither possible nor natural for a slender stalk to support a heavy branch, so a small republic cannot take control of cities or kingdoms stronger or larger than itself. Even if it conquers them, its fate will be like that of a tree with a branch thicker than its trunk. It will carry its burden only with great effort, and any little breeze will snap it. This is what happened to Sparta. She conquered all the cities of Greece, but as soon as Thebes rebelled against her, so did all the other cities.[30] The trunk was left standing with the branches torn off it. This could not happen to Rome, for her trunk was so thick she could easily support any branch. These policies, then, along with the others I will discuss below, made Rome large and immensely powerful. Livy made the point economically when he said: "Meanwhile Rome grew on the ruins of Alba."

Chapter Fifteen: On how weak states always have trouble making up their minds, and on how delays in decision making are always dangerous.

While we are on this subject, and still discussing the beginning of the war between the Latins and the Romans, it is worth noting that, whenever one has to take a decision, it is best to come straight to the particular issue one has to resolve; one should not allow uncertainties to develop or allow time to pass without reaching a decision. This is very apparent from the decision the Latins reached when they were planning to break with the Romans. For the Romans had caught wind of the hostile attitude that had spread among the Latin peoples. In order to confirm their assessment, and in order to see if they could regain the support of the Latins without resorting to arms, they told them to send eight of their citizens to Rome so they could consult with them. The Latins, hearing this, and well aware they had done numerous

30.   379 B.C.

things the Romans had not wanted, held a meeting to decide who should go to Rome and to give them instructions as to what they should say. While the council was debating what to decide, Annius, their praetor, said the following: "In my view it is of foremost importance for the conduct of our affairs that you decide what ought to be done rather than what ought to be said. It will be easy, once you have decided what you want to achieve, to choose words to fit your deeds."[31]

There is no doubt this argument is absolutely correct, and every ruler and every republic should consider its implications. For if you are confused or uncertain as to what you want to do, then you will not know what to say; but once you have made up your mind and have decided what policy to implement, then it is easy to find the right words. I have been all the keener to draw attention to this remark because I have often noticed that such uncertainties have handicapped public policy making, to the detriment and disgrace of our republic. It will always be the case that when difficult decisions have to be taken, and when you need courage to make up your mind, then uncertainties will flourish so long as weak men debate the issues and make the decisions. Slow and late decisions are every bit as harmful as ambiguous ones, especially when a decision has to be made as to whether to help a friend. For delay does no good to anyone and brings harm to you. Late and poorly-formulated decisions are the result of either lack of courage and strength or the ill will of those who have to take the decision. They, driven by their own passions, want to ruin the state or accomplish some other private objective. They do not let debate reach a conclusion but obstruct it and waylay it.

Good citizens, by contrast, even if they see popular enthusiasm building up for a mistaken decision, never try to delay decision making, particularly in cases where delay will have evil consequences. When Hieronymus, tyrant of Syracuse, died while a major war was going on between the Carthaginians and the Romans, the Syracusans began to disagree among themselves as to whether they should ally themselves with the Romans or the Carthaginians. Both sides were so intransigent that the decision hung in the balance, and no decision was actually taken until Apollonides, one of the leading citizens of Syracuse, made a speech full of wisdom, maintaining one ought not to criticize those who thought the Syracusans should ally with the Romans or those who thought they should ally with the Carthaginians, but one certainly should have no patience with uncertainty and delay in reaching a

31. Livy, bk. 8, ch. 4. The year is 341 B.C.

decision, for he feared such uncertainty could lead to the ruin of the republic; but once a decision had been taken, no matter what it was, one could hope some good might come of it.[32]

Livy could not have made clearer than he does in this passage the dangers that accompany indecision. He points them out again in the section on the Latins, for when the Latins asked the Lavinians for help against the Romans, the Lavinians put off making a decision so long that when they finally marched out of their city to come to the Latins' aid, no sooner had they passed the gate than news arrived that the Latins had been defeated. Milionius their praetor then said this: "You're going to have pay a high price to the Roman people for marching this short distance."[33] They should have made up their minds earlier either to help or not to help the Latins. If they had decided not to help them they would not have angered the Romans, while if they had decided to help them, and their help had come in time, then their additional troops might have been enough to secure victory; but by delay they ensured they lost out no matter what happened, as proved to be the case.

If the Florentines had taken note of this passage, they would not have had so much trouble with the French as they had when King Louis XII of France marched into Italy to attack Ludovico, Duke of Milan,[34] nor would they have suffered such losses at their hands. For the king, when he was planning his advance, asked the Florentines for permission to cross their land. The Florentine ambassadors at the French court agreed with Louis that Florence would stay neutral, and the king when he invaded Italy would support Florence if she were attacked and extend his protection to her. It was agreed that the city should have one month in which to ratify this undertaking. Ratification, however, was delayed by those who were foolish enough to support the cause of Ludovico, until the king was on the point of victory. Only then did the Florentines want to ratify the agreement, but their proposal was rejected, for it was evident to the king that the Florentines had been forced to become his allies and had not done so voluntarily. This cost the city of Florence a good deal of money and put its government at risk—on a later occasion it did, indeed, fall in similar circumstances.[35] This policy was all the more misconceived because it did not even provide any assistance to Duke Ludovico. If he had won, he would

32. Livy, bk. 24, ch. 28. The year is 215 B.C.
33. Livy, bk. 8, ch. 11. The year is 340 B.C.
34. In 1499.
35. In 1512, when the Medici were restored with Spanish help.

have been even more hostile in his behavior towards the Florentines than the King of France was. Although I have discussed in an earlier chapter the evil consequences that this feebleness had for the republic, nevertheless, since I had another occasion to mention it while discussing a different topic, I wanted to repeat myself, for I think this is a matter of the greatest importance that ought to be noted by all republics like ours.

Chapter Sixteen: On how soldiers in our day do not come up to
the standards of classical times.

The most important battle the Romans ever fought—in any war, with any enemy—was the battle with the Latin peoples that took place during the consulship of Torquatus and Decius.[36] For there is no reason to doubt that, just as the Latins were enslaved because they had lost the battle, so the Romans would have been enslaved if they had not won it. Livy takes this view, and at every point he stresses the two armies were equal: in discipline, skill [*virtù*], determination, and numbers. The only difference was that the commanders of the Roman army were more skillful [*virtuosi*] than those of the Latin army.

One may remark how, in the course of this battle, two things happened that had not happened before and rarely happened afterwards. Both consuls sought to keep their soldiers in good spirit, obedient to their commands, and determined to fight. To achieve this, one of them killed himself, and the other killed his own son.[37] If, as Livy stresses, the two armies were indistinguishable, it was because they had fought alongside each other as allies for a long time. They had the same language, the same training, the same weapons. Their battle formations were identical, and their military units and officers had the same names and titles. It was therefore necessary, since they were equal in strength and skill [*virtù*], that some extraordinary event should take place that would improve the morale of one side and make it more determined than its opponent, for, as I have said before, it is determination that decides the outcome of a battle; as long as the individual soldiers who are fighting are determined the army will never retreat. And in order to ensure the Romans remained determined longer than the Latins,

36. In 340 B.C.

37. The consuls had vowed to kill themselves if their troops retreated. This Decius did, while the son of Manlius Torquatus disobeyed orders and was executed on his instructions.

a combination of chance and the skill [*virtù*] of the consuls brought it about that Torquatus had to kill his son, and Decius himself.

Livy describes, in explaining the equality of the two armies, the organization of the Roman army, both while on the march and in battle. Since he describes this at length I will not repeat what he says. I will only discuss the lesson that I think is to be learned from it. Because it has been neglected by all the military commanders of modern times the result has been poor organization, both in armies on the march and in the field. Let me point out, then, that from Livy's text we can gather that the Roman army had three principal divisions, or, in Tuscan terminology, three "ranks." They called the first *Hastati* (lancers), the second *Principes*,[38] the third *Triarii*,[39] and each rank had its own cavalry. In drawing up their troops on the battlefield, they put their *Hastati* in front; behind them, standing right by their shoulders, they placed the *Principes*; in the third rank, still directly behind them, they placed the *Triarii*. The cavalry of all these formations were placed to the right and to the left of the three divisions; the ranks of the cavalry, because of how they were organized and where they were placed, were called *alae*, because they looked like two wings attached to the main body.

They organized the first division, the *Hastati*, which was in front, in a tight formation so they could push forward and take the brunt of an enemy charge. The second division, the *Principes*, because it was not the first to engage the enemy, but was needed to give support to the front division if it was broken or buckled, they did not draw up in close formation. They kept its ranks spread out, so it could absorb the first division into its lines without becoming disordered, should the enemy attack oblige the first division to retreat. The third division, the *Triarii*, had its ranks even more spread out than the second, so it could absorb, if necessary, the first two divisions, the *Hastati* and the *Principes*. With these divisions drawn up in this way they entered into the fight; and if the *Hastati* were pushed back or broken, then they withdrew into the open lines of the *Principes*, and, all joined together, having turned the two divisions into one body, they returned to the fray; if this new formation was beaten back yet again, then, under pressure, they all retreated into the open lines of the *Triarii*, and all three divisions having become one body reentered the battle. If they were then overwhelmed, having nothing more to fall back on, they lost the battle. And because every time this last division, the *Triarii*, was thrown into the battle it meant the army was in danger of defeat,

38.   I.e., the first division.
39.   I.e., the third division.

there came to be a proverbial saying: "There's nothing left but the *Triarii*," which is the equivalent of our Tuscan proverb, "We're betting everything on the outcome."

The military commanders of our own day, just as they have given up all the other practices and no longer observe any aspect at all of the old military procedures, so they have given up this, too. Which is of no small consequence, for if you draw up your troops so that you can regroup yourselves three times during the course of a battle, then you can face the prospect of defeat three times, and three times you have the chance to show you have the determination [*virtù*] to fight back against the odds. But if you are drawn up to withstand only a first charge, as all Christian armies are these days, you can easily be defeated, because any defect in your organization, any limitations in your skill [*virtù*] can deprive you of victory.

Our armies are unable to regroup three times because they have forgotten how to absorb one division into another. This is because nowadays people draw up battle formations in one of two unsatisfactory ways: either they put their divisions shoulder to shoulder, so that they have a battle line that is wide, but thin, which means it is weak, because there is little between front and rear; or, in order to strengthen their formation, they concentrate on a narrower front so as to have the strength in depth of the Romans. But still, if the first division is broken, because they are not organized so as to be able to absorb it into the second, they all get tangled up together and destroy their own formation. For if the front division is driven back, it crashes into the second; if the second wants to advance, it is blocked by the first. The result is the first bangs into the second, and the second into the third, and total confusion breaks out. Thus, a small setback can often destroy a whole army.

According to the standards of our day, the Battle of Ravenna, where the Count of Foix, the commander of the French forces, was killed, was a rather well-fought event.[40] The French and Spanish armies drew themselves up in one of the formations I have just described: That is, both armies spread all their troops out in a line, with the result neither army had any troops in reserve, and both formations were aimed more at width than at depth. This is what they always do when, as at Ravenna, they have a large space in which to maneuver. For, knowing the disorder that results if they retreat into each other, they try to avoid it by drawing themselves up in a single line, as I have described, whenever they have the space for a broad front. But when the lay of the land constricts them,

40. 11 April 1512. The French won, but, without Foix, were soon in retreat.

then they draw themselves up in the other unsatisfactory arrangement I described, and yet have no plan for avoiding the evil consequences. In this same unsatisfactory formation they march through hostile territory, whether they are plundering or engaged in some other military maneuver.

At Santo Regolo, in the territory of Pisa,[41] and elsewhere when the Florentines were defeated by the Pisans during the war between Florence and Pisa that began when Pisa rebelled after King Charles of France brought his troops into Italy, defeat was simply brought about by the Florentine's own cavalry. They were in front and were driven back by the enemy straight into the ranks of the Florentine infantry, who broke, with the result that all the rest of the troops turned and fled. Mr. Ciriaco dal Borgo, formerly commander of the Florentine infantry, has often said, as I can testify, that they would never have been beaten had they not had to face their own cavalry. The Swiss, who are the best of modern soldiers, when they fight as allies of the French, always take the greatest care to ensure they stand to one side of the allied cavalry, so if they are forced to retreat they will not charge into them.

Although this seems easy to understand and easy to prevent, nevertheless, we have yet to see a modern commander who is prepared to imitate classical methods or to correct the defects of contemporary ones. It is true they have divided their armies into three, calling one part the vanguard, another the battalion, and the third the rearguard, but they do not make any use of this division except when it comes to assigning sleeping quarters; when it actually comes to fighting it is rare, as I have said, for the whole army not to be forced to submit to a single fate.

Many, in order to justify their ignorance, claim the introduction of artillery makes it impossible to adopt many of the practices of the ancients in our own times. So I want, in the next chapter, to discuss this question and to ask whether artillery fire makes it impossible to use ancient techniques [*virtù*].

Chapter Nineteen: On how republics that acquire new territory do themselves much more harm than good, unless they have good institutions and a Roman efficiency [*virtù*].

These opinions [that cavalry are better than infantry], though at odds with the truth, are justified by appealing to bad examples that have

41.   21 May 1498.

become the norm in these centuries of corruption. They ensure men do not think of deviating from their accustomed procedures. How could one have convinced an Italian of thirty years ago that ten thousand infantry could attack, across a plain, ten thousand cavalry and as many infantry and not only hold their own but defeat them? Yet we have seen this can indeed happen. I have already referred several times to the lessons to be learned from the Battle of Novara. Although the history books are full of such examples, until recently nobody would have believed they really happened; and if they did believe they happened they would have said that in these days the heavy cavalry are better armed, and a squadron of cavalry would be able to cut through a rock face, let alone some infantry. Such misconceived excuses would have distorted their judgment. They would have given no weight to the fact that Lucullus with only a few infantry broke an army of one hundred fifty thousand cavalry under Tigranes, and among those cavalry there was a sort of horseman almost identical to our own heavy cavalry.[42] So it has been left to the northerners to show in practice that this view is mistaken. But now we can see that what is said about the infantry in the history books is nothing less than the truth. We ought to conclude that everything else they say about classical military tactics and political institutions is true and useful.

If we took this approach, then republics and rulers would make fewer mistakes. In particular, they would be stronger in standing firm against a cavalry charge; they would not think their best hope lay in running away. And those who are in charge of a participatory political system would have a better idea of how to manage it, whether their goal was to acquire new territory or hang on to what they had. They would recognize the sound policies that would make a republic great and enable it to acquire an empire are the following: to increase the number of inhabitants in the capital city; to acquire fellow citizens and not subjects; to send out colonies to hold down newly acquired territory; to make plunder a capital offense; to defeat the enemy with raids and with pitched battles and not with sieges; to keep the state wealthy and the individual poor; and to put every effort into keeping up a high level of military training. And if the pursuit of territorial expansion by means of these policies did not please them, they would pause to consider that acquisitions made by any other means bring about the ruin of a republic. So they would put a stop to all ambitious plans, would regulate the internal affairs of their city well with good laws and good customs, and would prohibit territorial expansion, thinking only of defense. They

42. In Armenia, 69 B.C.

would keep their defenses in good order, as the republics of Germany do. They live according to these principles and have been able to maintain their freedom for some considerable time.

Nevertheless, as I said earlier when discussing the difference between organizing yourself for conquest and organizing yourself for defense, it is not possible for a republic to succeed in peacefully enjoying its liberty within a small territory, for if she does not attack anyone else, then someone will attack her. If she is attacked, she will want and need to conquer. Even if she did not have an enemy abroad, she would find enemies within, for it seems this is inevitable in all large cities. So if the republics of Germany can get by on the basis of this policy and have been able to survive for some time, then this is because of certain exceptional circumstances that are to be found in that geographical region and do not occur elsewhere; without these circumstances such a strategy cannot succeed.

The region of Germany I am talking about was part of the Roman empire, just as France and Spain were. But when Rome declined, and when the title of emperor came to be held by someone whose authority was confined to Germany, then the more powerful German cities, seizing on the weakness or necessities of the Holy Roman Emperors, began to lay claim to independence, purchasing their liberty by agreeing to pay the emperor a small annual tax. So, little by little, all those cities that were under the immediate authority of the emperor and were not subject to any intermediate prince, bought their freedom in this way. At the same time as these cities were buying their freedom, a number of communities that were under the authority of the Duke of Austria rebelled against him, among them being Fribourg, the Swiss communes, and others like them.[43] They prospered from the beginning, and little by little their strength grew to the extent that, far from being reconquered by the Austrians, they have become a source of fear to all their neighbors. These are the people we call the Swiss. So the province of Germany came to be divided between the Swiss, a number of republics that are called free states, the princes, and the emperor.

The reason why, among so many different political systems, there are not many wars, or, when there are wars, they do not last long, is because of the vestigial authority of the emperor. It is true he has little power, but he has such status among them that he is able to function as a conciliator. He uses his authority to interpose as a mediator between the parties and, so, quickly brings every conflict to an end. The greatest and longest wars in Germany have been those between the Swiss and

43. The first Swiss confederation was formed in 1291.

the Duke of Austria; and although for many years now, the emperor
and the Duke of Austria have been one and same person, nevertheless,
he has never been able to overpower the bold Swiss, and there has
never been any way of bringing about a settlement between them
except by force. The rest of Germany has not been eager to come to his
support. The free cities have no desire to attack people who want to
live in freedom as they do; and as for the princes, some of them are
unable to help because they are too poor, and others have no desire
to help because they are jealous of the emperor's power. So these cities
are able to survive. They content themselves with the small territories
they control, for they have no reason, given the limited extent of the
emperor's authority, to want more. They have to live in unity within
their city walls, for their enemy is close at hand and would seize the
opportunity to occupy them if they fell out among themselves. If the
province of Germany were structured differently, then they would
need to try to extend their territory, and they would no longer be able to
live in peace. Because elsewhere the same circumstances do not apply,
other states cannot adopt this way of life. They must either increase
their power by forming alliances or grow as the Romans did.

Anyone who acts differently from the Romans is not trying to survive but to bring about his own death and ruination. For conquests are
dangerous in a thousand ways and for a thousand reasons. It is all too
easy to acquire territory without acquiring new strength, and if you
acquire territory without at the same time building up your strength,
you are heading for destruction. You cannot increase your strength if
you impoverish yourself by expenditure on war, even if you win, for
then your acquisitions are costing you more than you are gaining by
them. This is what happened to the Venetians and to the Florentines.
The Venetians were much weaker when they controlled Lombardy[44]
and the Florentines much weaker when they controlled Tuscany[45] than
they were when the Venetians were content to rule the sea and the
Florentines to control the territory within six miles of their city walls.
Their problems derived from wanting to expand without knowing how
to do it; and they deserve to be all the more criticized because they
had so little excuse, for they had the example of the Romans to follow
and could have imitated them had they chosen to. The Romans, on
the other hand, had no model to copy but worked out what to do
through their own wisdom.

In addition, acquisitions are capable of doing significant harm to

---

44. I.e., in the second half of the fifteenth century.
45. In the last quarter of the fifteenth century.

even a well-organized republic when one acquires a city or a province that is full of delights. There one is in danger of picking up the manners of the conquered from the dealings one has with them. This happened to the Romans when they conquered Capua;[46] and then happened to Hannibal when he did the same.[47] If Capua had been further from Rome, so the failings of her soldiers could not rapidly be put right, or if Rome had been at all corrupt, then without doubt the acquisition of Capua would have been the ruin of the Roman republic. And Livy says as much when he says this: "Even then life in Capua was far from favorable to the maintenance of military discipline, for every pleasure was to be encountered there, and the weary soldiers began to forget their homeland."[48] Such cities and provinces have their revenge on their conquerors without a fight and without bloodshed, for they infect them with their wicked habits and leave them ready to be defeated by the first attacker. Juvenal could not have expressed the situation better when he says in his *Satires* that the conquest of foreign lands had led the Romans to adopt foreign customs, and instead of the parsimony and other excellent virtues [*virtù*] they had exemplified, "they became given over to greed and luxury, so that the conquered globe had its revenge."[49]

If, then, acquiring new territories could be dangerous for the Romans in the days when their policies were shaped by such remarkable wisdom and virtue [*virtù*], what will happen to those who conquer without imitating their policies? Especially to those who, leaving aside the other mistakes they make, about which I have already said enough, employ soldiers who are either mercenaries or auxiliaries? The harm that often results will be briefly discussed in the next chapter.

Chapter Twenty: On the risks a ruler or a republic runs by using
auxiliary or mercenary troops.

If I had not discussed at length in another book of mine how useless mercenary and auxiliary troops are, and how necessary it is to have an army of one's own subjects,[50] I would discuss the matter in more detail in this chapter than I will do. But since I have talked in detail about

---

46.   343 B.C.
47.   216 B.C.
48.   Livy, bk. 7, ch. 38.
49.   *Satires*, bk. 6, ll. 291–92.
50.   *The Prince*, ch. twelve.

it elsewhere I will be brief here. I did not think, however, I could completely omit the question, having found so many instances of the use of auxiliary troops in Livy. Let me explain that auxiliary troops are those another ruler or republic lends to you, while he provides their commanding officers and their pay. Turning to the text of Livy, I note that the Romans, on two separate occasions, defeated Samnite armies with their own, which they had sent to help the Capuans.[51] By this assistance they put an end to Samnite aggression against the Capuans. They wanted to withdraw their troops and bring them back to Rome, and were concerned that the Capuans, without an army to defend them, would once again be attacked and defeated by the Samnites. So they left two legions behind in the territory of Capua to defend them. These legions, with time on their hands, began to enjoy living a life of leisure, so much so that they forgot their homeland and their duty of obedience to the senate. It occurred to them that they could take up their arms and seize control of the territory they had already, through their courage and skill [*virtù*], defended. They felt the inhabitants were not worthy to own the property they had been incapable of protecting. Realizing what was happening, Rome took the necessary steps, and in the chapter on conspiracies I will discuss what happened in detail.

For now I want to repeat that, of all the types of soldier, auxiliaries are the greatest liability. For the ruler or the republic who uses them to fight on his side has no control over them. Only the authorities in their homeland can control them. For auxiliary soldiers, as I said, are troops sent to you by another ruler. He supplies their commanders and pays their wages, and it is his standard they fight under. An example is the army we have been discussing that the Romans sent to Capua. Such soldiers, if they win the war, usually plunder impartially those they were fighting for and those they were fighting against; they do so, sometimes because the ruler who has sent them has evil intentions, sometimes because they have their own plans. The Romans had no intention of breaking the alliance and the agreements they had made with the Capuans; nevertheless, the Roman troops thought it would be so easy to crush them they began to think of seizing their land from them and establishing their own government.

One could give plenty of other examples like this; but I want to make do with this one, and with the example of the inhabitants of Rhegium.[52] They had their lives and their land taken from them by a Roman legion that had been sent to protect them. So a ruler (or a

---

51. Livy, bk. 7, chs. 32–41. The battles were in 443–42 B.C.
52. Polybius, bk. 1, ch. 7, in 279 B.C.

republic) ought to do anything rather than resort to bringing auxiliary troops onto his territory to fight in his defense in circumstances where he will be completely dependent on them. Any agreement, any treaty, no matter how harsh, that you can reach with the enemy will be more favorable to you than such a policy. If you study history carefully and analyze contemporary events, you will find that for every occasion on which such a policy has paid off there have been innumerable occasions when it has failed. A monarchy or a republic that is keen to expand cannot hope for a better opportunity to occupy a city or a region than to receive a request to send one of its armies to defend it. While someone who is so keen to acquire new territory that he calls on such assistance, not merely to defend himself, but to attack someone else, is trying to acquire territory he cannot hope to hold, that can easily be taken from him by the ally that acquires it for him.

Yet men are so eaten up with ambition that in their eagerness to get something they want here and now, they do not pause to think about the evil consequences they are storing up for themselves in the not-too-distant future. Neither do they pay attention to the examples provided by ancient history on this subject and on the others discussed in this book; for if they paid attention they would see that the more generous a state appears to be towards its neighbors, and the more it seems to have no interest at all in gobbling them up, the more likely it is to be successful in taking them over, as I will point out below in discussing the case of the Capuans.

Chapter Twenty-Seven: On how wise princes and republics will be satisfied with winning; for those who want more usually lose.

You usually insult your enemy because you have become overconfident, either as a result of victory, or because you mistakenly feel sure of victory. Such overconfidence makes men not only say, but also do, things they will come to regret. For this overconfidence, when it gets a hold on men's minds, makes them overstep the limit and often causes them to pass up a chance to acquire a guaranteed benefit in the hope of acquiring something better, but something that may prove to be beyond their grasp. This problem of knowing where to draw the line deserves consideration, for people often make mistakes in this matter and damage their political interests as a result. I think it is best illustrated by a consideration of ancient and modern examples, for it cannot be so clearly portrayed if one discusses it in abstract terms.

Hannibal, after he had defeated the Romans at Cannae, sent his ambassadors to Carthage to tell them of the victory and to ask for assistance.[53] The Carthaginian senate debated what to do. Hanno, an experienced and prudent citizen, advised that they make intelligent use of this victory to make peace with the Romans, for they could obtain peace on favorable terms, given that they were for the moment the victors, while they would not be able to obtain comparable terms once they had been defeated. The goal of the Carthaginians ought to be to demonstrate to the Romans that they were capable of standing up to them; having won a victory they should not run the risk of losing merely because they had some hope of making further gains. This view was not adopted, but the Carthaginian senate later had to recognize just how wise it was, by which time it was too late to act on it.

Another example: when Alexander the Great had conquered the whole of Asia, the republic of Tyre—which was in those days a great city and was powerful because, like Venice, it was a city built on the water—having seen how successful Alexander was, sent ambassadors to tell him they wanted to become his faithful servants and to obey him in any way he wanted, but they were not ready to allow either him or his troops to enter their territories.[54] Alexander, indignant that a city would dare to close its gates to him when everyone else was opening theirs, turned them away: He rejected their proposal, and laid siege to Tyre. The city was surrounded by water, and well stocked with food and with the ordnance necessary for its defense. After four months Alexander had to admit a single city was holding up his advance longer than a whole series of conquests had done. He decided to try to reach a settlement with them and to agree to the terms they themselves had proposed. But the citizens of Tyre had grown conceited and not only did not want to reach a settlement, but killed the ambassadors sent to negotiate it. Alexander was enraged and renewed the attack with such overwhelming force he overran the defenses and destroyed the city, killing and enslaving the men.

In 1512, a Spanish army marched across Florentine territory in order to restore the Medici to power in Florence and to hold the city to ransom. They were led by Florentine citizens who had encouraged them to believe that as soon as they crossed the Florentine frontier the people would take up arms in their support. Having advanced to the plain without anyone having declared for them, they found themselves short of provisions and tried to negotiate a settlement. This success made the people of Florence disdainful, and they rejected the

---

53.   216 B.C.

54.   333 B.C. The source is probably Quintus Curtius.

offer. The consequence was their defeat at Prato and the collapse of the government.

Rulers who are attacked, if their attackers are immeasurably more powerful than they are, can make no error greater than that of rejecting a settlement on any terms, especially when one is actually offered to them. For there is no proposal, no matter how unfavorable, that is not in some respect to their advantage, and so any proposal may be considered a partial victory. It ought to have been sufficient for the people of Tyre that Alexander was prepared to accept conditions he had earlier rejected. It should have been victory enough for them to have forced such a man to give in to their wishes by taking arms against him. The people of Florence, similarly, ought to have been satisfied, ought to have regarded themselves as victorious enough, if the Spanish army would agree to only one of their demands and did not simply do as it pleased. For the Spanish intended to overthrow the government of Florence, force Florence to abandon her French alliance, and force her to pay a ransom. If the Spanish had been prepared to settle for only two of these three objectives, provided they were the last two, and the people of Florence had been able to achieve only one of theirs, which was the preservation of their political system, then each party would have emerged with some honor and grounds for satisfaction. It would have been wrong for the people to worry about the two concessions they would have had to make, for they would have survived as a people. Even if they thought they were almost certain of achieving better terms by holding out, they should not have been prepared to gamble on the outcome, for their own destruction was a possibility. No wise man will risk everything unless he is forced to do so.

When Hannibal left Italy, where he had campaigned for sixteen glorious years, because he had been recalled to defend Carthage, his own homeland, he found Hasdrubal and Syphax defeated, the kingdom of Numidia lost, and Carthage no longer in control of any territory outside her own city walls.[55] He and his army were their only hope. Realizing his homeland's survival was at stake, he did not want to risk a battle until he had tried every possible alternative. He was not ashamed to sue for peace, believing that if his homeland had any chance of surviving it was through a negotiated settlement, not through war. When the enemy refused to negotiate, he was determined to put up a fight, though he seemed bound to lose. He reckoned that perhaps he could win against the odds, or, if he was defeated, he would go down to defeat covered in glory. If Hannibal, who was so skillful [*virtuoso*]

55. 202 B.C.

and whose army was intact, tried to negotiate peace before going into battle when he saw that his homeland would be enslaved if he was defeated in the field, what should someone else do, someone who is less skillful [*virtù*] and less experienced than he? But the men who make this mistake are those who do not know how to keep their hopes within bounds; they plan as if their hopes were bound to be realized, and, having failed to calculate the odds, they are destroyed.

Chapter Twenty-Nine: On how fortune blinds men's minds when she does not want them to thwart her plans.

If you will think sensibly about how people's lives are shaped, you will see that often events and accidents occur against which the heavens were determined we should have no protection. Seeing this sort of thing happened to the Romans, who were so skillful [*virtù*], pious, and well-organized, it is not surprising that it happens much more often to cities or regions who lack these advantages. Because this subject is a rather good one if one wants to show the influence of the heavens in human affairs, Livy discusses it at length and most eloquently.[56]

He says that, because the heavens had some reason for wanting the Romans to recognize their power, they first made those Fabii who had been sent as ambassadors to the French make mistakes, with the result that their efforts served to incite the French to make war against the Romans, and then they ensured the Romans fell way below their normal standards when it came to making preparations for war. Fate had ensured that Camillus, who would have been able to handle such a difficult situation single-handedly, but for whose abilities there was no substitute, had been banished to Ardea. When the French began to march on Rome, the Romans, who had often appointed a dictator when faced with attacks by the Volsci and other hostile neighbors, failed to appoint one to deal with the French. Moreover, when it came to choosing soldiers, they chose poorly and without making any real effort. They were so slow to muster that they were only just in time to block the French advance where it had to cross the river Allia, a mere ten miles from Rome. There the tribunes pitched camp without taking any of the normal precautions. They did not reconnoiter the site, nor did they surround the camp with a ditch and palisade. In fact, they did not employ any precautions, either natural or supernatural. When it came to drawing up the battle lines they spread the ranks out

56. Livy, bk. 5, chs. 37–38.

so they were thin and weak. Neither soldiers nor officers lived up to the standards of the Roman army. The battle itself was bloodless, for the Romans fled before they were attacked, the bulk of the army making for Veii, while the rest withdrew to Rome.[57] When they arrived in Rome they did not even stop by their houses but made straight for the Capitol, with the result the senate did not give any thought to defending the city, did not even bother to close the gates, but some of them fled, and others went with the rest into the Capitol. However, when it came to defending the Capitol, they finally began to get organized. They did not hamper the defense by admitting people who would be useless, while they stockpiled all the grain they could collect so they could withstand a siege. Of the vast numbers of those who were useless—the old, women, and children—the majority fled into the surrounding countryside, while the rest remained in Rome at the mercy of the French.

Anyone who read about all the Romans had achieved over the preceding years and then came to read about these events, would be quite incapable of believing these were the same people. When Livy has described this whole series of errors, he concludes with the remark: "So one can see the extent to which fortune will blind men's minds when she does not want them to deflect her onward momentum."[58] This conclusion is as true as could be. It follows that men who regularly encounter extreme adversity or have the habit of success deserve less praise or less blame than one might think. For usually you will find they have been led to either tragedy or triumph because the heavens have pushed them decisively either one way or the other, either making it easy or virtually impossible for them to be able to act effectively [*virtuosamente*].

One thing fortune does is select someone, when she wants him to accomplish great things, who will be sufficiently bold and skillful [*virtù*] to recognize the opportunities she makes for him. In the same way, when she wants to bring about someone's destruction, she chooses a man who will help bring about his own undoing. If there is someone around who might get in her way, then she kills him, or deprives him of all the resources he would need to do any good. You can see this clearly in Livy's account. Fortune, in order to make Rome all the greater and build her up to the power she eventually attained, judged it necessary to give her a nasty shock (I will describe all that happened at length at the beginning of the next book), but did not want, at this point, to destroy her completely. That is why she had Camillus banished, but not killed; had Rome seized by the enemy, but not the

57.   390 B.C.
58.   Livy, bk. 5, ch. 37.

Capitol; determined that the Romans did nothing right when it came to defending Rome, but did everything right when it came to defending the Capitol. So that Rome would fall to the enemy, she ensured the bulk of the forces that had been defeated at the Allia would make for Veii, thus destroying any opportunity of defending the city. But in bringing this about she also laid the ground for Rome's liberation. A complete Roman army stood ready at Veii, and Camillus was nearby at Ardea. So they were able to make a determined effort to liberate their homeland under the command of a general whose reputation was not tarnished by defeat but was unblemished.

Perhaps I should add, in support of what I have said, an example from modern history; but I do not think it necessary, for this one example should be sufficient to satisfy anyone, and so I will move on. But I want to repeat that this is absolutely true, and all history testifies to it. Men can help fortune along, but they cannot resist it; they can swim with the tide, but they can never make headway against it. Of course, they should never give up, for they can never know what fortune has in mind. Her path is often crooked, her route obscure. So there is always reason to hope, and if one has hope one will never give up, no matter how hostile fortune may be, no matter how dreadful the situation in which one finds oneself.

Book Three

Chapter One:[1] On how, if you want a [political or religious] movement or a state to survive for long you must repeatedly bring it back to its founding principles.

It is certainly true that everything in the world has a natural life expectancy. But usually creatures live out the full cycle the heavens have determined for them only if they do not abuse their bodies, but keep them in such good shape they either remain unchanged, or if they change it is to get healthier, not weaker. Now my subject is collective bodies, such as republics, political parties, and religious sects, and my claim is that those changes are healthy that bring them back to their founding principles. Consequently, the best constructed organizations, those that will live longest, are those that are organized in such a way they can be frequently reformed; it amounts to the same thing if, for some external reason independent of their structure, reform is thrust

---

1. This chapter serves as preface to Book Three.

upon them. It is clearer than daylight that if organizations are not reformed they cannot survive.

The way to reform an organization is, as I just said, to bring it back to its founding principles. For all political and religious movements, all republics and monarchies must have some good in them at the start. Otherwise, they would not be able to start out with a favorable reputation, nor would they be able to make progress in the early days. But as time goes by, that original goodness becomes corrupted, and, unless something happens that brings them back to first principles, corruption inevitably destroys the organization. Medical doctors say, speaking of the human body, "Everyday it takes in something that, in the end, requires treatment."

This return to founding principles, in the case of states, occurs either through some external accident or through domestic wisdom. As for the first, you can see it was necessary for Rome to fall to the French[2] if she was to have a hope of being reborn; being reborn, she acquired new strength and new skill [*virtù*], committing herself once again to respect for religion and justice, which, in the old Rome, had begun to be corrupted. This is very evident in Livy's history, when he points out that when they marched out with an army against the French and when they created tribunes with consular authority they did not perform any religious ceremonies. Even more strikingly, not only did they not punish the three Fabii who, contrary to the law of nations, had attacked the French, but they appointed them tribunes. One can reasonably presume the other sound laws that had been introduced by Romulus and by Rome's other wise rulers were increasingly treated with less respect than was reasonable and, indeed, necessary if Rome was to preserve political freedom.

Then this shock came from the outside so that all the institutions of the city could be renewed. It was made evident to the people that it was not only necessary to uphold religion and justice, but also to have respect for good citizens and to place more value on their judgment [*virtù*] than on the interests they felt they would have to sacrifice if they adopted their policies. And this is, indeed, exactly what happened, for as soon as Rome recovered, they renewed all her old religious ordinances; punished the Fabii for beginning a conflict contrary to the law of nations; and moreover held the judgment [*virtù*] and goodness of Camillus in such esteem the senate and everyone else put their jealousy to one side and entrusted to him the leadership of the republic.

So it is necessary, as I have said, that men who live together in any

2. In 390 B.C.

sort of institution regularly take stock of themselves, either as a result of external shocks or of internal factors. As far as this second type of reform is concerned, it best arises either as a result of a legal require-ment that the members of an institution frequently take stock, or because one good man appears among them and, by his own example and his skillful [*virtuose*] policies, has the same effect as such a law. So this improvement takes place in a state, either because of the skill [*virtù*] of a man, or because of the effect [*virtù*] of a law.

As far as legal authorities are concerned, the institutions that drew the Roman republic back to its first principles were the tribunes of the people, the censors, together with all those laws that were a barrier to the ambition and the insolence of men. Such laws and institutions have to be given life through the will power [*virtù*] of an individual citizen who determinedly sets out to enforce the laws despite the powerful opposition of those who seek to ignore them. Among such cases of the laws' being enforced, prior to the sack of Rome by the French, one may note the death of the sons of Brutus, the death of the ten citizens, and that of Maelius the corn dealer.[3] After the sack of Rome, there is the death of Manlius Capitolinus, the death of the son of Manlius Torquatus, the prosecution brought by Papirius Cursor against Fabius, his commander of cavalry, and the charges brought against the Scipios.[4] These cases involved going to extremes and caught people's attention. Whenever such a case occurred, it made men take stock; and as they became less common there was more opportunity for men to become corrupt, and reform became accompanied by ever greater danger and ever increasing conflict. For between two such dramatic legal decisions no more than ten years ought to go by. If the gap is longer men begin to develop bad habits and to break the laws; and if nothing happens to remind them of the penalties and to reawaken their sense of fear, there are soon so many lawbreakers springing up all over the place that it is no longer possible to punish them without endangering stability.

Those who were in charge of the Florentine state from 1434 to 1494[5] used to say, when discussing this subject, that it was necessary to retake power every five years, otherwise power would slip away from them. What they meant by "retaking power" was inspiring the same

3. Respectively 509 B.C.; 449 B.C. (in fact the Ten were only exiled); 440 B.C.

4. Respectively 384 B.C.; 340 B.C.; 326 B.C.; and 189 B.C., the two being Scipio Africanus and his brother Lucius.

5. The Medici.

fear and terror in their subjects they had inspired when they first came to power, when they had set out to crush those who had acted badly by the standards of the new system of government. But as the memory of that clampdown faded, people began to be emboldened to attempt innovations and to speak ill of their rulers. So it was necessary to provide a remedy by bringing matters back to first principles.

This reform of governments according to their first principles is sometimes the result of the simple virtue [*virtù*] of one man, without being based on any law that inspires him to act rigorously; such men are so respected and admired that good men want to imitate them, and bad men are ashamed to live according to principles at odds with theirs. The individuals in Roman history who are notable for having had such good effects are Horatius Cocles, Scaevola, Fabricius, the two Decii, Regulus Attilius, along with a few others. By their remarkable and virtuous [*virtuosi*] examples they had almost the same effects on their fellow citizens as good laws and good institutions had. If the individual instances of law enforcement I have mentioned, together with the examples provided by admirable individuals, had occurred at least every ten years in Rome, then it would certainly have been the case that Rome would never have become corrupt. But as both punishments and role models became less frequent, corruption began to spread. After Marcus Regulus there is not a single exemplary individual to be found. It is true the two Catos came along later, but there was such a long gap between Regulus and the first Cato, and then between the first and the second, and they were such isolated instances, that they could not by their own good example have any good effects.[6] This is particularly true of the second Cato, who found the city very generally corrupted and could not by his own example improve the behavior of his fellow citizens. This is all I need to say about republics.

But we should consider movements. We can see similar reforms are necessary if we take the example of our own religion. If this had not been brought back to first principles by St. Francis and St. Dominic it would have completely died away.[7] They, by living lives of poverty and imitating the life of Christ, renewed religion in the minds of men at a time when they had lost all commitment to it. The new orders they founded were so effective that it is only because of them that the

6.   Regulus died in 250 B.C., Cato the Elder in 149 B.C., Cato the Younger in 46 B.C..

7.   St. Francis founded the Franciscans in 1210; St. Dominic the Dominicans in 1216.

dishonesty of the prelates and of the hierarchy does not destroy the church, for the friars continue to live in poverty and have such influence with the people as a result of hearing confession and preaching that they persuade them it is wrong to criticize evil, and it is right quietly to obey the church authorities, and, if they make mistakes, to leave their punishment to God. And so the clergy do as much harm as they can, for they do not fear a punishment they do not see and in which they do not believe. Thus, this reform movement preserved, and continues to preserve, the Christian religion.

Kingdoms, too, need to renew themselves and to reform their laws so they accord with their original principles. One can see what a good effect this policy has in the Kingdom of France. That kingdom lives according to its laws and respects its institutions more than any other kingdom. These laws and institutions are upheld by the *parlements*, and especially the *Parlement* of Paris. They give them new life every time they enforce them against a prince of the kingdom or condemn the king in one of their judgments. So far, the *parlements* have maintained their role by being determined enforcers of the laws whenever the nobility break them; but should they ever leave first one and then more and more noblemen unpunished, the result would certainly be that they would either have to put things right by provoking a major crisis, or the whole system of government would break down.

One can therefore conclude that there is nothing more essential in any form of communal life, whether of a movement, a kingdom, or a republic, than to restore to it the reputation it had when it was first founded, and to strive to ensure there are either good institutions or good men who can bring this about, so that one is not dependent on having some external intervention before reform can occur. For although an external intervention is sometimes the best remedy, as it proved for Rome, it is so dangerous there are no circumstances in which one should hope for it.

In order to show you how the deeds of individuals made Rome great and had numerous good consequences for that city, I will turn to an account of individual leaders and a commentary on their actions. This third and final section of my commentary on the first ten books of Livy will deal with this subject. And although the kings of Rome did great and remarkable things, nevertheless, since history discusses them at length, I will leave them to one side and will say nothing more about them, except for mentioning one or two things they did in pursuit of their own private interests. I will begin, instead, by talking about Brutus, the father of Roman liberty.

Chapter Three: On how it is necessary, if one wants to preserve
                liberty when it has been newly won, to kill the
                sons of Brutus.

The harsh methods Brutus employed to preserve the liberty he had
won for Rome were not merely useful, but necessary. His example is
an exceptional one, with few parallels throughout history: a father
sitting in judgment and not only condemning his sons to death, but
supervising their execution.[8] Those who study classical history will
always learn from this that after a change in the system of government,
whether it be from republic to tyranny, or from tyranny to republic,
it is necessary to act decisively and in public against those who want
to overthrow the new government. Anyone who sets up a tyranny and
does not kill Brutus, anyone who introduces self-government and does
not kill the sons of Brutus, cannot expect to survive long. Because I
have already discussed this at length and in detail, I refer you to what
I have already said on the subject.

I will simply add one memorable example that occurred in our own
time and in our own country, that of Piero Soderini. He believed that
he could overcome through patience and kindness the desire the sons
of Brutus[9] had to restore a different system of government. He was
mistaken. Although he had wisdom enough to recognize the need to
act, and although circumstances and the ambition of those who opposed
him gave him the opportunity to eliminate them, nevertheless, he never
resolved to do it. For not only did he believe he could overcome hostility through patience and kindness, and could buy off some of his enemies with rewards, he was of the view (and he often affirmed as much to
his friends) that if he set out to attack his opponents boldly and to
destroy his adversaries, he would have to claim extraordinary powers
and set aside not only the laws but the principle of political equality.
Even if he did not go on to make tyrannical use of his powers, he
believed such an action would have so dismayed public opinion that
after he died people would never agree again to appoint a gonfaloniere
for life; and he believed this office was one that ought to be preserved
and strengthened.

This was a genuine and significant consideration. But one should
never put up with an evil consequence for the sake of some benefit if
the evil consequence is more than likely to eliminate the benefit. He
ought to have decided that since his deeds and his intentions would

---

8. See Livy, bk. 2, ch. 5. The date is 509 B.C.
9. I.e., in this case, the supporters of the Medici.

be judged by their outcome (assuming he lived long enough, and circumstances were not too unfavorable), he would be able, in due course, to demonstrate to everyone that he had acted in order to ensure the safety of the homeland and not out of private ambition. He ought to have been able to take steps to ensure no successor of his would be able to do for corrupt motives what he had done for patriotic ones. But he failed to see the mistake in his original view. He did not recognize that hostility is not overcome by time or bought off by gifts. So, because he did not know how to imitate Brutus, he fell from power, lost his reputation, and was forced into exile.

It is difficult to preserve a free state; but it is equally difficult to preserve a monarchy, as I will show in the next chapter.

Chapter Seven: On why it happens that some revolutions, when liberty is replaced by servitude, or servitude by liberty, are bloodless, while others are bloody.

Perhaps someone wonders why, of the many revolutions and coups d'état that occur, when political liberty is replaced by tyranny or vice versa, some are bloody, others bloodless. For history records that, in what would appear to be similar political upheavals, sometimes innumerable men are killed, and other times no one is hurt. For example, in the revolution in which monarchy was replaced in Rome by the rule of the consuls, the Tarquins were the only people expelled from the city, and nobody else was hurt at all.

The crucial factor is this: The government that is being overthrown was either created through violence or was not. If it was established through violence, then the likelihood is that many people suffered by it; and, consequently, when it is brought down those who suffered want their revenge, and this desire for revenge leads to bloodshed and killing. But when the government was established by the common agreement of the community, working together to make it powerful, then when it is brought down the community has no need to attack anyone except the head of state. This was the case with the government of Rome and the expulsion of the Tarquins, just as it was the case with the government of the Medici in Florence. When they were driven out of power in 1494, they were the only ones who were attacked. Such revolutions, consequently, do not turn out to be very dangerous; but those carried out by people with a desire to exact revenge are extremely dangerous. They have always been enough to appall anyone who reads about them, let alone lives through them. And because history is full of examples that make my point, I will say no more.

Chapter Eight: On how, if you want to overthrow a republic, you
                  ought to take account of its inhabitants.

I have already discussed how a wicked citizen can do no harm, except
in a republic that is corrupt. Further evidence in support of this view,
beyond what I have already given, is provided by the cases of Spurius
Cassius and of Manlius Capitolinus. Spurius was ambitious and wanted
to acquire unconstitutional power in Rome. He sought to win the
support of the populace by doing numerous things to benefit them,
such as sharing out among them the agricultural land the Romans had
seized from the Hernici. The senators began to suspect his true motives
and reported them to the populace, who became so distrustful of him
that when he addressed it, offering to hand over to it the proceeds
from the sale of the grain the government had imported from Sicily,
it was determined to reject his proposal, for it believed Spurius was
trying to buy from it its liberty. But if the Roman populace had been
corrupt, then it would not have turned the money down and would
have allowed him to take a step towards establishing a tyranny, instead
of blocking his path.[10]
    An even more important example of this is that of Manlius Capi-
tolinus.[11] His case enables us to see how strength [*virtù*] of body and
mind, and good works done in favor of the homeland, become worthless once one has demonstrated a disgusting desire to seize power.
This desire grew in him, it seems, because he was jealous of the honors
received by Camillus.[12] He was so blinded by ambition that, giving no
thought to the political culture of the day, paying no attention to the
inhabitants of the city, who were not yet ready to give their support to
an evil constitution, he set out to provoke demonstrations in Rome
against the senate and against the fundamental laws. What happened
demonstrates the excellence of that city and the goodness of her inhabitants. For in this case not a single member of the nobility, who usually
did not hesitate to come to each other's defense, declared support for
him; even among his relatives no one moved a finger to help him. It
was customary for an accused man's relatives to appear at his trial
looking disheveled and sorrowful, dressed in black as if in mourning,
in order to evoke pity for the accused; there were no mourners when
Manlius stood trial. The tribunes of the people, who usually gave their
support to anything that seemed likely to help the populace, and were

10. He was executed in 486 B.C.
11. Executed 384 B.C.
12. Who had defeated the French: cf. above, bk. 2, ch. 29.

especially keen to support anything that seemed likely to harm the nobility, in this case made common cause with the nobility to eliminate a threat
to them all. The populace of Rome, which was all too keen to defend its
own interests and quick to approve of anything that was disadvantageous
to the nobility, had given its backing to Manlius in the past; nevertheless,
when the Tribunes charged him, and handed him over to the populace to
be judged, the populace, sitting in judgment on the man it had supported,
showed no partiality at all as it condemned him to death.

I do not think there is another case in this history book better suited
to illustrate the excellence of all the traditions of that republic. Not a
single person in that city came to the defense of a citizen who had every
good quality [*virtù*], someone who had done, in public life and in private
life, very many admirable deeds. For in each of them the love of country
counted for more than anything else, and each of them was more concerned about the present danger Manlius represented than about his
past accomplishments. They wanted him to die so they might be free.
Livy says: "So died a man who, if he had not been born in a free city,
would have left his mark on history."[13] There are two things to think
about here: In the first place, we see the strategies you must employ to
achieve glory in a city that is corrupt differ from those that work in a city
that still lives in freedom; secondly (but the point is almost the same),
men should think about the times they live in and adapt how they behave
to the circumstances in which they find themselves, particularly if they
are trying to accomplish something important. Those who do not fit in
with their times, either because they make the wrong decisions or because
their temperaments are unsuited, usually live unhappy lives, and everything they try to do comes out badly. The opposite is true of those who
meet the needs of the day.

There is no doubt that we can conclude, from the sentence of Livy I
just quoted, that if Manlius had been born in the days of Marius and
Sulla,[14] when the Romans were already corrupt, and when they would
have been responsive to his ambitions, then his plans would have had as
much support and success as those of Marius and Sulla and of all the
others who aspired to establish tyrannies after they had shown the way.
By the same token, if Marius and Sulla had been born in the days of
Manlius, then they would have been crushed almost before their plots
had begun to take shape. For a man's behavior and evil talk can begin to
corrupt the inhabitants of a city, but there is no way in which one man
can live long enough for him to corrupt them sufficiently to gain the

13. Livy, bk. 6, ch. 20.
14. I.e., three hundred years later.

benefits himself. Indeed, even if it were possible for him to live that long, success would be at odds with human nature. Men are impatient, and they cannot put off trying to satisfy their desires for year after year. So they make mistakes in the management of their affairs and especially in trying to obtain the things they greatly desire. Either for lack of patience or because of bad judgment, someone who set out to corrupt his city would try to seize power too soon and would come to a bad end.

If you want to take power in a republic and change its constitution for the worse, you will only succeed if the citizens have long been corrupt, if, little by little, for generation after generation, decay has set in. Now this is bound to happen, as I have explained, whenever the republic is not regularly renewed by the exemplary conduct of good citizens or is not brought back to first principles with new laws. We have seen why Manlius would have left his mark on history if he had been born in a corrupt city. The moral is that citizens who try to accomplish anything in a republic, whether in favor of liberty or of tyranny, ought to give some thought to their fellow inhabitants, and, in the light of their assessment of them, decide whether their undertaking is likely to succeed. It is just as difficult and dangerous to try to free a people who want to live in slavery as it is to try to enslave a people who want to live in freedom. I have just said men in making their plans should take into account the nature of the times and adapt themselves to them. We will discuss this point at greater length in the next chapter.

Chapter Nine: On how you have to change with the times, if you
                        want always to have good fortune.

I have pointed out several times that whether men have good or bad fortune depends on whether they adjust their style of behavior to suit the times. It is evident that some men set about doing what they want impetuously, while others act cautiously and carefully. Both styles are mistaken, for in both one behaves inappropriately, and deviates from the best path. But, as I have said, the mistake is less important and you will still encounter good fortune if the times are suited to your style and if you always act as nature urges you.

Everyone knows how Fabius Maximus proceeded cautiously and care-fully, keeping his army out of battle and avoiding any display of Roman audacity.[15] It was his good fortune that his style corresponded well to the needs of the time. For Hannibal was a young man when he marched into Italy, things were going his way, and he had already defeated the Roman

15.   After the defeat at Lake Trasimene in 217 B.C.

armies twice. Since Rome had lost most of her best soldiers and was demoralized, she was extremely lucky to acquire a general whose delay and caution slowed the enemy down. Nor could Fabius have found himself in circumstances better suited to his style, with the result that he was covered in glory. It is evident Fabius acted in this way because it came naturally to him, not because he had made a conscious choice. For when Scipio wanted to invade Africa with the Roman armies in order to bring the war to an end, Fabius was strongly opposed to his plan.[16] He could not break with his past habits and adopt a different style. If it had been left to him, Hannibal would still be in Italy, for he could not recognize that circumstances had changed, and he needed to change his style of warfare. If Fabius had been King of Rome he might well have lost the war, for he would not have known to change his style of behavior as the times changed. But he was born in a republic, where numerous citizens, all with different temperaments, had a say. So, just as they had Fabius to lead them when he was the best man to avoid defeat, so they had Scipio when he was the best man to ensure victory.

One can see a republic should survive longer and should more frequently have fortune on its side, than a monarchy, for a republic can adapt itself more easily to changing circumstances because it can call on citizens of differing characters. Someone who is used to proceeding in a particular way will never change, as I have already pointed out, so it is inevitable that when the times change and become unsuitable for his particular style, he will be ruined.

Piero Soderini, as I have already mentioned on several occasions, always proceeded with kindness and patience. Both he and his country did well while the times favored his style of behavior; but when the circumstances were such that he needed to stop being patient and kind, he did not know how to do it; and he and his country were destroyed. Julius II, during the whole time he was pope, proceeded impatiently and always acted in the heat of the moment; and, since the times suited such behavior, he succeeded in all his undertakings. But in other circumstances, when different policies were needed, he would inevitably have brought about his own downfall, for he would not have changed his style of behavior or pursued different policies.

There are two reasons why we are unable to change when we need to: In the first place, we cannot help being what nature has made us; in the second, if one style of behavior has worked well for us in the past, we cannot be persuaded we would be better off acting differently. The consequence is that one's fortune changes, for the times change,

16. In 205 B.C.

and one's behavior does not. Another consequence is that cities are destroyed, for the institutions of a republic are never modified to suit changing circumstances, as I have pointed out at length already. Change comes too late because it is too difficult to accomplish. In order to bring it about the whole society must feel endangered; it is not enough for just one individual to change his methods.

Since I have mentioned Fabius Maximus, who kept Hannibal at bay, I think I will discuss in the next chapter whether a general who is determined to engage the enemy in battle can be prevented from doing so by his opposite number.

Chapter Twenty-Two: On how the harshness of Manlius
Torquatus and the gentleness of Valerius
Corvinus won the same amount of glory
for them both.

There were two excellent generals in Rome at the same time: Manlius Torquatus and Valerius Corvinus.[17] They were equally skillful [*virtù*], were rewarded with the same triumphs, and each obtained as much glory as the other. Each of them, in his dealings with the enemy, demonstrated the same level of skill [*virtù*]. But they behaved very differently in the treatment of their soldiers and the management of their armies. For Manlius always relied on harshness when commanding his soldiers; he always worked them hard and punished them severely. Valerius, by contrast, always treated his with every possible kindness and behaved towards them as if they were his personal friends. In order to ensure the obedience of his soldiers, one of them killed his own son, while the other never did any harm to anyone. Nevertheless, despite their quite different modes of behavior, they were both equally successful. They were equally effective against the enemy and equally good at pursuing their country's interests and their own. Not a single soldier in either of their armies ever refused to fight or mutinied against them; both were obeyed implicitly. Manlius's command, however, was so harsh that all other commanders who exceeded the limits were called Manlians. One should ask oneself the following: First, why was Manlius obliged to behave so harshly? Second, how was Valerius able to get away with being so kind? Third, why did these contrasting ways of proceeding have the same effect? Lastly, which of them is the better and more useful to imitate?

If you pay attention to Manlius's character, from the moment when

17. Manlius was dictator in 353, 349, and 320 B.C.; Valerius in 343 and 301.

Livy first begins to mention him, you will find he was a very strong man, devoted to his father and his country, and extremely respectful towards his superiors. You can tell as much from the death of the Frenchman, from his defense of his father before the tribunes, and from the fact that before he went to fight with the Frenchman he came to the consul and said, "Unless you command me to, I will never fight against the enemy, even if I am certain of victory."[18] When a man like this is put in charge he wants everyone under him to be like him, and his strength of spirit makes him push his men to the limit and makes him want to be obeyed without question. It is an infallible rule that if you ask the virtually impossible, then you must be implacable in demanding obedience; otherwise, you will find yourself let down. You should note that if you want to be obeyed you must know how to command. You will know how to command if you compare your qualities with those of the men who have to obey you. You must give commands when you know you are their superior but keep silent when you are not.

For this reason a wise man said that if you are going to keep power through violence you have to be able to overpower those whom you expect to submit. As long as you are able to do this your hold on power is secure; but as soon as those you are trying to overpower become stronger than you, then you must expect to lose power at any moment.

Getting back to our subject, my claim is that if you are going to push your troops to the limit you must be capable of doing what you ask them to do. If you are as tough as any of them and command them to do things only the tough can do, then you will not get them to obey by being gentle with them. But if you do not have this strength of will, then you should avoid making exceptional demands on your troops. If your demands are modest, on the other hand, you can rely on kindness, for commanders are not held responsible for run-of-the-mill punishments; the laws and the institutions take the blame. So one is bound to think Manlius was obliged to proceed so harshly because he made exceptional demands of his troops, and that he was inclined to do this because it was in his character. Such demands are useful in a republic, because they bring its institutions back to their founding principles and restore their original virtue [*virtù*]. If, as I have already said, a republic was lucky enough often to have people who, by their example, gave new vigor to the laws, and who not only put a brake on its descent into the abyss but pulled it back up the slope, then it would last forever. Manlius was one of those who, by the harshness of their command, preserved military discipline in Rome; he was compelled to it first by

18. Livy, bk. 7, ch. 10; 361 B.C.

his character and second by his desire to see obeyed the commands that his instincts had caused him to give. On the other hand, Valerius could rely on kindness, for it was enough for him if his soldiers did the things Roman soldiers normally did. Because the army's traditions were good ones, respect for them was enough to win him admiration. It was not difficult to obey him, and Valerius had no need to punish those who disobeyed—for either everyone obeyed, or, if some disobeyed, their punishment was, as I have said, blamed on the code of discipline and not on the commander. So Valerius could give free rein to his instinct for kindness, which enabled him to acquire the goodwill of his soldiers and to ensure their contentment. Thus, both commanders could rely on the obedience of their soldiers, and consequently both, despite following different policies, could achieve the same results. But those who want to imitate them must also beware of falling into the vices that provoke disdain and hatred, the ones I referred to above when discussing Hannibal and Scipio. In order to escape these vices you must have exceptional qualities [*virtù*]; without them you cannot succeed.

There remains the question which of these styles of command is the more praiseworthy. There are, I gather, two points of view on this, for some writers praise one, others the other. Nevertheless, those who discuss how a ruler ought to govern lean more in the direction of Valerius than of Manlius. Thus, one may compare the many examples Xenophon (whom I had occasion to cite earlier) gives of the kindness of Cyrus with what Livy says about Valerius.[19] When Valerius was made consul in the war against the Samnites, and when the day of battle came, he spoke to his troops with the affection typical of his command. After reporting his speech, Livy says: "There was never a general who was on better terms with his soldiers. He did not hesitate to help out with the tasks of the lowest ranks and did so without complaint. Moreover, on the sports field, when the soldiers competed one against the other in trials of speed and tests of strength, he was as cheerful and comradely if he won or if he lost, and he never held it against anyone if they boasted they were as good as he. He was as generous as circumstances permitted, and when talking to people was as mindful of the fact that they were free citizens as of the fact that he was in command. Nothing made him more popular than that he continued to display the same attitudes after he became a commander as he had when seeking promotion."[20]

Livy speaks equally well of Manlius, pointing out that when he was

19. Xenophon, *Cyropaedeia*, bks. 4 and 5.
20. Livy, bk. 7, ch. 33.

consul his severity in executing his son made his army remarkably obedient, and this made it possible for the Romans to defeat the Latins. He goes so far in praising him that, after reporting Manlius's victory, after describing the order of battle, and pointing out all the dangers the Romans faced and the difficulties that had to be overcome in order to win, he draws the conclusion that Manlius's vigor [*virtù*] was alone responsible for the Roman victory. When he compares the strength of the two armies, he asserts that whichever side was commanded by Manlius was bound to win. So, taking into account everything the various authors say about such men, it would seem to be difficult to choose between them.

Nevertheless, so as to eliminate uncertainty, I would say that in a citizen that lives under the laws of a republic I take Manlius's methods to be less dangerous and more praiseworthy. For this approach is entirely directed at the public benefit and is completely unconcerned with private advantage. For by such policies you cannot hope to acquire "party members." You will not win those personal allies whom we call "party members" by treating everyone harshly and acting solely out of love of the public good. So this form of behavior is extremely useful and entirely to be encouraged in a republic, since it serves the public good and cannot be suspected of being directed at building up private power. Valerius's style of behavior is the opposite. It may bring about the same public benefits, but it gives rise to real concerns as a result of the personal loyalty such a commander builds up among his soldiers. If he is in command for long, then the consequences for liberty can be serious. It is true such evil consequences did not result from the command of Publicola,[21] but then the Romans had not yet been corrupted, and he was not long or continuously in command.

But if we are considering the qualities that should be found in a ruler, as Xenophon is, then we cannot fully approve of Valerius, but we can recommend Manlius even less. For a ruler should seek to have his soldiers and his subjects both obedient and loving. They will be obedient if he respects the laws and is thought to be a good ruler [*virtuoso*]; they will be loving if he is friendly, gentle, compassionate, and has the other qualities that Valerius had and that Xenophon describes Cyrus as having had. For it is perfectly compatible with the other aspects of his government for a ruler to be someone for whom his subjects feel personal affection, and for him to have an army made up of his loyal supporters. But to have a citizen with an army made up of his own loyal supporters is at odds with the other aspects of a

21. Valerius Publicola, consul in 509 B.C.

republican government which requires its citizens to live under the laws and obey the authorities.

In the records of the early history of the Venetian republic I have read of an occasion when the Venetian galleys returned to their home port. Some dispute broke out between those who had been on the galleys and the populace, and it escalated from shouts to armed conflict. It proved impossible to restore order; neither the brute force of the local guards, nor respect for the citizens, nor fear of the magistrates could do the job. All of a sudden a gentleman who the year before had had command of the rioting sailors came forward, and out of love of him they withdrew and abandoned the fight. This obedience made the senate so suspicious that shortly afterwards the Venetians neutralized him, either by locking him up or killing him.[22]

So I conclude Valerius's style of command is useful in a ruler and dangerous in a citizen; dangerous not only to his country but to himself. To his country, because this style of command gives him an opportunity to establish a tyranny; to himself, because when his city comes to be suspicious of his methods it will be obliged to neutralize him to his own prejudice. On the other hand, I hold that Manlius's style of command is disadvantageous for a ruler and useful in a citizen, and that his homeland especially benefits from it. You are unlikely to suffer from being thought of as a harsh commander unless you have so many fine qualities [*virtù*] that the hatred your severity provokes is reinforced by suspicion of the immense reputation you have won for yourself. I will describe below how this happened to Camillus.

Chapter Twenty-Nine: On how rulers are responsible for the failings of their subjects.

Princes should not complain of any failings to be found in the people over whom they rule. For such failings are likely to be caused either by their own negligence or because they themselves have the same faults. If you think of the peoples who in our own day have been thought of as being given over to robbery and such crimes, you will see their faults were entirely derived from those who ruled them and had the same failings. The Romagna, before Pope Alexander VI eliminated the nobles who ruled over it, was well known for every type of crime. People knew that on the slightest excuse, murders and mayhem

---

22.   This may be a garbled account of events involving the Venetian admiral Vettor Pisani, who was imprisoned in 1379 and defeated the Genoese in 1380, the year of his death.

took place there. The cause of this was the wickedness of the rulers, not the incorrigible wickedness of their subjects, as the rulers claimed. For the rulers of the Romagna were poor but wanted to live as if they were rich. So they had to turn to plunder and invented various types of exaction. One of the dishonest methods they turned to was to pass laws prohibiting some activity or other. Then they encouraged people to ignore the laws and never punished those who broke them. Only when they were sure lots of people had put themselves in the wrong did they start enforcing the laws; not because they wanted people to be law-abiding, but because they wanted to collect the fines. Such policies had many evil consequences; above all, they impoverished the people without improving their behavior. Those who had been impoverished put their minds to ways of getting the better of those who were weaker than themselves. The result was all those evils I began by mentioning, all of which were caused by the rulers.

The truth of this is apparent from Livy's account of how, when the Roman legates were bringing the plunder they had taken from Veii as an offering to Apollo, they were seized by pirates from Lipari in Sicily and taken there as prisoners. When Timasitheus, their ruler, heard what sort of cargo this was, where it was going and who had sent it, he behaved as if he were a Roman though he had been born in Lipari, and explained to his people how wicked it would be to seize a religious offering. So, with popular approval, he let the legates continue on their journey with all their possessions. Our historian says: "Timasitheus inspired in the populace, who always copy their rulers, respect for religion."[23] And Lorenzo de' Medici made the same point, remarking: "What the ruler does one day, many others do the next, for they all have their eyes on him."[24]

Chapter Thirty: On how a citizen who wants to use his personal authority to do some good deed in his republic must first overcome other people's jealousy; and on how, when the enemy attack, one should organize a city's defense.

The Roman senate was informed that the whole of Tuscany had raised an army to attack Rome, and the Latins and the Hernici, who had previously been allies of the Romans, had reached an understanding with the Volsci, who had always been Rome's enemies. They gathered

23. Livy, bk. 5, ch. 28.
24. Lorenzo de' Medici, *Opere*, ed. A. Simioni (Bari, 1914), vol. 2, 100.

the coming war was going to be dangerous. Camillus was tribune at the time, with consular authority, which caused them to think they could get by without creating a dictator, provided the other tribunes who were his colleagues would agree to transfer to him all their authority. This the tribunes were perfectly willing to do. "Neither did they think," says Livy, "that they were losing status by virtue of giving it to him."[25] So Camillus, taking these expressions of obedience literally, ordered that three armies be enrolled. He wanted to be in command of the first himself, which would fight the Tuscans. He made Quintius Servilius commander of the second and ordered him to remain close to Rome so he could obstruct the Latins and the Hernici if they advanced. He put Lucius Quintus in charge of the third army, which he enrolled to garrison the city and to defend the gates and the city-center no matter what happened. In addition, he ordered Horatius, one of his colleagues, to stockpile weapons, grain, and the other supplies needed in time of war. He placed Cornelius, another colleague, in charge of the senate and the public assembly, so he could take advice on those things that had to be done day by day. This is how, in those days, the tribunes were prepared both to take command and to obey in order to protect the homeland.

This passage gives an indication of what a good and wise man can do, how much he can accomplish, and how useful he can be to his homeland, provided that his goodness and skill [*virtu*] have been able to overcome the envy of others. For envy often prevents men from achieving what they might have; it resists their having the authority necessary in crucial situations. There are two ways in which such envy is eliminated. One is for people to find themselves in a dangerous and difficult situation. Everyone faces the prospect of death, lays ambition aside, and eagerly agrees to obey whoever they think has the skill [*virtù*] required to rescue them. This is what happened to Camillus. Everyone was familiar with the reports of his extraordinary abilities. He had been dictator three times, and each time he had used his office to benefit the public, not to advance his own interests, with the result that no one feared being harmed if power was concentrated in his hands. Because Camillus was so admired and so important no one thought it shameful to take orders from him (hence Livy's wise remark that I have just quoted).

Another situation in which envy is eliminated is when those who have been your competitors in pursuit of status and office die, whether by violence or by natural causes. For when they were alive, they would

25. Livy, bk. 6, ch. 6; 389 B.C.

never have been able to acquiesce in your being better thought of than they, neither would they have patiently put up with it. Such men, if they are accustomed to living in a corrupt city, where their upbringing has not given them any generous qualities, will never under any circumstances be prepared to abandon the competition. To get their own way and satisfy their perverse desires, they will be happy to see the destruction of their homeland. There is no cure for envy like this other than the death of those who are eaten up with it. If fortune smiles on an able [*virtuoso*] man, his envious opponents die naturally, and he can become illustrious without provoking a crisis, for then he can demonstrate his abilities [*virtù*] without opposition and without giving offense. But if he does not have this stroke of luck, then he must try to think of any possible way to get rid of them. Before he does anything he must find a way of solving this problem.

If you read the Bible at all sensibly you will see Moses was obliged, in order to have his laws accepted and his proposals adopted, to murder vast numbers of men, men who opposed his plans for no other reason but envy.[26] Friar Girolamo Savonarola clearly recognized the need to take such action; so, too, did Piero Soderini, Gonfaloniere of Florence. The first, the friar, could not overcome the problem because he did not have an office that gave him authority to do it, and because his intentions were not well understood by his followers who were in a position to take action. Nevertheless, it was not his fault nothing was done, and his sermons are full of attacks on the worldly-wise—that is what he called those who were jealous of him and opposed his plans— and of invectives directed against them. Soderini believed that with time, with kindness, with good luck, with the occasional favor, he would be able to overcome this jealousy. He was fairly young and constantly winning new supporters with his style of government, so he thought he would eventually be able to overcome all those who opposed him out of envy and to do so without a crisis, without conflict or violence. He did not realize that time does not stand still, that goodness is not enough, that good luck changes to bad, and that there is no bribe that will buy off hatred. So both these men were ruined, and their destruction was caused by their not having known how to overcome jealousy, or not having had the opportunity to put their knowledge to work.

Also worth noting are the arrangements Camillus made for the protection of Rome, both within the city and without. Good historians, like our Livy, are right to deal with certain situations in detail and with care, so that future generations can learn from them how they ought

26. Exodus, 32.25–8.

to defend themselves if they find themselves similarly placed. In this passage, one should note there is no more dangerous and more worthless defense than one thrown together in a hurry without adequate planning. This is apparent from the case of the third army that Camillus enrolled so they could remain in Rome as a garrison for the city. Many must have thought, and would still think, that this decision was unnecessary. The Roman people were used to bearing arms and were always keen to fight, so many would conclude there was no need to enroll them in an army. All one had to do was arm them when the need arose. But Camillus thought differently, and anyone who had his good sense would have agreed with him. One should never allow a mob to arm itself; there must always be an organization and a plan. So anyone who is put in charge of the defense of a city should learn from this example that one should avoid like the plague having men arm themselves in a disorderly way; first, you must select and enroll those you want to be armed, appoint their officers, decide where they are to muster, and choose where they are to be posted. Those you do not enroll you must instruct to remain in their own houses, guarding their own possessions. If you adopt this procedure in a city that is under attack, you will have no difficulty in defending it; if you do not, you will not be following Camillus's example, and your defense will fail.

Chapter Thirty-One: On how strong republics and fine men
                                    sustain the same outlook, no matter what
                                    happens, and never lose their dignity.

Our historian has Camillus do and say magnificent things in order to show us how a fine man ought to behave. One example is the following statement that he puts into his mouth: "Being dictator did not make me more self-confident, and being in exile will not make me doubt myself."[27] From this you can see how great men are always themselves, no matter what happens to them. Their luck may change, and one moment they may be lifted up to the heights, the next crushed, but they themselves do not change, but always remain determined and seem so comfortable with their own style of behavior that everyone can easily see fortune has no power over them. Weak men behave very differently. For they become conceited and overexcited when they have good fortune, presuming that everything good that happens to them is a reward for excellent qualities [*virtù*] they do not, in fact, have. The

27.   Livy, bk. 6, ch. 7.

result is they become intolerable and hateful to all those who have to deal with them. And this causes their luck to change quickly, and, as soon as they stare ill fortune in the face, they quickly develop the opposite vices, becoming inadequate and unselfconfident. Rulers who have weak characters like this are quicker to think of flight than of self-defense when times become tough, but then, since they have misused their period of good fortune, they have made no preparations against attack.

This virtue [*virtù*] of strength of character, and this vice of weakness of character, which I have been describing in individuals, can also be found in republics. One may take the Romans and the Venetians as examples. As for the first, no bad luck ever made them demoralized; and no good fortune ever made them overconfident, as is evident from their behavior after their army was routed at Cannae and after their victory fighting against Antiochus. After the rout, although it was extremely serious, for it was their third defeat,[28] they never allowed themselves to feel inadequate. They sent armies into the field. They refused to ransom those of their soldiers who had been made prisoner, for this would have been a breach with tradition. They did not send emissaries to either Hannibal or Carthage to beg for peace. But, turning their backs on all such feeble policies, they thought only of carrying on the war, arming, since they were short of soldiers, old men and slaves. When Hanno the Carthaginian learned of this, he pointed out to the Carthaginian senate, as I have already mentioned, just how little they had gained by their victory at Cannae. So you can see how hard times did not dismay them or humiliate them.

On the other hand good fortune did not make them overconfident. Antiochus had sent ambassadors to Scipio to seek peace before the battle that he was to lose.[29] Scipio had stated certain conditions for a settlement. They were that he must withdraw into Syria and that all other outstanding matters must be left to the decision of the Roman state. Antiochus rejected these terms. After he had fought the battle and lost he sent new ambassadors to Scipio with instructions to accept whatever conditions the victor chose to impose. The conditions Scipio offered them were exactly the same as those he had offered before the battle. He only added these words: "For the Romans, if they are beaten in battle, do not lose heart; and, if they win, they do not make a habit of being overconfident."[30]

---

28. Following Ticinus in 218 B.C. and Lake Trasimene in 217 B.C.
29. Livy, bk. 37, chs. 35–45; 190 B.C.
30. An invented quotation. The nearest equivalent is in Livy, bk. 37, ch. 45.

We have seen the Venetians exemplify the opposite characteristics. When things were going their way they thought they had made gains because of their own excellent qualities [*virtù*], which in fact they did not have. They became so full of themselves they called the King of France the son of St. Mark;[31] they showed no respect towards the church; their aspirations extended far beyond Italy; and they had begun to dream of having an empire like that of the Romans. Then, when their luck turned, and they were half-defeated at Vailà by the King of France, they not only lost control of the whole of their territory because their subjects rebelled, but they ceded large parts of it to the pope and to the King of Spain out of feebleness and inadequacy.[32] They sank so low they sent ambassadors to the emperor offering to be his vassals; they wrote letters to the pope full of cowardice and of submission in an attempt to persuade him to have pity on them. They were reduced to this miserable condition in four days after a semi-defeat, for after the battle their army, in retreat, was attacked, and about half of it destroyed.

Nevertheless, one of their generals who escaped reached Verona with more than twenty-five thousand soldiers, counting both infantry and cavalry. If the Venetians and their institutions had had any decent qualities [*virtù*], they could have regrouped and stood up to look fortune in the eye. There was still time for them either to win or lose more gloriously, or to obtain a more honorable settlement. But their feeble spirits, which had been shaped by the character of their institutions, which were unsatisfactory when it came to war, made them lose in one and the same moment both their territory and their self-confidence.

And this will always happen to anyone who behaves as they did. For this pattern of becoming overconfident at times of good fortune and inadequate at times of bad is a result of your habits of behavior and of your upbringing. If your education was foolish and weak, then you will be, too; if it was the opposite, then you will be the opposite. If you are brought up to have a decent understanding of the world, then you will be less inclined to get overexcited when things go well or to get dismayed when things go badly. If this is true of an individual it is also true of a group of people living together in the same state; they have the qualities that result from their society's habits of behavior.

Although earlier on I said that all states depend upon having a good

31. St. Mark is the patron saint of Venice.
32. In 1509.

army, and that if you do not have a good army you cannot hope to have either good laws or anything else worth having, I think it bears repeating. For at every point, as we read this history book, the importance of this fundamental requirement becomes apparent. And we see an army cannot be good if it is not kept in training, and you cannot keep it in training if it is not composed of your own subjects. States are not always at war, nor could they withstand it if they were. So you must be able to train your army during peacetime; but it is far too expensive to train an army in peacetime unless it consists of your own subjects.

Camillus, as I have said, had marched out with an army against the Tuscans. When his soldiers saw the size of the enemy army they were all dismayed, for it seemed to them they were so badly outnumbered that they would not be able to stand up to an enemy charge. When Camillus came to hear of the low morale among his soldiers, he went out and walked around the camp, chatting to a soldier here, another there, and got them to express their fears. In the end, without altering any of the dispositions he had made, he said, "Let each man do what he knows how to do, what he is used to doing."[33] If you think about what he said and the way in which he set out to give his soldiers courage to face the enemy, you will realize you could not say this or pursue this sort of policy with an army that had not first been organized and trained, both in time of peace and in time of war. For a general who has soldiers who have never learned anything cannot trust them or expect them to do anything worthwhile; even if they had a second Hannibal in command, they would be defeated under him. For a commander cannot be everywhere while the battle takes place. So he is bound to be defeated unless he has first ensured there will be men throughout the army who share his outlook and have a good understanding of his routines and methods.

If a whole city is armed and organized as Rome was, so that every day its citizens, both in private and in public, have occasion to experience both the extent of their own strength [*virtù*] and the power of fortune, the result will always be that they will maintain the same attitude whatever happens to them and will always keep up their dignity without wavering. But if they are disarmed, and they put their trust in the tides of fortune and not in their own strength, then their temperament will change as their luck changes, and they will inevitably make a spectacle of themselves, just as the Venetians did.

33. Livy, bk. 7, ch. 6.

Chapter Thirty-Four: On the role of rumor, word of mouth, and
public opinion in deciding whether the
people begin to support a particular citizen;
and on whether the people make wiser
appointments to government offices than
individual rulers do.

Earlier on we were discussing how Titus Manlius, who was later called Torquatus, successfully rescued Lucius Manlius, his father, from an accusation brought against him by Marcus Pomponius, tribune of the people;[34] and although the way in which he rescued him was somewhat violent and exceptional, nevertheless, his filial piety towards his father was so strongly approved of by everybody that not only was he not criticized for what he had done, but, when they came to elect the tribunes of the legions, Titus Manlius was elected in second place. This achievement invites us to consider how the people make judgments about men they are considering for public office; and it enables us to test the conclusion I put forward above, that the people are a better judge of whom to appoint than is an individual ruler.

In my view, the people, in deciding whether to appoint someone, do not simply rely on what rumor and gossip say about him. If they do not have enough information about things he himself has done, then they judge by presumption or on the basis of the opinion they have of him. Presumptions are based on their knowledge of the candidate's father. If he has been a great man and accomplished a great deal in public life, then people believe his sons ought to take after him, at least until their own deeds establish this is not the case. Opinions are based on the characteristic behavior of the candidate himself. The best type of behavior is the following: to be a companion of men who are serious, well-behaved, and believed by everyone to be wise. There is no better indication of the sort of person someone is than the company he keeps, so it is right that someone who keeps good company acquires a good reputation, for it is inevitable he will have some similarity to those with whom he associates. On the other hand, you can acquire a public reputation through some extraordinary and remarkable thing you yourself have done, and that has won honor for you, even if it was an action in your private life.

Of all these three factors that give someone a good reputation before he enters public life, none is more influential than this last. The first factor, a presumption based on the character of your father and your

34. *Discourses*, bk. 1, ch. 11; bk. 3, ch. 22.

relatives, is so unreliable people are reluctant to place much store by it; and it has little continuing significance if the qualities of the candidate himself prove not to live up to it. The second, which judges you on the basis of your associates, is better than the first but is not nearly as good as the third, for so long as you are not being judged on the basis of something you yourself have done, your reputation is based on assumptions, and it is easy for them to be proved mistaken. But the third, being begun and maintained by your own deeds and actions, gives you from the beginning such a secure reputation you need to do many things that are at odds with this reputation before you can change it. So men who are born in a republic ought to take advantage of this and ought to make every effort to come to the public's attention through some remarkable achievement. Many men in Rome succeeded in this while they were still young. Perhaps they proposed a law from which the public stood to benefit; or they charged some prominent citizen with breaking the law; or they did some other similar action that was novel and remarkable, and was bound to be widely discussed.

Not only are such actions necessary if you want to begin to acquire a reputation, but they are also essential if you want to preserve one and strengthen it. If you want to do this, you must be always doing new things, as Titus Manlius was throughout his life. For, after he had defended his father so successfully and so remarkably, and had thereby acquired the beginnings of his reputation, a few years later he fought with the Frenchman and, having killed him, took from him a necklace of gold, which resulted in his being called Torquatus.[35] He did not stop there, for in middle age he killed his son for having fought without his permission, even though he had defeated his enemy. These three deeds gave him a greater reputation at the time and have made him more famous through the centuries, than any of his triumphs or any of his other victories, although he had as many of these as any other Roman. The reason is that there are many others besides Manlius who had such victories; but in these particular deeds, there were none or few with whom he could be compared.

Scipio the elder did not win more glory from all his triumphs than he got from having, when he was still young, defended his father during the battle of Ticinus and from having, after the defeat of Cannae, boldly, bloody sword in hand, made a group of younger Romans swear they would not abandon Italy, as they earlier had been discussing among themselves. These two deeds were the start of his reputation and were steps on the way to the triumphs of Spain and of Africa. He

35. I.e., necklace-wearer.

improved his public reputation even further when, in Spain, he returned a daughter to her father, a wife to her husband.[36]

This type of behavior is not only necessary for citizens who want to acquire fame in order to win places of honor within their own republic, but it is also necessary for rulers who want to maintain their reputations in their own states, for nothing causes a ruler to be more admired than doing or saying something exceptional that benefits the public and is quoted as a remarkable example to others. By such actions a ruler shows himself to be magnanimous, or generous, or fair; and he becomes a byword for such qualities among his subjects.

But to go back to the subject with which we began this chapter, I claim that the people, when they first appoint one of their citizens to an office, if they rely on one of the three factors I have described, are employing the right criteria. But later, when someone has established a record that ensures he is well known for his good actions, then their decision is even more soundly based, for in such cases they scarcely ever make a mistake. However, I am only talking about those appointments that are given to men at the beginning of their careers, before they have done enough for people to have a secure knowledge of their character, or before it has become apparent they are capable of doing an admirable thing one day, and a disgraceful thing the next. In such circumstances the people will always be a better judge than a ruler, for they will be less easily misled, and less liable to corruption.

Of course it is true a community may be misled by the fame, the reputation, and the deeds of an individual, and may think him better than in fact he is, while a ruler may avoid such errors because his advisers point out his mistake to him; for this reason, the wise founders of republics have sought to ensure that the people, too, should have their advisers. They have decreed that when people are to be appointed to the highest offices in the city, to which it would be dangerous to appoint men who were unsuitable, if any citizen believes public opinion is about to bring about the appointment of such a person, then he is entitled to declare in the public assembly the faults of this individual so that the people, having the advantage of his knowledge, may reach a better judgment. To stand in this way against the tide of opinion should be seen as a noble action.

Such a practice existed in Rome, as we can see from the speech Fabius Maximus made to the people during the Second Punic War, when, during the election of the consuls, public opinion seemed to be favoring the appointment of Titus Otacilius. Fabius thought he was

36. Livy, bk. 26, ch. 50.

not up to the job of being consul in such circumstances and spoke against his appointment, pointing out his defects.[37] By so doing he prevented his being elected and ensured the people elected someone better. So we can see the people, when they are appointing to offices, make their decisions on the basis of those indications that are the most reliable guides to men's characters; when they can be advised as princes are, then they make fewer mistakes than princes do; and a citizen who wants to begin to have the people's good will must do something remarkable to win it, as Titus Manlius did.

Chapter Forty-One: On how one should defend one's homeland whether one wins shame or glory by it; one should employ whatever defense will work.

The consul and the Roman army were, as I explained above, under siege by the Samnites, who had proposed they surrender ignominiously; they wanted to make them pass under the yoke[38] and send them disarmed back to Rome. The consuls were shocked by this, and the whole army was in despair. Lucius Lentulus, a Roman ambassador, said that in his view one should not reject any terms if they would make possible the defense of the homeland. Rome's survival depended on the survival of this army, so he thought one should do anything necessary to ensure the army's survival. The homeland is well defended by any methods that work, whether one wins shame or glory by them. For if this army escaped destruction, then Rome would have a chance to undo the disgrace it had incurred; but if it did not escape, even if it died gloriously, then Rome and her political freedom were doomed. So his advice was followed.[39]

This deserves to be noted and is an example to be imitated by any citizen who finds himself called on to advise his country. If you are discussing nothing less than the safety of the homeland, then you should pay no attention to what is just or what is unjust, or to what is kind or cruel, or to what is praiseworthy or shameful. You should put every other consideration aside, and you should adopt wholeheartedly the policy most likely to save your homeland's life and preserve her liberty. The words and the deeds of the French, when it comes to defending the majesty of their king and the power of their kingdom,

---

37. Livy, bk. 24, ch. 8; 215 B.C.
38. A form of ritual humiliation.
39. Livy, bk. 9, ch. 4; 321 B.C.

show that they understand this principle. There is nobody they are more impatient with than someone who stands up and says, "Such a proposal is beneath the dignity of the king," for they say that nothing the king does can bring shame on him, whether in the end it succeeds or fails, for whether he loses or wins, whatever the king does is said to be a matter of state.

Chapter Forty-Three: On how the men who are born in a particular region scarcely change in character over the course of centuries.

Wise men often say, and not without good reason, that if you want to predict the future you should look at the past, for everything that happens, no matter where or when, has its analogue in past history. The reason for this is that men have and always have had the same passions, so it inevitably follows that their passions have the same effects, and their deeds do not change. It is true that what they do varies from place to place. In one region they are more effective [*virtuose*] than in another and still more successful in a third, depending on the upbringing that has shaped the way of life of that particular people. It is also easy to predict the future on the basis of the past if one recognizes that nations retain the same habits of life over long periods. They are always miserly, or always dishonest, or have some other similar vice or virtue [*virtù*].

If you read about the past history of our own city of Florence and also consider those things that have happened in the last few years, then you will find the German and French peoples are full of avarice, pride, ferocity, and untrustworthiness; for our city has suffered greatly from each of these four qualities of theirs at different times. As far as their unreliability is concerned, everyone knows how often we gave money to King Charles VIII, in return for which he promised to hand back the fortress of Pisa; yet he never gave it back.[40] This behavior shows just how unreliable and greedy this king was. But let us leave to one side these recent injuries, the memory of which is still fresh.

Everyone will have heard of what happened during the war between the Florentines and the Visconti, dukes of Milan. Florence, having run out of options, thought of persuading the emperor to march into Italy so he could attack Lombardy; his reputation, it was thought, would be as intimidating as his army. The emperor gave his promise to come with an adequate number of troops, and to join in the war against the

40.   1494.

Visconti, and also to defend Florence from the enemy forces, provided Florence gave him one hundred thousand ducats to enroll an army and a further hundred thousand once he had reached Italy. The Florentines accepted these terms and paid him both installments. But, once he had reached Verona, he turned back without having done anything, complaining he had had to call a halt because the Florentines had not lived up to the agreements between them.[41]

The Florentines may have been forced by circumstances or overcome by passion, but if they had studied and understood the ancient habits of the barbarians, they would not have been taken in, either on this occasion or on numerous others. For they have always been the same, and everywhere they have gone, and no matter with whom they have been dealing, they have always behaved in the same way. An example is their behavior in classical times towards the Tuscans who were being oppressed by the Romans, had been defeated by them several times, and been put to rout. They realized their troops could not withstand the Roman legions, and so they reached an agreement with those French who lived on this side of the Alps, in Italy, that, in return for a certain sum of money, they would be committed to join forces with them and march against the Romans. What happened was that the French took the money but then did not want to fight on their behalf, saying they had been paid, not to fight Tuscany's enemies but to give up plundering the Tuscan countryside.[42] So the Tuscans, because of the greed and unreliability of the French, found themselves deprived simultaneously of their own money and of the help they had hoped to receive from the French. So you can see, from this example from classical history involving the Tuscans and from the more recent case of the Florentines, that the French have always behaved in the same way, and so it is easy to work out to what extent other rulers can afford to trust them.

41. 1401.
42. 300 B.C.

INDEX